ISBN 978-1-333-92435-5
PIBN 10639442

This book is a reproduction of an important historical work. Forgotten Books uses state-of-the-art technology to digitally reconstruct the work, preserving the original format whilst repairing imperfections present in the aged copy. In rare cases, an imperfection in the original, such as a blemish or missing page, may be replicated in our edition. We do, however, repair the vast majority of imperfections successfully; any imperfections that remain are intentionally left to preserve the state of such historical works.

1 MONTH OF
FREE
READING

at

www.ForgottenBooks.com

By purchasing this book you are eligible for one month membership to ForgottenBooks.com, giving you unlimited access to our entire collection of over 1,000,000 titles via our web site and mobile apps.

To claim your free month visit:
www.forgottenbooks.com/free639442

English
Français
Deutsche
Italiano
Español
Português

www.forgottenbooks.com

Mythology Photography **Fiction**
Fishing Christianity **Art** Cooking
Essays Buddhism Freemasonry
Medicine **Biology** Music **Ancient
Egypt** Evolution Carpentry Physics
Dance Geology **Mathematics** Fitness
Shakespeare **Folklore** Yoga Marketing
Confidence Immortality Biographies
Poetry **Psychology** Witchcraft
Electronics Chemistry History **Law**
Accounting **Philosophy** Anthropology
Alchemy Drama Quantum Mechanics
Atheism Sexual Health **Ancient History**
Entrepreneurship Languages Sport
Paleontology Needlework Islam
Metaphysics Investment Archaeology
Parenting Statistics Criminology
Motivational

MY NAVAL CAREER

AND TRAVELS

BY

ADMIRAL OF THE FLEET

THE RIGHT HON. SIR EDWARD H. SEYMOUR

WITH ILLUSTRATIONS

NEW YORK

E. P. DUTTON & COMPANY

31 WEST TWENTY-THIRD STREET

1911.

" Let decision and execution be the same, and though success may not always follow, defeat is oft times left behind."

DEDICATION

PREFACE

PROBABLY no one can write his Memoirs without being open to the charge of egotism. If so I shall attempt no defence, being satisfied with the reasons that led me to do it, and feeling that as a memoirist I am at least in some good company.

My hope is to be read by young naval officers, who may be interested to see the changes in what is probably the finest profession in the world—viz. the British Navy.

I have tried to avoid all mention of my private life; because however interesting to myself, I cannot suppose it would be so to others.

E. H. SEYMOUR,

QUEEN ANNE'S MANSIONS,
ST. JAMES'S PARK,
LONDON, S.W.
April 1911.

CONTENTS

CHAPTER I

H.M.S. *ENCOUNTER*

CHAPTER II

H.M.S. *TERRIBLE*

CHAPTER III

H.M.S. *TERRIBLE* (continued)

CHAPTER IV

H.M.S. *TERRIBLE* (continued)

CHAPTER V

H.M.S. *CRUIZER*

CONTENTS

CHAPTER VI

H.M.S. *CALCUTTA*

CHAPTER VII

H.M.S. *PIQUE, MERSEY,* AND *IMPERIEUSE*

CHAPTER VIII

H.M.S. *CHESAPEAKE, COWPER,* AND *WATERMAN*

CHAPTER IX

H.M.S. *SPHINX* AND *IMPERIEUSE*

CHAPTER X

FLAG-LIEUTENANT

CHAPTER XI

THE *MAZINTHIEN*

CONTENTS

CHAPTER XII

THE COASTGUARD

CHAPTER XIII

H.M.S. *GROWLER*

CHAPTER XIV

COMMANDER—H.M.S. *LIVELY*—CAPTAIN

CHAPTER XV

H.M.S. *ORONTES*

CHAPTER XVI

CAPTAIN

CHAPTER XVII

H.M.S. *IRIS*

CONTENTS

CHAPTER XVIII

H.M.S. *INFLEXIBLE*

CHAPTER XIX

CAPTAIN—H.M.S. *OREGON*—CAPTAIN

CHAPTER XX

FLAG-CAPTAIN—NAVAL RESERVES

CHAPTER XXI

REAR-ADMIRAL

CHAPTER XXII

REAR-ADMIRAL (continued)

CHAPTER XXIII

REAR-ADMIRAL (continued)

CONTENTS

CHAPTER XXIV

SECOND IN COMMAND CHANNEL SQUADRON

CHAPTER XXV

SECOND IN COMMAND CHANNEL SQUADRON (continued)

CHAPTER XXVI

ADMIRAL-SUPERINTENDENT OF NAVAL RESERVES

CHAPTER XXVII

CHINA COMMAND

CHAPTER XXVIII

CHINA COMMAND (continued)

CHAPTER XXIX

CHINA COMMAND (continued)

CHAPTER XXX

CHINA COMMAND (continued)

CONTENTS

CHAPTER XXXI

CHINA COMMAND (continued)

CHAPTER XXXII

CHINA COMMAND (continued)

CHAPTER XXXIII

CHINA COMMAND (continued)

CHAPTER XXXIV

ADMIRAL

CHAPTER XXXV

PLYMOUTH COMMAND

CHAPTER XXXVI

ADMIRAL OF THE FLEET

CONTENTS

CHAPTER XXXVII

ADMIRAL OF THE FLEET (continued)

CHAPTER XXXVIII

H.M.S. *INFLEXIBLE* AND NEW YORK

CHAPTER XXXIX

ENVOI

LIST OF ILLUSTRATIONS

MY NAVAL CAREER

AND TRAVELS

CHAPTER I

H.M.S. *ENCOUNTER*

Entering the Navy—H.M.S. *Encounter*.

PROBABLY no one profession in England has given so many of its sons to serve the State as what is commonly called ' The Church.'

My father was a clergyman, Rector of Kinwarton, Warwickshire, and Canon of Worcester Cathedral.

I was born at Kinwarton in April 1840, and as soon as I had sense enough to form a real wish it was to go to sea—a choice I have never regretted.

On 11th November 1852 I entered H.M. Navy.

The procedure then was very different from what it is now. The age for entry was 12 to 14, the examination was held in the old Naval College at Portsmouth, and lasted only one day; it consisted of arithmetic, including the 'rule of three,' no fractions, and dictation of twenty lines from the *Spectator* : three spelling mistakes turned the candidate back for good, no second trial being allowed.

In September 1852 (the month and year the great Duke of Wellington died), I, being at school at Radley, got the offer of a nomination as naval cadet in H.M.S. *Encounter* just commissioned. I accepted, and was sent to a 'crammer' in Britain Street, Portsea.

Our preceptor there was Mr. Eastman, a retired naval instructor, his house only held about ten lodgers, and the rest, I for one, were billeted about St. George's Square.

We had no facilities for games, and had to pass our leisure time as we could. My chief recollection is an arranged fight between myself and another boy named Herbert in the small back yard. We were separated by our master's wife armed with a broom, and my opponent, a most promising young officer, was killed at the attack on the Peiho forts in 1859.

On 10th November I went through my examination at the old Naval College, and next day received my passing certificate and an order to join my ship at Spithead, which I did on 12th November.

The *Encounter* was a screw corvette, full ship rigged, carrying fourteen 32-pounder guns, and able to steam 9 to 10 knots at best, a fairly high speed in those days. Her complement was 180 officers and men, and I was the only naval cadet on board.

Naval officers will appreciate how different the signal service of the Navy was then, when I say that on arriving on board the first thing the

First Lieutenant said to me was, 'You will take charge of the signals of this ship,' of which I, of course, knew nothing.

The signal staff consisted of myself aged $12\frac{1}{2}$, and a first class boy aged about 16, no signal man being allowed to the ship, nor were spy glasses of any sort allowed by the service, but had to be purchased at the officers' private expense.

The *Encounter* was on 'particular service' in home waters; the first time I went to sea was on a trip to Queenstown and back directly after I joined. We fell into a south-west gale and had to put in both to Torbay and to Falmouth for shelter; the ship rolled quickly and heavily, but curiously enough, though I was often sea-sick afterwards, the excitement of my first voyage prevented my being so then.

We went to bring back the navigating crew of the *Ajax*, and on our return the midshipmen's berth was well filled, and I had my first experience of a cheerful musical evening, enlivened by grog and by some songs by a jovial old second master, which do not all bear repeating.

Perhaps I should here say that a 'second master' was of the same rank as a then 'mate' (now sub-lieutenant) and was the same intermediate step between master assistant and master that a mate then was between midshipman and lieutenant.

Our First Lieutenant was Roderick Dew, a man full of energy and life, with a sense of humour often displayed, and with a command of strong language rarely equalled.

No greater change has come in the service than the cessation of swearing at the men. In the 'fifties no exercise aloft ever went on without it in most ships ; and many officers would have thought a youngster wanting in zeal who never accentuated his orders and appeals to the men. Indeed in those days many officers might well have kept in mind the third verse of the 141st Psalm.

In those days the chief things required in a man-of-war were smart men aloft, cleanliness of the ship, her hammocks, and her boats. Her gunnery was quite a secondary thing. I have heard very good officers of that date say that if a ship's boats and hammocks were in first-rate order you might depend that all was well with her.

Target practice in those days was carried out as follows. The ship was anchored, and the target, often a cask with a flag on it, was laid out and moored at exactly so many yards from the ship, measured by sextant angle of her mast-head from the boat with the target, probably at about 600 yards.

The range being then well known, firing was steadily conducted. Anything less like an action between two ships can hardly be imagined. We certainly manage these matters better now.

Our next service was to lie guardship to H.M. the Queen at Cowes at Christmas time, a period then spent by the Court at Osborne. After that we were ordered to Bristol to enter seamen for the Navy.

4

My readers must remember this was before the continuous service days of the Navy, and that when ships commissioned they had to enter men how they could, and a seaman, whatever his rating, belonged to the service for that ship's commission, whether it was for one year or five years or more, and then was as free as if he had never served at all.

To Bristol we went, and passed up the river under where the Clifton suspension bridge now is; a hawser only was then stretched across, with a basket in which some adventurous people were hauled over. We passed through the Cumberland basin and into the river beyond, and lay there two or three weeks, probably the only man-of-war that ever lay in the Avon.

We were often with the Channel Fleet, then all sailing vessels, and exercise aloft was frequent.

The *Encounter* was, I think, the smartest ship aloft with her spars and sails that I ever served in. After drill aloft with the Channel Squadron, I have seen her sometimes so much in advance, and finished so long before the other ships, that the Captain proposed to turn the hands up to see the other ships finish.

During the winter of 1852–3 we were more than once at anchor at Spithead with the Channel Squadron, in a gale of wind with lower yards and topmasts struck, and no communication with the shore for a whole day. In those days no steamboats existed.

In April the ship went into dockyard hands at Portsmouth to ship new boilers, and we were all put to live in the *Dryad* hulk. She was an old frigate moored close to the logs in front of the Hard. In her we spent a few weeks with discipline much relaxed, and very varied visitors from the shore.[1]

I think young officers of the present day cannot imagine what life in a midshipmen's berth was then sometimes like. If they want to form a just idea, let them read some of Smollett, or a description in ' Rattlin the Reefer ' of his joining his ship.

In the 'fifties many convicts worked in Portsmouth dockyard, and lived at night in two hulks moored just inside Blockhouse point. They were herded in cells holding several men, and could look through the gun ports, which were strongly barred. I have known naval officers pull round these hulks and chaff the gaol birds, who were not backward in repartee, more forcible than refined.

There was a story told of an empty mud barge returning into Portsmouth Harbour, and as she passed close by a man-of-war, some one on board the latter very improperly called out to the two bargees, ' There's a rat in your fore-chains,' which was well-known barge chaff. The only reply made was by one bargee saying to the other loud enough to be heard in the ship, ' Bill,

[1] If anyone wishes to get an idea of life in a midshipmen's mess at that time, let them read the first chapter of *Hurrah for the Life of a Sailor*—which I recommend,—written by my old messmate and friend, Admiral Sir William Kennedy.

it's werry 'ard we seldom comes into Portsmouth Harbour without meeting with a —— fool ! '

I was only eight months in the *Encounter*, and as she had no naval instructor I was then moved to a ship that carried one.

CHAPTER II

H.M.S. *TERRIBLE*

Naval Review — Sir Edmund Lyons — Sinope — Odessa — Ship grounding — Russian Steamer — Wreck of *Tiger* — Off Sevastopol—The Cholera.

IN July 1853 I joined H.M.S. *Terrible*, then fitting out at Woolwich, which in those days was one of our dockyards. Arriving by train one evening, a boat with a few boys were sent to bring me off ; the tide was low and covered the bottom of a long flight of stone steps, to what depth I knew not ; my chest with all my possessions in it took charge of the boys and all plunged into the water at the bottom, but luckily found it only a foot or so deep ; this was chance and good luck.

The *Terrible* was a paddle-wheel steam frigate of 21 guns. Built about 1846, she was always the finest paddle-wheel man-of-war in our Navy. Her tonnage was 1847, her horse-power 800 nominal, her extreme full speed nearly 13 knots, then wonderful for a man-of-war. Her guns seven 68-pounders 95 cwt., the heaviest in the service or anywhere, four 10-inch hollow shot 84-cwt. guns, and ten 8-inch hollow shot ones. Complement of men 300. When built, indeed, she

8

was the most powerfully armed steamship afloat. This was her third commission.

Her Captain was J. J. McCleverty, and a more cool and courageous man never I believe wore the British uniform, as one or two occasions in that ship showed.

We took part in the Naval Review at Spithead, on 11th August 1853, in the presence of H.M. Queen Victoria, the chief naval interest being centred in H.M.S. *Duke of Wellington*, 121 guns, a new ship and the first screw three-decker in the world. She was launched at Pembroke in 1852 as the *Windsor Castle*, but on the death of the Duke of Wellington in September of that year, the Queen ordered the ship to be named after that splendid soldier.

It may interest naval officers to hear that the first appearance of semaphore on board ship was at the above review, when one was fitted on the taffrails of the steamers to assist in keeping station. We had one; but directly the review was over they were all landed, and were not adopted as a service fitting till about 1870.

At the end of August we were one of the ships accompanying Her Majesty in the *Victoria and Albert* from Holyhead to Kingstown to open the Dublin Exhibition. The *Terrible* was the fastest ship of war that could be found, but the highest speed we were able to go on the run across was 12·8 knots. The Royal Yacht went one or two knots faster. The other three escorting men-of-war were left hull down before we got to Kingstown.

In October 1853 we were ordered to the

Mediterranean station, and to proceed to Spithead to embark Rear-Admiral Sir Edmund Lyons, Bart., and his staff for passage, and to be second in command on that station.

This was in view of the war clouds gathering in the East, and foreshadowing the Crimean War. Sir Edmund Lyons was at that time just 63 years old; he had been made commander at 21, and a captain at 23 in 1814, but was $35\frac{1}{2}$ years on the captains' list, and therefore not made a rear-admiral till he was over 59 years old.

When this is considered one sees how bad was the system of providing officers for the highest ranks of the service. In the early 'fifties there could be no rear-admirals under nearly sixty; the result was that it was often necessary to make first-class commodores instead; which rank is a standing insult to the rear-admirals' list. Sir David Milne was in his eighty-first year while still Commander-in-Chief at Devonport, and many other such cases could be cited.

Mr. Childers rendered a great service to the country by his age retirement scheme. No man after fifty becomes *more* fit in any way in my opinion to perform the duties of an admiral in command at sea, especially if under the strain of war. Some men no doubt last longer than others, but if I hear a man over sixty say he is as fit for the above as he was at forty, I say he is evidently too old already.

Sir Edmund Lyons had just had the experience (for the naval officer on the active list an extraordinary one) of a diplomatic career, having been our Minister at Athens since 1835, a service he had admirably performed.

But in these days we cannot imagine a naval officer, after nearly twenty years on shore, hoisting his flag at sea!

However, changes in ships went slowly in those days, and Admiral Benbow might have taken command of a sailing line-of-battle ship in 1853 and only remarked that she was larger, and the guns heavier, than he had been used to.

We called at Gibraltar, my first foreign port, and at Malta; and passing Constantinople, joined the allied French and English Fleets at anchor in Beikos Bay on 24th November. On the arrival of H.M.S. *Agamemnon*, Sir Edmund Lyons shifted his flag to her on 28th December.

By this time few could doubt that war must follow. On 30th November occurred the Sinope [1] affair when a Russian squadron under Admiral Nachimoff entered the harbour of Sinope, and destroyed a Turkish squadron of very inferior force at anchor there.

This action on the part of Russia has been severely criticised, but the two countries were virtually at war, and so I consider it was legitimate; the only questions being: Should the Turkish squadron have been given a fair chance of surrendering? and, Did the Russians continue their fire longer than was necessary when resistance had ceased?

---

[1] Readers of Thackeray's *Rose and the Ring* may not be aware that Sinope is the ancient Paflagonia where King Valoroso XXIV reigned.

On 4th January 1854 we accompanied the combined English and French Fleets into the Black Sea for a short cruise, and then returned to the Bosphorus ; this was a very definite demonstration to Russia of our intention to support Turkey.

On the 6th we visited Sinope, and I was much interested at seeing for the first time the result of a fight, in the wrecks of the Turkish squadron, and their demolished batteries.

On 24th March the combined Fleet left the Bosphorus for good, and proceeded to Kavarna Bay, which now became their principal rendezvous till the expedition left for the invasion of the Crimea.

On 9th April a general signal from the *Britannia* told us that war was declared against Russia, and it was of course received with cheers.

On the 17th the Fleet left for Odessa and anchored off it on the 20th, it being decided to bombard that place. I am aware that this proceeding has been adversely criticised by some ; but I think it was quite justified by two things : first, that a flag of truce sent in by the *Furious* just before we heard of war, to bring away our Consul, had been fired on ; and, second, that many English and French merchant ships trading to Odessa when war was declared were not allowed to leave. Several of them under cover of our attack succeeded in escaping.

On 22nd April 1854 the first shot in the war may be said to have been fired. The bombardment was conducted by five English paddle-

BOMBARDMENT OF ODESSA, BEING THE FIRST ACTION IN THE CRIMEAN WAR

H.M.S. Terrible in the foreground

1854

wheel steamers, viz. the *Sampson*, *Retribution*, *Tiger*, *Furious*, and *Terrible*, and three French ones, viz. the *Mogador*, *Vauban*, and *Descartes*. We were divided into two divisions, the idea being that all would not be engaged at once. The action began about 6.30 A.M. and lasted with intervals till after 4 P.M., partly under way and partly at anchor.

At about 1.30 P.M. the magazine on the Mole blew up, a fine sight to us.

Besides the steamers some rocket boats were sent in from the Fleet to set fire to the shipping ; and a pretty episode resembling olden days took place in the *Arethusa*, a 50-gun sailing frigate, then commanded by Captain W. R. Mends,[1] standing in under sail and engaging the outer batteries ; this being, I believe, the last time that an English man-of-war was ever in action under sail.

One's first experience of warfare is not the less impressive on the mind, if it occurs when one is not quite fourteen years old.

On 25th April we left for Constantinople, chiefly to take despatches, and on 4th May we rejoined the Fleet cruising off Sevastopol. This was our first sight of that great sea fortress, of which really very little was known to the world at large, and I firmly believe that if in the year 1853 you had asked at an ordinary London dinner party, ' What and where is Sevastopol ? ' very few people could have given you a proper answer.

We were very ill informed as to the number

---

[1] Afterwards Admiral Sir William Mends, G.C.B., and the splendid organiser of the trooping and transport service generally.

of Russian troops in the Crimea. In those days of innocence, ignorance, or indifference — which was it?—intelligence departments existed not with us, and the world generally was not as occupied with military matters as it is now.

The allied fleets cruised off Sevastopol for several days under sail, often in thick fog, and I remember one day a French line-of-battle ship looming out of the fog close to our starboard beam, both ships barely moving and ours just clearing her by putting men in our paddle-wheels to turn them, the wheels being of course disconnected from the engines. The Russian ships remained inside their harbour.

At this time we heard the sad news of the loss of H.M.S. *Tiger* on 12th May. In a thick fog she ran on shore under a high cliff four miles from Odessa. The Russians soon saw her and opened fire with field-pieces and small-arms, which she could hardly return.

It was soon evident she could not be saved, so her Captain (H. W. Giffard) ordered the ship to be set on fire and the crew to land. They were, of course, made prisoners. Among other casualties the Captain was mortally wounded and his nephew, a midshipman of the same name, was killed.

During the summer of 1854 we were chiefly employed in reconnoitring Sevastopol, in company with one or two other ships, English or French. We generally arranged so as to appear off the harbour at daylight, so as to close it as near as their guns' range allowed, before a superior force of ships could be sent to drive us off.

On one occasion, on 23rd August, we were nearly lost like the *Tiger*. We, with the *Fury* in company, arrived off Sevastopol early one morning, and finding some of their line-of-battle ships outside, we were running to the northward along the coast. After going a few miles we saw a boat pulling in for the land, and, wishing to cut her off, we edged a little more in shore.

It was my morning watch and I was on the forecastle getting a gun pointed on the boat, when suddenly I felt the deck rise under me, and heard a noise like the beaching of a boat on shingle.

We had struck on a shoal running out from the land. The ship rolled but held her way.

One's immediate thought was, Shall we be a second *Tiger*? And the alternatives between being killed in defending the ship, or put in a Russian prison, loomed before us ; but happily our ship being at full speed saved us, and we got clear over the reef though with much damage to the keel and planking near it. Such moments are anxious ones, especially to those in command.

On 15th June off Sevastopol in company with the *Furious* we found the Russian squadron at sea with six men-of-war steamers. These last stood toward us and we let them come within range. The wind was blowing towards Sevastopol, so their sailing ships could only stand out close hauled.

The steamers hoisted Russian ensigns at their mast-heads, and all looked promising for a sea fight. Much enthusiasm existed on board us, officers got their pistols ready and non-executive officers volunteered to fight the boats' brass guns.

However, after mutually exchanging shots for about two hours, the Russians seemed to think they were getting too far from their fleet, and turned back to rejoin their line-of-battle ships, we following as far as was reasonable, on account of the latter.

This was the only case in the Black Sea during the war of vessels under way engaging each other.

Our frequent reconnoitring duty was to count the ships in Sevastopol; their entire fleet seemed to be three three-deckers, ten two-deckers, five frigates, and six steamers. The land defences of the south side looked very slight indeed, as was found, at first, to be the case.

On 8th July in the evening we arrived off the Sulina mouth of the Danube a few hours too late to take part in an attack by the boats of the *Firebrand* and *Vesuvius* on some Russian works just inside the river. This operation was commanded by Captain Hyde Parker of the *Firebrand*, who, while leading his men with great gallantry, was shot through the heart.

On 13th July we and the *Furious* went to Cape Fontane, where the *Tiger* was lost, and opened fire on her wreck in order to destroy the machinery, lest the Russians should make use of it.

They brought field-pieces to the edge of the cliffs and returned our fire, but we succeeded in silencing them, and then did what we wanted. As soon as the field-pieces retired, and the Russians saw that our fire was only continued on the wreck, the cliffs were covered with people, many women among them, to watch the proceedings, as if all was friendliness.

It was a very pretty sight to arrive off Sevastopol early on a lovely summer morning, and see the fine white town girt as to its sea shores with massive grey granite forts ; and beyond the town on the south side the ground sloping upwards, and often covered with many white tents, where the allied armies' lines and batteries were soon to be made.

The harbour displaying a fine fleet all ready for sea, and all as it were smiling in the sunny morning, and as little foretelling the really awful destruction of life and property, and the frightful human suffering, which a few months was to witness there.

Tolstoy's ' Sevastopol ' is a work half history, half novel, but to my mind it puts very vividly before its reader what life in the town was like during the siege.

Our cruises off Sevastopol were varied by lying at anchor off Baljick in Kavarna Bay, some fifteen miles to the eastward of Varna, where the allied armies were assembling.

In July the cholera broke out among the troops, commencing with the French, who eventually lost most men by it, and soon after, in August, it attacked the ships also.

The *Britannia*, the flagship of our Commander-in-Chief, Vice-Admiral Sir James Dundas, lost 50 in one night, and 10 the next day ; and three of the French three-deckers lost respectively 152, 120, and 80 men.

The transports were beginning to assemble to take the army to the Crimea; and when our line-of-battle ships went out for a cruise in hopes of improving the men's health, our ship and another were left to guard the transports.

In a few days our ships returned with the cholera no less on board, and I and others were employed in going alongside the large ships and taking the men ill, some dying with cholera, in our boats to the transports. This, however, did not give the cholera to any of our men, which, added to my further experience in other parts of the world, has made me regard that disease as non-infectious. No doubt others in the same locality and conditions of air or water may be liable for the same reasons to take it, but vicinity to patients does not, by my experience, seem to give it.

In all the ships that had the epidemic the proportion of officers affected was very small indeed.

CHAPTER III

Expedition to the Crimea—Battle of the Alma—Siege begins 17th October—Bombardment of Sevastopol.

ALL this time the preparations for the Crimean expedition were maturing at Varna : the transport part and the embarking and landing programme were progressing under the immediate supervision of Sir Edmund Lyons, his Flag Captain, Captain W. R. Mends, late of the *Arethusa*, being, I believe, really the chief hand in the naval part of the scheme and arrangements, his military colleague being, principally, Sir George Brown.

It is not my part or object to dwell on the general proceedings of this great expedition, which have been so well described by several historians. Everyone admits the almost perfect part played by our Navy in the embarkation, transporting, and landing of our troops.

Finally we left the anchorage off Baljick on 7th September with the Fleet and transports in company.

The next day we joined up with our allies, the French and Turkish Fleets at sea, about thirty miles south of Serpent Island, and, after about a week's passage the landing of the armies at Old Fort was completed by about the 18th September.

The disembarkation was on a low beach, without shelter from the sea, but the weather was on the whole favourable, and the enemy as is known attempted no opposition.

There was then no steamboats, which would now accelerate matters. Our paddle-box boats were much the largest in the service, they drew very little water and were most useful for landing men and horses ; a platform was in many cases built on two boats placed side by side, and on this a large number of soldiers stood and were thus conveyed to the shore.

During this time we were often off Sevastopol watching the Russian ships. Some people have, I believe, blamed them for not coming out and attacking the transports ; but, when the comparative force of the allied squadrons and of the Russians is considered, I think any such charge is absurd.

It seems now very curious that opinions were much divided as to where the landing in the Crimea should be—from Eupatoria even to Kaffa places were suggested ; but such variety of opinions may be expected in the case of allied forces of different nations.

On 19th September the armies moved towards Sevastopol, the Fleet accompanying them, if the term may be allowed; that is, keeping abreast along the coast. On the 20th the Battle of the Alma was fought, so called after the small river of that name.

We on board the ships had a very fair side view of the battle, which, considering its import- ance, occupied a very short time. The Crimean campaign is now 'ancient history' and therefore public opinion is probably but lukewarm about it. It is not for me to criticise, but I have no hesitation in saying that after the Battle of the Alma, the allies could have gone straight into the north side, and thus captured Sevastopol with very little, if any, further loss.

I know this not only from reading, but from talking in after years with French and with Russian officers who were present there.

The result of our not doing so, but sitting down before the place for a siege, was no doubt to bleed Russia through an extremity. But that was not what the expedition was sent for. It was to take Sevastopol, and capture or destroy the Russian Fleet, and when commanders, naval or military, are by their Governments, or superiors, ordered to do a thing, I presume their duty is to do it — if they can — and as quickly and with as little loss to their own forces as may be.

Any student of the Crimean campaign can see various errors that were committed; but at least two brilliant facts stand out: one, that, on the whole, good relations were maintained between the allied commanders and forces; and, second, the great courage generally displayed by the troops of both the allies and of the Russians.

After the Battle of the Alma the French Commander-in-Chief, Marshal St. Arnaud, became so ill that he had to leave for home and was succeeded by General Canrobert, and the flank march, so called, to move round the town towards Balaklava and invest the south side of Sevastopol was carried out.

It would seem that the allied commanders did not know they could have at once taken the north side, and if so the southern position for a long siege had this immense indisputable advantage, that it gave the allies Balaklava harbour and the Kazatch and Kameish creeks as sheltered places for shipping and landing operations ; none such existing to the north side.

For the Russians the advantage of the above was, that during all the siege, reinforcements and supplies could be, and were, constantly arriving by land. The south side of Sevastopol had but scanty land defences ; evidently a sea attack was what had always been expected and prepared for, and I believe that if the city had been at once stormed on the south side, it would have been taken. I form my opinions partly from what Russian officers, who were there, have told me.

I will not attempt any account of the operations, which can be very well obtained from various well-known works ; but only say that, it being decided that the English should take the right attack and the French the left, we were given

Balaklava as our principal port, and the French took Kameish creek, which is to the westward of the city; we also having a smaller one, the Kazatch creek, which is again west of Kameish.

The allies now set to work to prepare their siege batteries, which were armed very greatly with ships' guns, manned by a Naval Brigade from the Fleet, as well as by the military siege train worked by artillerymen.

The Russians under that great soldier General Todleben at the same time threw up bastions, which were also principally armed with guns from their ships.

Comparatively little fire was exchanged until the 17th October, which date the Russians still celebrate as the real opening of the siege.

The question of what active part the ships should take in the attack on the forts was, I believe, found difficult to settle; I will only say that the Admirals decided to bombard the sea defences on the day that the shore batteries opened fire. During that time the allied fleets were mostly at anchor off the Katcha River to the north-east of Sevastopol.

At times the *Terrible* and other steamers passed by the north shore of Sevastopol to reconnoitre, and exchanged long shots with the earthworks on the cliff. There was one especially noted called the 'Wasp.' We had four 68-pounders 95 cwt. mounted on broadside carriages, on the main deck.

These we got up on deck, and cut the carriages so as to give them greater elevation, when we got them to carry about 4000 yards in distance—then thought extraordinary. The 'Wasp's' guns ranged about the same distance.

About daybreak on the 17th the allied batteries opened fire, and were at once replied to by the Russians with great vigour.

It had at first been proposed that the ships should also go into action early in the day, but this was deferred to midday, and I think wisely, as it was desired not to expend too much ammunition at first, which a whole day's firing would have done ; and to have begun early in the day, and retired at midday after a few hours, would have seemed like a defeat, which it did not do when they only hauled out as night came on.

The sea bombardment of Sevastopol did not hasten the fall of the place by one hour, but I think it was right to have it, as its result could not be certainly foretold, and its object greatly was to force the Russians to have a large number of men employed in manning the sea defences.

The bombardment by the ships began about 1 P.M. on the 17th, the Russians first firing on the leading French ships.

At 1.15 the Admiral signalled 'Sampson, Tribune and Terrible engage the enemy,' and our Fleet moved into action. We began firing, and at dark returned to our anchorage off the Katcha River, with the Fleets.

There was a good deal of unpleasant talk as to the part played by some vessels, and the positions they took up during the action, but of this I shall say nothing except that the English ships which occupied the best position for damaging the enemy were the *Agamemnon* (flagship of Sir Edmund Lyons) and the *Sans Pareil* (Captain Sydney Dacres). These were the only steam line-of-battle ships in our Fleet, which of course gave them great manœuvring advantages.

Human nature does not alter much, and I imagine that in past days after every general action opinions were divided as to who played the best part. I have, however, little sympathy with those who try to enhance their own prowess by running down the conduct of others.

I cannot refrain from mentioning the gallant performance of the *Circassia*, a small paddle-wheel tugboat brought into the service and commanded by Mr. Ball, a second master.[1]

She steamed in ahead of the *Agamemnon*, sounding carefully and signalling the depth of water, to prevent the latter from running on the shoals off the north side of the harbour's mouth. All the sailing line-of-battle ships had steam men-of-war lashed alongside them to tow.

The general formation of the combined Fleets was a crescent, the French being to the south-west, the English to the north-east, and the Turkish ships between the two. The shoals off the northern point of the mouth of the harbour were a great danger, and one or two of our ships actually touched on them.

The *Agamemnon* claimed to have been within 800 yards of Fort Constantine, which was a large stone fort close to the water on the north side.

---

[1] Equal in rank to a navigating sub-lieutenant.

After the bombardment we observed men at work repairing some of the forts, especially Fort Constantine.

Had it been decided that *coûte que coûte* the sea defences of Sevastopol should be disabled by the fire of the ships, I suppose the way would have been to provide plenty of ammunition, and then, dividing the allied fleets into three divisions, continue the attack during daylight hours till the object was attained, hoping then to enter the harbour and isolate the south side of the city from the north.

I have little personal to say about the action; a naval cadet hardly can have. I was stationed at the fore main deck quarters, and from the bridle ports at times had a pretty good view. It was certainly the greatest noise I have ever heard, and when one considers that all the allied land breaching batteries, and some twenty-three sail of the line, besides smaller vessels, were firing away as hard as they could, and that the Russians from hundreds of guns were replying, the noise made may be imagined.

Shells in those days were but playthings compared to modern projectiles, but I remember one coming into our quarters and bursting, and, besides the actual harm it did, filling the place with such thick smoke that for a few minutes nothing could be seen at the quarters.

The Russians fired some mortar shells at the ships, but very few hit—I only remember that one fell on a French ship and burst; they would, of course, be first rate against modern armour-plated ships, and, as we know, most sea defence citadels now have guns for that purpose.

It had been expected by the Generals that the bombardment of the 17th would be followed shortly by an assault on the town ; but I suppose the Russian strength, indicated by their return fire, deterred the allies from the attempt.

Probably the first apparent injury done was the destruction of the white stone tower on the Malakoff, which a very few hours' firing brought down.[1]

The next great event in the Crimea was the Battle of Balaklava on 25th October, but its history is no part of my memoir. I will only say that some field-pieces lent by us to the Turks to assist in the defence of Balaklava were captured by the Russians. I have seen them at the Kremlin in Moscow. They were, I believe, the only guns lost by us during the war.

As regards the Turks, no braver private soldiers, when properly led, than they are—unless it be the Japanese—probably exist, as is well known ; but as regards the Sevastopol part of the war, neither by land nor sea did the Turks play a conspicuous part.

The third, and most severe, field fight was the Battle of Inkerman on 5th November ; this very distantly by spy-glasses could be seen from

---

[1] Some achieve mundane immortality—so called—in odd ways. The Malakoff hill, I believe, is named after a purser in the Russian Navy of that name, who having been dismissed the service set up a drink shop at the above place ; the Russians being thirsty souls frequented it, and it acquired the name of its publican.

some of the ships, but it is not for me to relate this hard-won fight, a ' soldiers' battle ' as it was.

A desperate struggle in which our troops being on the right or east side of the allied camps bore the first and, perhaps, the chief part of the day's strife ; but had we not been splendidly reinforced and supported by the French, the day would have gone very hard with us.

CHAPTER IV

H.M.S. *TERRIBLE* (continued)

Fourteenth November Gale of Wind—Off Sevastopol—The
Commanders—Night Attack—Kertch—The Trenches—The
Siege—Fall of Sevastopol—Kinburn.

'Du sublime au ridicule il n'y a qu'un pas,' though
not so for me on the 11th November, when I was
rated midshipman, having been two years in the
Navy, and I much doubt if any subsequent promotion has given me more, or even as much
pleasure.

The 14th November was a day to us nearly as
exciting as the 17th October, for on it occurred
the great gale of wind. Till then we were at
anchor off the Katcha River as close in as
possible to protect the watering-place from the
Cossacks, which for the moment was our special
duty.

Speaking of the Cossacks reminds me of how
ubiquitous they seemed to be: usually when we
neared the coast of the Crimea, almost anywhere,
two Cossacks mounted on small horses appeared
patrolling the cliffs or sea shore. From the

Katcha the Fleet obtained fresh water to drink. Most of our vessels were sailing ships, and in steamers at that date distilling fresh water was in a very elementary and crude condition.

The great gale of the 14th was from the westward. It began at about 9.0 A.M. where we were. We let go a second anchor, veered nearly all the cable we could, got up steam and began steaming slowly ahead to take the strain off our cables. This has saved many a ship, but is a difficult thing to do, without at times bringing a heavy jerk on the cables. We being close in shore were almost in the breakers.

Next outside us lay the *Sampson*, a paddle-wheel ship. The line-of-battle ships were further out, and many sailing transports were also anchored at intervals among the Fleet.

By 10.30 the gale was at its highest, and several transports were dragging their anchors and going on shore without any possibility of saving them.

About this time a transport ahead of the *Sampson* began drifting, and fouled another, which then also broke adrift. Both these ships came athwart the hawse of the *Sampson* as I was watching it. The *Sampson* gave a dive, and her bowsprit striking the transport turned up at a right angle. Next moment all three of her lower masts gave way and fell aft, reminding me of the dominoes which a child sometimes puts up to knock each other over.

The transports then drifted clear of the

Sampson, and went on shore. The *Sampson,* wonderful to relate, held on and was saved.

Her captain, a grand old sailor,[1] as soon as possible cleared the wreck of his masts, hoisted an ensign and pennant on jury spars, and asked leave by signal to fire on the Cossacks.

Our turn was soon to come.

It had been my forenoon watch, during which the wind was so strong that it was really hard at times to walk forward in the teeth of it. In those days midshipmen dined at 12 o'clock on what they could get to eat, in our case while blockading Sevastopol not much beyond ship's allowance.

I had just finished dinner and was sitting in the midshipmen's berth talking to my messmate, Armand Powlett,[2] when we felt a heavy shock, and heard water pouring down the large hatchway just outside us in the steerage. We jumped up and ran up the ladders on deck as fast as we could, went over to the starboard side of the quarter deck and held on to the main topsail halliards. The ship was nearly broadside on to the sea, rolling heavily, and the waves were sweeping over her and rushing below. It seemed as if she could not be saved, and onlookers from the other ships thought so.

What had happened was that, while steaming ahead to take the strain off the cables, they had got slack and a sea striking the ship on her starboard bow, had paid her head off to port, the best bower cable (i.e. the starboard one) had

---

[1] Afterwards Admiral Sir Lewis Tobias Jones.
[2] Now Admiral.

parted, and, as our only chance, the other was slipped, the helm put hard down, and the engines moved ahead at full speed. Relieving tackles were on the tiller below, without which, owing to a mishap to the wheel on deck, the helm could not have been kept down.

Our Captain had got on the starboard paddle-box, which was the weather one. He was as cool as if in a snug harbour, or a dead calm. A tremendous sea now struck the ship nearly on her broadside, lifting the starboard paddle-box boat, throwing it in amidships, and knocking the Captain off the paddle-box on to the deck where, fortunately, he was not hurt, but at once climbed up again.

The ship was now almost in the breakers and her keel could not have been far from the bottom; however, she responded to her helm, and her bow came up head to wind and sea. Then she began to go ahead, got out to sea and was saved.

So much water, however, had been shipped that in the stokehold thirteen out of our total of twenty-four fires were put out, and probably all would have been extinguished and the ship lost had not the chief engineer, with great presence of mind, ordered the stokehold plates on which the stokers stood to be unshipped, which allowed the water to get down into the bilges. It was what is called ' a very narrow squeak,' but all was well.

The great gale of 14th November was felt disastrously chiefly where we were, off Balaklava, and at Eupatoria. At the latter place was lost the *Henri Quatre*, a very fine two-decked French line-of-battle ship of 100 guns. The beach she was driven on was of shifting sand; no one was drowned, but the ship was driven up so high, broadside on, that I have walked along a brow stretched from her lower deck port to the shore.

Off Balaklava, that is outside it, the loss of ships and of life was terrible. The anchorage was very deep; anchors were often let go in 40 fathoms, and the shore was, in fact, cliffs of rock, 'steep to' as the expression is. Against these precipices several transports were driven, fortunately without troops on board, but their hapless crews were there, and were nearly all lost.

The *Prince*, a large steamer, was one so lost. She had, only a few days before, arrived from England with the 46th Regiment on board, and a quantity of ammunition and warm clothing. By an odd chance I had myself been sent on board her on her arrival, but not to remain there. Happily she had time to land the regiment before the gale came on, but almost all her cargo and nearly all of the crew were lost. Great misery was caused to the troops on shore. They were almost entirely in tents, many of which were blown down, and even blown away.

At Eupatoria, where several men-of-war and transports were lying, besides the *Henri Quatre* already mentioned, a Turkish line-of-battle ship, a French man-of-war steamer, and several merchant ships were lost.

The total loss of ships of all sorts during the gale of the 14th was about forty-two. It was a great satisfaction to us that no English man-of-war was lost.

The winter was now upon us, it was a dreary time for everyone both ashore and afloat. The Generals had decided to put off the next assault *sine die*, and only to invest the south side of the city by land.

The Fleet's duty was to blockade closely by sea.

We were frequently at anchor off the harbour's mouth day and night with steam all but up, a small anchor down, guns cleared away and loaded, and at night the watch lying down near their quarters in case a Russian ship ventured out.

On 7th December early in the afternoon the *Vladimir*, the most powerful of the Russian steamers, did come out far enough to shell the western French camp, but returned before she could be cut off. None of our ships were off the harbour at the moment; we were coaling, but our steam was nearly up, and we were soon off to help to drive her in, the *Valorous* just ahead of us.

On 20th December, Vice-Admiral Dundas, Commander-in-Chief on the station, his three years having expired, gave up the command to Sir Edmund Lyons, and sailed in the *Furious* on his way home.

Admiral Dundas, on the breaking out of the war, found himself in a very awkward position, as he felt his age and failing strength unequal to the work now imposed upon him.

His successor, Sir Edmund Lyons then 64 years old, was wonderfully active for his age. We all greatly admired him, and to me and my mess-mate, Armand Powlett, he showed much kindness.

Letters from Sir Edmund's Flag-captain speak with great affection and admiration of him, but show that he also felt the burden of his years, and that, though a better officer for the post could probably not have been found, he would ten years earlier have been even more efficient.

My experience makes me a great advocate of age retirement, and indeed I believe the country would greatly benefit if such a regulation existed for ALL paid servants of the State under the Crown.

Many men as they get old ' lose their nerve,' as it is called; how should I define it ? A more lively apprehension of the possibility of mishap perhaps fits it. As regards the Crimean Generals, there were three English Commanders-in-Chief and also three French, as is well known. The first French one had to leave for ill-health after the Alma; the second, a brave man, could not bear the responsibility; the third, General Pelissier, was in my opinion the great soldier of the allied forces, strong and determined.

As regards our three Generals, the first, Lord Raglan, was a most high-minded and gallant gentleman, but his age, and perhaps the strain of having lost his right arm, were against his con-stantly being out and about. The second was but a short time in command ; of him I will say no more. The third had no real opportunity of doing much.

D 2

But to return to my story.

Night attacks by single ships, or two or three in company, were occasionally made on the sea batteries, in which we at times took part. Lights were placed on buoys laid down for the purpose of guiding the ships where to go, and we steamed in a curve in front of the harbour, delivering one or two broadsides towards the town; and as we did so our ships were occasionally hit by the return fire.

The *Valorous* was the first ship to make a night attack, and one of her shells passed through the room in which the famous General Todleben was sleeping.

On the night of 18th June, Captain Lyons, of the *Miranda*, the son of Sir Edmund, while so engaged was severely wounded in the leg, and died a few days after. This was a terrible grief to our beloved Admiral.

Early in April we were sent to assist in laying the submarine electric telegraph cable from Varna to St. George's Monastery, the western point of the Crimea. In those days submarine cables were rare things.

Off Cape Kaliakra we lay several days, and used to visit there the ruins of a grand old Genoese castle, built on a high rocky point—a relic of the long-departed power of Genoa.

Early in May we accompanied the first expedition towards Kertch, the objects being to take that place, enter the Sea of Azoff, destroy Russian stores of food and do all we could to prevent supplies reaching Sevastopol from that direction.

This expedition, owing to the fickleness of General Canrobert, the French Commander-in-Chief, was recalled before it got to the Straits of Yenkale at the entrance of the Sea of Azoff.

On General Pelissier succeeding to the command of the French army a second Kertch expedition was at once arranged. We carried French troop horses. The expedition consisted of about 15,000 troops, which were landed without opposition on 24th May. In fact our force was overwhelming compared to the enemy's.

Kertch was pillaged and looted by the allies. I remember entering its museum; the building was still standing, but its contents destroyed or taken away. Outside the doors was the inscription in French to the effect that we were at war with the present and not with antiquity, &c. The notice taken of it was to carry off what people could, and smash the rest. This, however, was only in keeping with what has usually happened in war.

The Sea of Azoff is very shallow, and is getting shallower by degrees. Our light vessels went into it and did what destruction they could.

Off Sevastopol, at times during the summer of 1855, I and others got leave to visit the camps for a few days and to go into the trenches. This was, of course, a great treat for us. I used to stay with the 93rd Sutherland Highlanders, a splendid set of men to my recollection, and their brigade was under the command of no less a man than Colin Campbell, the future Lord Clyde.

In the Crimea for most of the time, at least

until wooden huts came out, the regimental officers' messes did not exist. A few of the officers, some five or six, formed a scratch mess and fared as best they could. I remember the names of those I used to stay with. Some were killed in the Mutiny in India, and I fear all have died ere now.

The guard of the trenches was changed every evening, for twenty-four hours; this was in order that they might be as fresh as possible during the night, when of course sorties from the city usually took place.

Some midshipmen used to try and raise their uniform caps on sticks above the parapet of the trench hoping the Russian sharpshooters might send bullets through them, so that the caps would show the narrow escape they had had. This, however, was not approved, as likely to draw fire on the trenches. In wet weather the trenches were misery, the choice at times being between standing in water, or getting no shelter.

On 18th June took place the first great assault on the city, preceded by a heavy bombardment from the allied land batteries. The ships were many of them under way off the harbour, and I believe their bombarding was arranged for, but prevented by the stormy wind blowing in.

We knew an assault was to take place, but, though we could hear heavy firing going on, we did not till next morning know that we had all been defeated, the French beaten off from the Malakoff and Bastion du Mât, and the English from the Great Redan.

On 28th June Lord Raglan died, his death, I believe, partly caused by anxiety, and by grief at our repulse in the assault of the 18th. His local funeral was a great ceremony, consisting of the embarkation of his body in H.M.S. *Caradoc* for conveyance to England.[1]

From June to September the siege went on without any very special incident. The leading spirit was the French Commander-in-Chief, partly from his commanding temperament, but also because the French army greatly outnumbered ours, being about double our force in numbers, and they had in consequence three-quarters of the whole land attack, that is all the left, or western, half of it, and the extreme right, or eastern, quarter ; we keeping the quarter between the French trenches.

This placed us still opposite the Redan, the French being opposed to the Malakoff on the right, and to the Bastion du Mât, or central bastion, on the left. I believe that either of the above three places if taken singly, and held, would have meant the fall of the city.

Towards the close of the siege the allies' mortar fire was much increased and was most efficacious. Our siege batteries too had increased from a total of about 80 guns at the beginning to about 200 before the end. But the French

---

[1] General Pelissier on hearing of Lord Raglan's death at once repaired to his headquarters, and there standing by the side of the departed soldier, who in early life had often fought against the French, and had lost his arm at ' King-making Waterloo,' the French Commander-in-Chief, a man of iron in the field, shed tears over the remains of his lamented colleague.

had done much more, and from 60 guns on 17th October 1854 had now over 300 on their original left-hand attack, and on our right had 260 ; or nearly 600 in all.

The Russians, who also used mortars, had two of 15 inches, our largest being 13-inch ones. The 15-inch shell passing overhead made a whistling sound owing, I believe, to the rings for lifting them up cutting the air. I have heard them. The men gave those mortars in consequence the name of 'Whistling Dick.'

The end was now near, and an assault on 8th September was decided on. On 3rd September all plans were settled.

As regards the Fleet it was intended they should be off the harbour on the 8th and, perhaps, bombard ; for the same object as previously, viz. to keep the sea forts manned, but in view of the allies penetrating into the town, the question of fire from our ships became a difficult one. When the day came, however, it was blowing in too hard from seaward to manœuvre the ships under the forts.

The preliminary bombardment from the batteries began on 5th September and continued on the 6th and 7th. It was heavier than any previons one, and seemed quite to dominate the Russian fire. In those three days they are said to have lost 4000 men.

It was arranged that the French should first storm the Malakoff, and if they succeeded make a signal, on seeing which we should storm the Redan.

At noon (on the 8th) the French made their attack, and got into the Malakoff; the Russians were somewhat taken by surprise, and fought furiously to turn their enemy out, but could not. I believe the Malakoff was a complete fort all round, and not open to the rear, which made it harder for them to pour in reinforcements. The taking of the Malakoff effected the capture of Sevastopol.

At about 12.10 we made our rush for the Redan, but two things were against us which the French had not. First the distance from their advanced trench to the position was only about thirty paces,[1] while we had 200 yards of the open to cross; second, the Russians were now all on the alert.

Some of our soldiers got into the Redan, but reinforcements of the enemy drove them out again. I think the siege of Sevastopol may be fairly and shortly summed up thus:

1. Neither we nor the French could have done it alone.

2. The English mainly bore the brunt of the field battles.

3. The French took Sevastopol.

As soon as the Russians found they could not retake the Malakoff, they decided to evacuate the south side (i.e. the city) and retreat to the north side by the bridge of boats which they had completed by the end of August.

This they did in remarkably good order, having

---

[1] I have stood on the Malakoff parapet and talked easily to a man on the French advanced trench position.

set fire to the city and forts in it, blown up the latter, and destroyed the dry docks.

The defence of Sevastopol was splendid and I doubt if in any other siege it has been surpassed. I have often spoken of it to Russians, whom I have always found justly proud, and ready to talk, of it. The morning of the 9th showed the city obscured by heavy smoke from the conflagration, and lit up with occasional explosions.

I had the opportunity of visiting the lines and the city of Sevastopol soon after its capture, and it was of course most interesting. Anyone doing so felt admiration for its defenders. The town was a ruin. The bastions—so called by the Russians—thrown up for the land defence in many cases had a platform of heavy beams, or timber, on which the guns were placed, and underneath were sort of subterranean passages and chambers, in which the men could find some rest and shelter, while still close to, in case of a sudden assault.

Coming out of the town late one evening with a messmate of mine we were caught in the dark and lost our way ; the rain began to fall. My messmate gave it up as a bad job, lay down and said he would stay there. I was very tired, too, and could not carry him ; but luckily found some privates of the 1st Royals who carried him to their camp, where we slept in a bell tent, some dozen in all, feet to the pole in the middle, and heads to the side, with one knapsack for our two heads.

Vermin infested the whole camp, officers'

quarters as well as the men's. These soldiers were most kind to us; money they would not take, but we afterwards managed to send them a case of wine, &c.

On 16th September we took to Odessa the Russian officer who had been in charge of St. George's Monastery near Cape Khersonese and his family, who had in fact been our prisoners. With them went Major Biddulph, R.A., who though in charge of them was himself captivated by a young lady of the family, whom he afterwards married.

The next operation was the taking of Kinburn, which was a fort built on a low narrow spit of land running out west-north-west and defending the entrance of the Bay of Kherson, into which ran the River Dnieper, up which is Nicholaief where all the Black Sea men-of-war were built.

Kinburn itself was a stone fort with casemates, and beyond it on the spit were two separate earthwork batteries.

On 17th October we bombarded the place; our force was perfectly overwhelming and in less than an hour the Russian fire was silenced and the place forced to surrender. About 1300 soldiers, 75 guns, and many mortars were taken.

The French had some floating batteries with ironclad sides engaged on the 11th; it was the first occasion of ironclads being in action.

We then returned to Kazatch near Sevastopol, after which we had very cold and trying work in embarking troops and horses at Eupatoria.

On 16th December we left the Crimea for

the Mediterranean, and first visiting Athens and Smyrna, went to Malta and lay there four months.

On arrival we youngsters felt quite rich with our allowance that could not be spent in the Crimea, but money soon burns a hole in a midshipman's pocket, and our riding and driving about the island had to give way to walking. In those days games were not arranged for as they are now, and their provision has been a great boon to all officers.

While at Malta we were docked and our bottom repaired from the serious injury done to it when we were on the shoal in August 1854.[1] It was remarkable that the ship had stood it so well, the *Teredo navalis* (a sea-worm) had eaten many holes in our timbers where the copper had been knocked off. This same worm was found to have greatly damaged the Russian ships sunk in the harbour of Sevastopol.

Early in June 1856 we returned to the Crimea. The armistice was now on, and much friendly intercourse was exchanged between the allies and the Russians.

I visited the north side of Sevastopol, which was very interesting, especially to see Fort Constantine, and go into the 'Wasp' battery on the north cliff, with which we had often exchanged shots ; and to see the marks of shell on some of the gun carriages, which might have been caused by the fire from our ship. The Russians were very friendly and some were wearing their richly earned Crimean medal.

[1] See p. 15.
44

The evacuation of the Crimea by the allies was now proceeding.

On 15th June we finally left the Crimea, with some Royal Artillery on board, and towing the *Queen*, a three-decker of 116 guns, on her way home also with troops on board. We were now ' homeward bound ' and occasionally passed other ships with bands playing ' Home, Sweet Home,' almost at times the most pathetic of tunes. On 19th July we reached Sheerness, and on 2nd August we were paid off, thus ending a not uneventful commission.

CHAPTER V

H.M.S. *CRUIZER*

Age retirement—Voyage to China—Gunboats.

Six weeks' leave soon passed, but it was as much holiday as a midshipman could expect between commissions. My uncle, Rear-Admiral Sir Michael Seymour, was then Commander-in-Chief of the China, East India, and Australian stations, which in those days were all combined together.

Owing to there being no age retirement the flag-officers were mostly elderly men ; the Mediterranean station generally had a vice-admiral as commander-in-chief, but the other foreign stations only a rear-admiral, or not seldom a commodore of the first class, in order to get young enough men.

My uncle being the Admiral in China it was natural I should wish to join his flagship, to which I was therefore appointed, and was ordered to go out in H.M.S. *Cruizer*.

The *Cruizer* was a full ship rigged sloop, of

about 750 tons, with an auxiliary screw able to drive her for a short time at 6 knots or so in a calm. She carried 17 light 32-pounders and had a complement of 165. Her commander was Charles Fellowes, a first-rate seaman.

I joined her at Portsmouth in September 1856, and at a little over 16 years old found myself the senior officer of the midshipmen's mess, which contained ten of us in all.

I think no one knew any of the others when we started, but we soon found that law and order were not our prevailing characteristics; and long before we reached China the mess-traps were nearly all broken, and what was called a 'radical mess' prevailed.

All ships commanded by officers above the rank of lieutenant in those days carried midshipmen.

The *Cruizer* was a first-rate specimen of how utterly youngsters were disregarded and neglected as to their instruction or care of any sort; and of their behaviour, so long as they did the work, deck, boat, or aloft, that was required of them. The results were, of course, often most unfortunate, and the percentage of those who came to grief was far larger than is ever known now.

Of my messmates in that ship three at least were turned out of the service, and only one besides myself ever became a commander.

We had to convoy to China three gunboats, the first that were ever sent abroad. They were small vessels of 60 horse-power with one screw and three masts, the foremast regularly stepped, the two after fixed in ' tabernacles.' They had only fore and aft standing sails, and a square foresail.

Their dimensions, &c., were as follows: Tonnage, 319; length, 94 feet; draft of water, 7 to 8 feet; highest speed, 7 to 8 knots; armament, two 32-pounders of 56 cwt. and two brass 12-pounders 6 cwt. howitzers. Their complement was 30. The officers were a lieutenant, a second master, and two engineers. As a lieutenant I have had casual command of more than one of them and they were the handiest vessels I ever knew.

The cables were worked by a deck tackle; if weighing in a crowded harbour you hove short, nearly up and down, then fleeted the deck tackle to the bows, manned it, gave the order, ' Away with the tackle, full speed ahead, hard over the helm,' and she turned almost as if she pivoted on her fore foot.

These vessels with us were the *Haughty*, the *Staunch*, and the *Forester*. The *Haughty* was commanded by the present Admiral Sir R. Vesey Hamilton, G.C.B., than whom no officer is more generally respected and liked in the Navy.

The *Cruizer* went first to Plymouth, where the gunboats awaited her, and starting with them put into Falmouth for bad weather. We sailed from there on 29th September 1856 and reached Hong-Kong on 29th April 1857, just seven months' voyage from England. We called at Teneriffe, Rio Janeiro, the Cape, Anger Point in Java, and Singapore.

Off Cape Frio at about 2 A.M. we had a bad

collision with a merchant barque, which kept us three weeks at Rio for repairs. The smash roused everyone up pretty effectually. Our 'master' (now called navigating officer), an elderly man for his position, and perhaps uncertain of his reckoning, ran on deck saying, ' We are on Cape Frio,' which is where the *Thetis* was lost in 1830 on her way home from the Pacific with $800,000 freight on board ; a very interesting account of this will be found in the life of Admiral Sir William Mends.

To return to our happily more trifling collision, the interval between seeing the barque and striking her was so short that the look-out on the starboard bow gun could only just call out and jump off it, when the gun was overboard.

This memoir pretends not to do justice to splendid scenery, nor ventures humbly to imitate ' Tom Cringle,' whose ' log ' is probably unsurpassed in its description of tropical scenery and storms. Were it otherwise Rio de Janeiro would certainly inspire me. But probably I was most interested in visiting the tomb of my grandfather, Admiral Sir Michael Seymour, who died while Commander-in-Chief on the South American and Pacific stations with his flag in H.M.S. *Spartiate*, and was buried at Rio. In those days the station included all the east coast of South America, and the Pacific coasts of both North and South America.

When we landed, or came off, in hired shore boats, they were pulled by black slaves chained to the thwarts to prevent their escaping.

From Rio we proceeded to Simon's Bay, then, as now, our naval headquarters in

South Africa. We there met the *Raleigh*, a 50-gun frigate commanded by Commodore Sir Henry Keppel, afterwards Admiral of the Fleet, on her way also to China.

While at Simon's Bay I and others went up to Cape Town by road; no railway then existing in Africa, south of Cairo. The well-known half-way house of Rathfelter with its quaint inscription was then in its glory—the inscription being:

Multum in parvo pro bono publico,
Entertainment for man and beast all in a row,
Lakker host as much as you please,
Very good beds without any fleas !
Nos patriam fugimus, now we are here
Vivamus, let us live by selling beer,
On donne à boire et à manger ici
Come in and try it whoever you be.

Our next port was Anger Point in Java, the south side of the Straits of Sunda, a place then called at by nearly all ships out to, and homeward from, China in the pre-Suez Canal days ; and where any amount of poultry and eggs could be got.

Our voyage to China was made nearly all under sail only, at which the gunboats were very poor hands, but, perhaps, equal to the ships of Columbus.

Our gunboats frequently parted company ; sometimes we towed them, or when we did not were reminded of the lines of the noble poet:

What leagues are lost before the dawn of day
Thus loitering pensive on the willing seas
The flapping sail hauled down to halt for logs like these.'

Life on board was diversified by more quarter-deck differences than I have known in my later ships ; opinions afloat differ as much as ashore, and the too close proximity of people not wholly in agreement magnifies their idiosyncrasies.

Over these I will draw a veil, and only remark that I fear we in the midshipmen's berth (then so called) were a rowdy set, and I no better than the rest. But our offences were but boyish freaks, and in after life I reckoned our Captain as one of my greatest friends, and when he died in command of the Channel Fleet I in company with many others greatly grieved for his loss.

We were favoured with the first of the south-west monsoons up the China Sea, and arriving at Hong-Kong on 29th April found there H.M.S. *Calcutta* with the Admiral on board.

CHAPTER VI

H.M.S. *CALCUTTA*

The *Arrow* Lorcha War at Canton—Fatshan Creek Action—
Capture of Canton—Viceroy Yeh—Move to the North—
Capture of Taku Forts—Tiensin.

ON 30th April 1857 I joined H.M.S. *Calcutta*, flagship of Rear-Admiral of the White—Sir Michael
Seymour, K.C.B.

At that time the three colours for admirals'
flags—red, white and blue—still existed. On
promotion to a new rank either rear-, vice-, or
(full) admiral an officer first hoisted the blue
flag, for the next advancement in his grade the
white, and in the upper grade of it the red.
The advantage of this was that if the fleet were
very large, it might be divided into three divisions
each flying an ensign of a different colour for
distinction. Commodores of the first class flew a
red swallow-tail 'burgee' and ensign, the commodores of the second class a blue one.

The *Calcutta* was a sailing two-decker of 84
guns, built in India of teak. Her figure-head
represented Sir Jamsetjee Jejeebhoy, and was
a very fierce-looking thing.

Teak is hard and durable, but slippery to stand on when wet ; so hard that I have heard my former Captain, McCleverty, who was a midshipman in the *Asia* at Navarino, say that some of the Turkish shot stuck in her sides, she being a sister ship to the *Calcutta*, and also built of teak.

It was a great change to the *Calcutta* as a much larger ship, and to a mess of about forty young officers.

In those days the lieutenants' mess was variously called a wardroom if in a line-of-battle ship, a gunroom if in a frigate or smaller vessel; while the midshipmen's mess was called the gunroom if in a liner, but the midshipmen's berth in all other ships. The origin of the term 'gunroom,' I believe, is that originally the seamen's muskets were kept there among the officers' for safety.

I am very fond of saying, ' There is no such thing as a trifle till you know its results.'

On 8th October 1856 the *Arrow*, Lorcha, flying British colours, arrived at Canton and was boarded by Chinese officials, who hauled down and insulted our flag and carried off most of the crew. And the above action on the part of some petty custom-house officers led to the very important events in China during the next few years.

Consul Parkes (afterwards Sir Harry Parkes), who was our very able representative at Canton, at once took the matter up. Yeh, the Viceroy of Kwang-Tung, would give no satisfaction, and so the Consul referred it to Sir John Bowring, our Governor of Hong-Kong. It was then placed in the hands of the naval Commander-in-Chief to deal with.

Sir Michael Seymour at once took action, and the Canton River was blockaded. The British factories at Shameen (Canton) were burnt by the Chinese, and much fighting ensued, the blockade of Canton by us continued, and in May 1857 the Admiral only waited reinforcements for further action.

I wish here to remark that this book has no pretence to be in any way the history of public events, but only a simple memoir of my life.

H.M.S. *Raleigh*, referred to above, had been wrecked by striking on an unknown rock off Macao on her arrival in China.

It then took nearly three months to get an answer from England, and the Admiral on his own responsibility retained Commodore Keppel[1] in command, and utilised him and his officers and men in various ways in the squadron.

At the end of May it was decided to attack the Chinese fleet of Mandarin junks lying up the Fatshan creek, partly protected by their own guns and also by a fort on Hyacinth Island.

This promised to be a very interesting affair, as it in fact turned out ; it was to be done by the boats of the squadron supported as far as the water permitted by the newly arrived gunboats; by the *Coromandel*, a paddle - wheel merchant steamer bought into the service by the Admiral and armed ; and by two paddle-wheel steamers

[1] The late Admiral of the Fleet the Hon. Sir Henry Keppel, G.C.B., O.M.

called the *Hong-Kong* and the *Sir Charles Forbes*, hired and armed and commanded respectively by Lieutenant J. G. Goodenough and Lieutenant Lord Gilford, both lately in the *Raleigh*.

The above armament assembled in the Canton River by the evening of 31st May. The whole force was under the personal command of the Admiral, but divided into two divisions, one led by Commodore the Hon. Henry Keppel and the other by Commodore the Hon. Charles Elliot of H.M.S. *Sybille*.

As regards myself, being signal midshipman I belonged to no boat, but I was of course most anxious to go, so I begged our Captain (W. King Hall [1]) to send me, and he being a very kind man did so, and sent me in our launch with Commander W. R. Rolland and a lieutenant.

We passed the night on board a gunboat, and long before daylight on 1st June were moving, first of all in tow of the gunboat. In those days ships' boats were only propelled by oars or sails. Our boat pulled 18 oars and was armed with a 24-pounder brass gun.

The *Coromandel* with the flag led, and first got into near action with the fort on Hyacinth Island, which was finally stormed and taken.

The Chinese force comprised about one hundred well-armed war junks, each carrying several guns, and with stink-pots up aloft to throw into their enemy's boats when close to. The junks were in two divisions, the lower one near the island, the other one three or four miles higher up.

---

[1] The late Admiral Sir William King Hall, K.C.B.

As we advanced up the creek the gunboats one after another grounded, and the boats had to take to their oars.

It was very exciting thus pulling up the creek, each boat trying to be first, the men cheering, and the enemy's shot flying by us. I was stationed by the gun in the bows, and as the fire was mostly ricochet the shot skipped over the water like what are called ' ducks and drakes,' and I remember thinking that with a cricket bat one might almost have hit them.

I have always thought that the most exciting thing in the world must be taking part in a cavalry charge in action, but to be in a boat propelled by oars, among other boats, the men pulling their hardest, shots flying by, men cheering, and guns firing, is also calculated to quicken the pulses.

After a bit the *Hong-Kong*, which was leading us, grounded and a slight check ensued.

Several shot now struck her ; but her Commander—afterwards the lamented Commodore Goodenough—backed her off the shoal. At that moment the boats, partly to get out of her way, turned their broadsides to the enemy. Commodore Keppel's galley was knocked to pieces and sunk, the Commodore being picked up by my cousin, Lieutenant Michael Culme-Seymour,[1] in our barge ; the launch in which I was at the same time got a round shot through her which sank her, and at the same moment also an officer of

---

[1] Now Sir Michael Culme-Seymour, Bart., G.C.B., Vice-Admiral of the United Kingdom.

the *Highflyer* was cut in half by a shot and his remains thrown over us.

This ended our boat's work for the day ; our first pinnace with a lieutenant and midshipman [1] in her ran alongside to offer us assistance. Meanwhile the Chinese kept up a hot fire and also shouted and beat their gongs, probably thinking they were about to win the day. But British dash prevailed, and so ended probably the hardest-fought boat action since the French War, except it may be the attack on Lagos in Africa in December 1851.

I am not sure our Admiral did not select the 1st June as being the anniversary of Lord Howe's glorious victory, in which my grandfather, the first Admiral Sir Michael Seymour, being then a lieutenant in the *Marlborough*, lost his arm.

The *Haughty* gunboat commanded by Lieutenant R. V. Hamilton [2] did such excellent service on this occasion that the Admiral being sent from the Admiralty a blank commander's commission to give to whoever he chose, gave it to Lieutenant Hamilton.

In consequence of the proceedings at Canton above referred to, Lord Elgin was sent out to China as plenipotentiary.

He arrived at Hong-Kong on 27th June in H.M.S. *Shannon*, commanded by Captain W. Peel. About this time the Sepoy Mutiny broke out in India, and the Admiral, seeing the extreme seriousness of it, at once sent the *Shannon* and

---

[1] Now Admiral Sir William Kennedy, K.C.B.
[2] Now Admiral Sir Vesey Hamilton, G.C.B.

the *Pearl* to Calcutta, which led to the glorious doings of the Naval Brigade under their gallant chief, Captain Sir William Peel.

I may also just remark how fortunate for us it was that some regiments *en route* to China were able to be stopped and almost at once landed in India.

The rest of the summer passed without any special incident with us, and as winter came on we moved up the Canton River to prepare to take Canton.

We anchored off Tiger Island, and our small arm and field-piece parties were constantly on shore there, drilling and preparing for our coming small campaign.

I was attached to three small brass Indian mountain guns, 12 pounders of only 3 cwt. each, under the command of Lieutenant J. G. Goodenough, late of the *Raleigh*, and now belonging to the *Calcutta* ; our other officer being A. K. Wilson,[1] then a midshipman.

In November our naval brigades left the ship, and moved up to Canton, where we were for many days lodged in a large ginger store belonging to a great Chinese merchant called Howqua, in the suburbs on the south side of the river opposite Canton.

While in Howqua's stores I remember we midshipmen by lighting a bonfire nearly burnt down one of the stores we lived in, but by climbing on the roofs and using a supply of water luckily kept up there, the fire was put out.

[1] Now Admiral of the Fleet Sir Arthur Wilson, V.C., G.C.B.

On Christmas Day 1857 I dined with the Admiral on board the *Coromandel*, and well remember the kindness of Captain W. T. Bate (of the *Actæon*). No officer was more respected and liked than he was, and his death four days later was regretted by all who knew him.

On the 29th Captain Bate, who was with the Admiral, and looking for a good place to attack the walls, was killed by a shot from them. The troops were commanded by General Van Straubenzie ; and Lord Elgin, who during the autumn had been at Calcutta, had now returned to conduct his duties as plenipotentiary in China.

On 28th December we were taken across the river and landed to the eastward of Canton city and slept in the open on the ground for the night, on the hills outside it. Next day we stormed the walls and gained possession of them, and the question now was what to do next.

In 1841, when our forces attacked Canton, we took a detached fort on a hill outside the walls to the north-east which bears with us the name of Gough's fort, because General Sir Hugh Gough was in command of the troops on that occasion. We did not then take and occupy the city, but only made terms, and exacted and obtained a ransom of five million dollars. This was very well in its way, but I believe the Chinese succeeded in making out to their Government, and China generally, that the barbarians failed to take Canton, and so obtain a real victory.

On the present occasion we did not intend there should be any delusion about it, so a few days after, on 5th January 1858, we left the walls and entered the city.

I should explain that the walls of Canton are both extensive, high, and massive, the sort of walls that in pre-artillery days, if well manned, would have been very difficult to storm.

Those who know Canton will remember the five-storey pagoda on the walls at the north part of the town, and the hill near it, also inside the walls, called ' Magazine Hill,' these parts of the walls we occupied at first, having stormed the walls to the eastward of those positions.

The Chinese Governor of Canton was the celebrated Yeh, a clever, middle-aged, strong-minded Mandarin, much trusted by his Emperor ; and who was said to have cut off more heads than any other Viceroy. He was credited with having had 100,000 cut off. His yamen or palace was in the middle of the city.

For that on 5th January our advanced force made, guided chiefly by Consul Parkes,[1] who, having been our Consul at Canton, and knowing both the Chinese and their language well, was the very man for the occasion. On our entering Yeh's yamen, one or two Chinese in turn came forward and said, ' I am Yeh,' but Parkes, who knew pretty well what Yeh was like from description, waved them aside and pushed on.

Captain A. C. Key,[2] R.N., hurried forward into the garden behind the yamen ; and seeing a stout middle-aged man in Mandarin's dress and

---

[1] Afterwards Sir Harry Parkes.
[2] Afterwards Admiral Sir Cooper Key, G.C.B.

hat, trying to escape and get over the garden wall, seized him by the pigtail, and compelled him to return into the yamen. Here he was seated in a chair, and various Chinamen were brought into his presence, on which they fell down and ' kow-towed,' i.e. prostrated themselves on their hands and knees and beat their heads on the ground.

This and other inquiries proved the captive to be Yeh, a point very important, but a little hard at first to settle. He was then put into a sedan chair and carried off as our prisoner.

One of the first questions put to him was, Where is Mr. Cowper ? I must explain that Mr. Cowper owned the dry dock at Whampoa, on the Canton River, some fifteen miles below Canton, where he lived on board a ' chop ' or floating houseboat. The previous autumn one evening after sunset a Chinese snake boat, i.e. one pulling many oars, came alongside, and the man in charge of it said he had an important letter which he must deliver only into Mr. Cowper's own hand.

Mr. Cowper came to get it; the Chinamen seized his hand, pulled him into the boat, and rowed off at once, and he was never heard of again.

Yeh at first pretended to know nothing about the above, but at last said something of the sort did occur, and Mr. Cowper gave a good deal of trouble, but at last died. His son ultimately had a money compensation from the Chinese Government.

The rest of Yeh's story is soon told. He was

sent to Calcutta as a prisoner of state, and in April 1859 he died there. His body was then brought back by us to Canton, but the Chinese said they did not want it as he had been degraded by the Emperor, and he was quietly buried; possibly on the same island in the Canton River as the great and good St. Francis Xavier. Who knows?

It now became a serious question what further steps to take in order that our dealings with China should be with the real Government, which alone could be satisfactory.

In 1793 Lord Macartney had visited Pekin as our ambassador, and had an audience of the Emperor, and in 1816 Lord Amherst had gone there on a like mission. The former embassy was not satisfactory and produced no good results, in which the latter failed even more, as no reception of our ambassador was accorded.

It was finally decided that an expedition should go north, to the Gulf of Pechili and the mouth of the Peiho River, and try to get into immediate touch with the Chinese Government at Pekin. On 25th March 1858 we left Hong-Kong for the north, still having the last of the north-east monsoon to contend with. In April we arrived off the mouth of the Peiho, where a considerable squadron of our own ships and gunboats assembled, as well as a small French squadron, with their Admiral's flag in the *Audacieuse*.

Our ambassador, Lord Elgin, lived on board the *Furious*, a paddle-wheel steam frigate. Even then the water was so shallow off the river's mouth that the larger ships had to lie seven or eight miles off the land, which being very low was hardly visible except from aloft. It is growing shallower now.

Negotiations were carried on for many days, and attempts made to get leave to enter the river, ascend it, and arrange some terms, but these failed. The spirit of Chinese diplomacy has always been procrastination.

The Taku forts then were almost entirely on the south side of the river's mouth, consisting mostly of large bastions of earth, or mud, and for those days heavily armed with large guns, many made of brass. Rifled ordnance was practically non-existent anywhere then. A boom of many wooden spars, chains, &c., was fixed across the river opposite the forts, and secured with large stakes firmly driven into the bottom.

I got leave to go in in a gunboat a few days before our action, when one of the *pourparlers* was going on. It was curious to be allowed to come in close in front of the forts, but many of their gunports were hidden by mantlets. The front of the fort was decorated with numberless flags, and a brave show kept up.

Till the morning of the 20th May it was uncertain if they would, or would not, let us enter the river, but failing a favourable reply then we had said we should open fire. None came, and so now our action began.

The French vessels were combined with ours ; and the unusual sight was seen of the admirals of both nations going into action on board the same vessel, viz. the *Slaney* gunboat, and with their flags both flying at the same masthead. Surely a novelty !

The *Cormorant* being the largest and heaviest vessel inside the bar was sent first to charge the boom, which she did and broke it. She was followed by the rest of our force, most of the gunboats towing the large ship's pulling boats, filled with the landing parties. Of these, I was in charge of a pinnace.

The Chinese kept up a good fire on us as we passed, which was well replied to by our side ; but our great object was to pass the forts, and land just above, and then to storm them, as it were, on their flank. This to a considerable degree we accomplished, and carried the position.

While towing in past the forts we were of course much exposed to their fire, and some casualties occurred. I remember a shot passing through a boat close to mine, in which a young seaman had lain down under what are called the stern sheets ; the shot must have very narrowly missed him, and as he did not reply when called to I thought he was killed ; examination showed he had escaped any injury, but was much frightened.

I think no one can often have been under fire without appreciating that some people value their life and limbs more highly than others do. Let me put it mildly in that way.

This leads on to the question of rewards for valour, which is a very difficult one. I know some

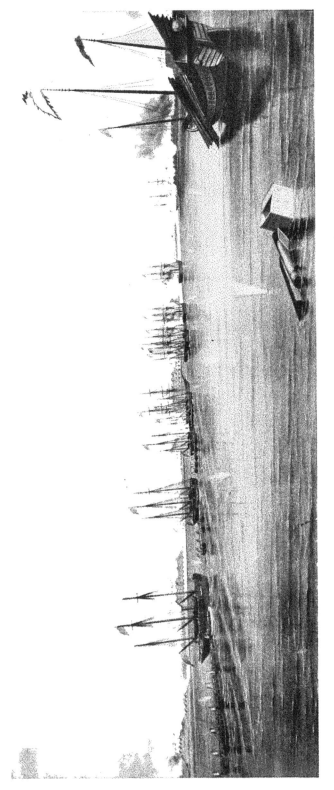

THE FIRST CAPTURE OF THE TAKU FORTS
1858

officers who disapprove of the institution of the Victoria Cross, about which I feel strongly as follows : it should have two classes or degrees— the first and highest for going out of your strict orders to do something of extra risk that positively assists to accomplish the service in hand ; and the second for incurring a gratuitous risk, not interfering of course with your proper duty, to save a comrade.

There is a rise and fall of tide of many feet in the Peiho River, and it was a question when to attack as regarded that. Our Admiral wisely chose the first of the flood, which meant our being lower down and many shots passing over us, as well as our having a fair current helping us in, and rising tide in case of grounding.

We had on landing to wade through soft mud quite up to our knees ; but as we neared the forts the Chinese fell back and ran away, their Mandarins or officers setting them the example.

A serious explosion occurred in the forts, perhaps owing to the carpenter warrant officer of the *Fury* smashing with a hammer a large chattie full of gunpowder and so striking a spark. He and many others fell victims ; and the sight of the terribly injured survivors, some with clothes and hair gone and blackened with powder, was shocking.

The next move was to go up the Peiho River to Tiensin and then see what would follow. We had now no more forts to stop us, and in a few days arrived at Tiensin. To the Chinese we must have been an extraordinary sight, as

unless some of the older people could remember
Lord Amherst, who forty-two years before arrived
in a ship and went up by boat, no one had
ever seen an 'Outer Barbarian' there, still less
steamers.

However, the Chinaman is not very demon-
strative in his astonishment, which is often
confined to 'Ay yah, what piecy pidgeon
that?'

It is a matter of history that at the end of
June a treaty of peace was signed at Tiensin by
Lord Elgin, Baron Gros (on the part of the
French), and a Chinese Mandarin called Keying,
which seemed to grant all that we required.

No doubt the Chinese all the time laughed
in their sleeves as the expression is (and Chinese
sleeves are loose and large), and with their usual
policy of procrastination said to themselves,
'We shall by this means get rid of the "foreign
devils" for the present, and the future must
look after itself.'

I was in my boat at Tiensin, I and her crew
sleeping in the *Coromandel*; the weather was of
course very hot, and the sun powerful.

Our Admiral had since he came on the station
allowed officers to wear a special sun hat made
of white pith, admirable against the sun's rays;
but I foolishly despised it, and only wore a
uniform cap.

The result was to me a sort of sunstroke, and
bad fever, necessitating my being sent down to
the ship. I suppose I nearly died, though I
did not somehow expect to. But it led to

my being sent to the *Pique*, which was going home.

I was very sorry to end my service under the flag of my uncle, Sir Michael Seymour, but the medical authorities advised my going home, and as all prospect of further fighting just then seemed—and was—over, it perhaps was not quite so much to be regretted.

Promotion in the China Squadron was rapid at that time. From the *Calcutta* alone while I was in her, one commander was made captain, and five lieutenants were made commanders, besides some junior promotions.

But I cannot leave the subject of the *Calcutta* without one or two remarks about her. Her midshipmen, generally, were more successful in the service than those of any other ship I ever heard of. About seventeen got on to the active list of captains, and at least eight on to the flag (or admirals') list. In after years on one day three of us were flying our flags in the same harbour. What was this due to? I will not pronounce, but our Captain, W. King Hall, took a real interest in his youngsters, who also had the benefit of a first-rate naval instructor, the present Professor Sir John Laughton.

I also look back with extreme respect and affection to our Commander, the late Commodore Goodenough, than whose example no one's ever was better, or impressed me so much.

We were devoted to him. He was strict, however, and often mastheaded us, or put us in watch and watch for so many days, i.e. to keep four hours on deck and four hours below alternately day and night. This with our other duty was no joke. But he was always just, and acted from the highest principles, and this we all felt. When I left the ship he wrote me a letter that gave me the greatest pleasure.

CHAPTER VII

H.M.S. *PIQUE, MERSEY,* AND *IMPERIEUSE*

The *Pique*—Long China Sea Passage—Gale of Wind—The *Mersey*—I pass for Rank of Lieutenant—A Smart Ship—The *Imperieuse*—Passage to China by Great Circle Track.

FROM the *Calcutta* off the Peiho River I and two other midshipmen from that ship joined H.M.S. *Pique* for passage to England. The *Pique* was a 40-gun sailing frigate, 167 feet in length, her main trunk being about the same height above the water, and with a complement of about three hundred.

She was a '*Symondite*' vessel, i.e. she was built from the designs of Admiral Symonds, and was first commissioned in 1835 to try her then new lines, which may shortly be described as greater beam than former ships of the same length, and carrying her extreme beam well above the water line.

She was the same ship that in 1835 was badly injured by grounding on the coast of Labrador, and then crossed the Atlantic with a rock sticking in her bottom, and that lost her masts in December 1840 in a gale of wind off the coast of Syria.

Our Captain had to consider how he could best get to England, having the prospect of the south-west monsoon in its full force against us all down the China Sea. In view of this it is quite possible that our quickest way would have been to cross the Pacific and go home round Cape Horn, but the usual route by the Cape of Good Hope was chosen, with the result that we were a good seven months on our way home.

We sailed from the Gulf of Pechili early in July 1858, were thirty days beating down to Hong-Kong, fifty days from there to Singapore, and twelve days thence to Anger Point in Java. In fact you might say we were over three months with the ' bow-lines hauled,' to use a nautical expression. But probably the modern naval officer has no idea what a bow-line is !— or was.

On joining the *Pique* I was an invalid, and her Captain, Sir Frederick Nicolson, kindly placed me at first in a cot in his fore-cabin; but youth quickly either dies or recovers, and before a fortnight I begged the Captain to treat and employ me like any other midshipman, which he did, and a month saw me as midshipman of the maintop aloft for a long time, beating into Hong-Kong in a blazing hot sun.

The *Pique* was one of our ships at Petropaulousky, and one of her officers, Lieutenant R——, told me this story of himself there.

They had landed to attack the Russian batteries, and our allied small-arm men, French and English, appear to have got somewhat scattered. Suddenly he saw a party of armed seamen near him, and one of them pointed his musket at him, and seemed about to fire. Lieutenant R—— was rather short-sighted, and taking the party for Frenchmen, held up his sword and called out, ' Ne tirez pas. Je suis Anglais.' This made the man for a moment hesitate, but apparently thinking better of it, he again pointed his musket and fired. Lieutenant R—— fortunately had on a belt with a pouch full of cartridges ; this the bullet hit, and so did not enter his body, but the blow doubled him up and knocked him down. The Russians ran up to finish him off, but luckily he was at the edge of the cliff, not precipitous but steep, and down this he rolled to the beach below, and so escaped.

A long sea voyage has not much of interest to relate ; to a mere passenger it is no doubt tedious, but to a real sailor, in the ship he belongs to, it means daily work and, in the good old sailing days, the delights of seamanship, and indeed of yachting on a grand scale.

In the *Pique* I learnt much seamanship, and at times the senior midshipmen, I being one, were allowed to keep ' officer's watch,' i.e. be in charge of the deck.

The excitement of tacking the ship was delightful. She had been over four years in commission with a fine ship's company, and things ' flew ' on board her, and for a boy to command nearly a hundred men, who rushed about at his order, was a proud position.

Even work aloft was exciting ; at the order

'reef topsails' for instance, with a strong breeze, the ship heeling over fifteen degrees or more, and the weather rigging as taut as a harp-string—to run up it followed by a crowd of top men was splendid. But this may not interest others, only I wish to record the sort of life sea work was then.

One of our officers had a small Pekin dog, which one morning at sea fell overboard; the Captain ordered the ship to be hove to, and a boat sent to try and pick it up. I was sent in charge, and when about to give up the search, we saw the wretched creature's head just visible in the trough of the waves, and it was saved.

We had one night in my middle watch one of the worst thunder-storms I ever saw, and on that occasion at the ends of two spars aloft were what are called 'St. Elmo's lights'; they look just like bright lanterns burning there, and are indeed electric lights, things then not invented by man, being caused by the immense amount of electricity in the air.

We lay a few days at Singapore and then went to Anger Point as mentioned above, where homeward-bound ships took in their stock of fowls and eggs for sea.

In the straits of Sunda between Java and Sumatra we fell in with the *Nankin*, a 50-gun sailing frigate, also homeward bound from China. The *Nankin* was a new ship that commission, and a beautiful vessel, finer lines than the *Pique* and more fitted for light winds than we were.

Her captain was senior to ours, and made

us a signal to close, and then to try the rate of sailing. For two or three days we did so, and as all yachtsmen know, trying one vessel against another is often exciting, and is the only way to find out what trim of the ship, and what point of sailing as regards the wind, best suit your own vessel. Finally, with the wind nearly a point before our beam in a fresh breeze and just able to carry topmast studding-sails, we walked away from the *Nankin*, and left her out of sight astern, but she arrived at Simon's Bay before us after all.

A few days before reaching Simon's Bay, when off Cape Agulhas, in the middle watch a heavy north-west gale of wind came on and lasted some twenty-four hours. It was an interesting experience, for the seas there are large : the ship was reduced to only close-reefed maintop-sail and forestay-sail and the former blew away. There was no real danger as we were not on a lee shore, and the ship was a good sea boat and well handled, but routine had to yield to the weather altogether, a variety much appreciated by many of us.

Our stay at Simon's Town was for a few days, enough for us to make a trip to Cape Town : the sort of holiday that perhaps only a sailor much at sea can really properly appreciate. From the Cape we went to St. Helena, running up there with the south-east trade wind blowing so steadily that the running ropes could be left quiescent, sufficiently for us to paint both the upper deck and even the yards aloft. I only mention this to show what the trade winds can be.

It was my first visit to St. Helena, where even the prosaic mind of the midshipman thinks of the once mighty Napoleon. Some of us rode out to Longwood and visited both the house and the tomb of that wonderful man.

Over the latter grew a willow tree; we were anxious to get some sprigs—or cuttings—of it to take to England, and plant there. For this purpose I climbed up the tree, and was soon attracted by a serious altercation between one of my messmates and an infuriated Frenchman, who was, or constituted himself, the guardian of the tomb and tree.

While lying here I remember a British merchant ship was also at anchor and flying a white ensign at her peak, instead of a red one. Our Captain, as was right, sent a boat on board her and brought the white ensign away. While on the subject I must say I am of opinion that the proper ensign of a man-of-war should be confined exclusively to H.M. ships ; not to yachts, except with a device added.

After St. Helena we called only at Ascension Island, which we took possession of in 1815 when Napoleon was placed in St. Helena, as a further security against any attempt to help him to escape.

Ascension Island is of volcanic origin, and probably Madeira ages ago was in much the same condition. Only the higher part of Ascension, called the Green Mountain, is now covered with vegetation, but what there is is gradually increasing and extending downwards.

Ascension, though only eight degrees south of the equator, is kept cool and airy by the south-east trade wind. The thermometer is usually not above 80°, and the place is very healthy. Its ' garrison,' or inhabitants, are entirely naval officers and men—seamen or marines—with their wives and families, and many of them get extremely fond of living there.

I never admired any ship I served in as a picture more than I did the *Pique*. In the modern ships I can see no beauty, except as a means—we hope—in case of war of bringing in the war indemnity. But ' the winged sea-girt citadel' was a thing of positive beauty: one could look at and regard her like one would a very fine animal, I had almost said a pretty woman!

Now do, or will, this or the next generation admire the modern armoured ship or torpedo boat—shall we also say submarine?—as much as we did the frigate, and some other vessels of the past? If so I can only say that there is no such thing as INANIMATE beauty, but it is only a question of what you are used to—a very low standard too. Ask the Royal Academy about this!

In February we got into the Channel, bent cables to the anchors, cables being kept unbent in the open ocean, and hove to for soundings with the deep-sea lead.

This in those days was almost a ceremony: the ship had to be hove to, the lead line passed forward outside the ship from aft, and when thrown in, the line was gradually quitted in turn by men all along the hammock netting, calling out in their turns, ' Watch, there, watch '—each waiting to see if the line was ' up and down,' meaning that the lead was on the bottom, and if so what depth was marked on the line. Now Lord Kelvin's admirable sounding machine has changed all that.

We anchored in Plymouth Sound, the ship having been five years away from England. Too long for several reasons ; many on board had long got quite tired of each other, and showed it plainly.

We paid off in the Hamoaze, i.e. Devonport Harbour, but first completely unrigged, dismantled and gutted the ship. Masts, guns, stores, and all movables were got out of her. Though a good sound ship she was never commissioned again, but now lies as a quarantine vessel (if so required) in Plymouth Sound.

To give an idea of the way money was kept owing to men in those days, I may mention that I remember one seaman receiving over £100 at the pay table.

I made no effort to select my next ship, and was appointed to the *Mersey*, fitting out at Portsmouth.

She was a new screw frigate, by far the largest and most powerful one in the service, and we all felt about as proud of her as if she had been the first *Dreadnought*.

She had 40 guns, the ones on the main deck all 10-inch—then the largest calibre—and on the

H.M.S. PIQUE
Forty-gun sailing frigate
1858

upper deck 68-pounders. She could steam 14 knots, then most unusual ; though this would not be thought much of now.

The *Mersey* as a lasting ship was a failure, her scantling was too slight for her engines and her guns. At full speed under steam her masts actually shook, and I have seen the topmast rigging flapping against the topmasts. Her seams to some degree opened and let the water through. She only lasted one sea-going commission. Perhaps the fact is that to stand the strains of powerful machinery and heavy ordnance a vessel should be built of iron, or better still of steel.

My time to pass for lieutenant was up six months before, but I had to wait for age, to become nineteen, which happened in a few weeks' time, and I passed in seamanship, on board the then new naval cadets' training-ship the *Illustrious* in Portsmouth Harbour. To show how different the examinations at that time were I may state that my Captain then said, ' I give you a month to get through gunnery and the College.'

For the first of them I was three or four weeks working on board the *Excellent* and living in the old Naval College in the dockyard, at which place I went afterwards through my examination in navigation, &c. For both the above examinations we used to 'cram' privately : for gunnery with a gunner of the *Excellent* in Portsea, who made a very good thing of it ; and for the College examination with a private mathematical instructor on shore.

In those days the examinations were what

would now be thought very easy, which was necessary, as our instruction in most ships was nil, or, if not quite that, shamefully neglected ; and if the examinations had been what they are now, nobody would have passed, and the Navy would have come to an end for want of officers ! Read Marryat's novels, and see his mention of examination for the rank of lieutenant ; it was then only before three captains, and an hour or little more metamorphosed the midshipman into a master's mate—now sub-lieutenant—and if his father was a peer, or influential M.P. on the then Government's side, probably at once into a full-blown lieutenant, with one ' swab ' or epaulette on his right shoulder.

Yet the Navy saved England, and saved Europe ; and fully justified Macaulay's famous remark, ' but the British Navy no misgovernment could ruin ' : and I believe it is the same now.

I served in five ships, as naval cadet and midshipman for a period of six and a half years—not including the *Mersey*—during which time I certainly had not the benefit of any naval instructor's tuition for over two years at most, and the *Calcutta* was the only ship I was in, in which any of the superior officers took any interest in whether we learnt anything or did not.

The *Pique*, carrying several youngsters, was over five years in commission, but never had a naval instructor, or anyone to teach them.

whatsaying this, I am only wishing to show In an extraordinary and beneficial change has come over the Navy as regards its young officers' training and teaching; and you cannot wonder that in those days many of them ' came to grief' as the expression is.

About my ' passing days ' I will mention no names, but I was with a luckless lot, none of whom rose in the service.

The ' Keppel's Head ' on the Hard is now a grand hotel, in its way ; its predecessor was a humble hostelry, much frequented by naval officers, and its landlord, George Clarke, respected and beloved by all who knew him.

The evening of the College examination I was in there, and we were comparing our answers to the different questions in the ' College sheet.' One officer said to me, ' Well, I fear you will be turned back (or ' goated ' as the expression was), for all my answers are different from yours and I believe mine are right.' This was not reassuring to me, but when we went in next day to hear the results the Clerk of the College said to my friend, ' Mr. H—— perhaps you would rather not see the Captain (who gave or refused the certificates) as you are turned back for the third time,' which meant dismissal from the service.

Another officer who had been acting-lieutenant on a foreign station for three years, and was trying to pass at the same time as myself, was turned back and lost all the above seniority ; and when he passed had to join a ship as a mate (now sub-lieutenant). In these days midshipmen whose time is up to pass are sent home as soon as possible for their examinations, which is quite right.

While I was at the College a large passenger sailing packet from India arrived one night at Spithead, and as she rounded the Nablight to bear up for her anchorage she somehow caught fire aft, the wind then fair, i.e. astern, fanned the flames, and she arrived about midnight burning fiercely. All that could be done was to save life, and the passengers came on shore in night attire.

A steam sloop was lying at Spithead about to sail for a foreign station, and after the wreck had become helpless this vessel was ordered to get under way and fire into her to sink her, but as she fired the burning wreck lightened, and drifted at last on shore off Haslar Hospital.

In June, having finished my examinations, I rejoined the *Mersey* as 'full-blown mate,' a fine old title that I was proud of. A few years after the Admiralty—in a fit of, shall we say snobbishness?—altered the title to sub-lieutenant, and on the same principle should have changed midshipman to ' Ensign de Vaisseau ' l

The *Mersey* belonged to the Channel Fleet; she was perhaps the best specimen of a man-of-war that I ever was in.

Both her captain and her executive officer—first-lieutenant in a frigate in those days—were noted as smart officers and good seamen. I am bound to say that the ship was called uncomfortable, owing to the amount of work on board, and the restriction of leave; but after all a smart ship is not only right, but is the most satisfactory one to serve in, and we had our diversions.

One evening lying in Plymouth Sound, I and a messmate tossed up who should at once jump overboard dressed as we were, and the other come after him to save him. It fell to my lot to go first, which of course I did, and I being in good odour with the superior powers my messmate, who was not so, also escaped blame.

In August we got the startling news of our defeat on the Peiho River, in our attempt to take the Taku forts. The naval excitement about it was very strong, and I was of course mad to go back to China at once, and having some interest I was appointed to the *Imperieuse*, just about to sail for Hong-Kong. The fight on the Peiho on 25th June 1859 came about thus. Mr. Bruce, Lord Elgin's brother, was sent to ratify the treaty made in 1858, which by mutual agreement was to be ratified at Tiensin within a year. Our Admiral, Sir James Hope, who had lately succeeded to the command in China, escorted Mr. Bruce with a squadron, though no force should have been required. The Chinese broke faith, and having restored the Taku forts and rearmed them, refused us admittance to the river. It became then the Admiral's duty to endeavour to force a passage in.

The boom proved too strong to be passed ; our people behaved with great pluck and energy, but kept before the guns of the forts the fire was too hot, and some of our vessels were sunk.

It was then resolved as a last resource to land, though in front of the forts, and try to carry them by assault—wading through deep soft mud.

It was probably a forlorn hope, and it failed; but we had incurred no dishonour. The Admiral was wounded, and many officers and men killed and wounded. The strength of the boom was really the determining factor. Of course I was not there, but as I not long after joined the *Chesapeake*, Admiral Hope's flagship, I have heard everything about it well discussed.

I joined the *Imperieuse* at Devonport, and remember for the first time in my life—though often after—being struck with the contrasts of ships' sizes, and how one gets to think whatever vessel you are in is the normal size, and that other ships are unduly large or small.

The *Imperieuse* was the first 51-gun screw frigate in our Navy. In 1853 she came to Spithead just commissioned, and I remember going on board her from the *Encounter* and thinking her enormous. When I joined her from the *Mersey* she looked quite cramped and small, yet the differences were not really very much.

She had been commissioned for the Channel Fleet, but in consequence of our disaster on the Peiho, was suddenly ordered to go to China to be flagship of Rear-Admiral Lewis Tobias Jones (mentioned before in the *Sampson* in the Black Sea), who had preceded us by mail to China, to take command if Admiral Hope did not recover from his wound, or if he did to be his second in command.

Our Captain was anxious to get out as quick as possible. We made most of the voyage under sail, steaming only when required. In those days steam was only looked on as an auxiliary.

We called at St. Vincent, Cape Verde Islands, for coal, and some of us had a sporting episode on shore which might have been more serious than it was.

We then made a sort of great circle track, going down far south of the Cape of Good Hope to get also the strong westerly winds of the South Atlantic and South Indian Oceans.

The seas there between 40° and 50° of south latitude are the heaviest in the world, and when running with a strong breeze aft or quarterly, it is fine to watch a following sea that, looking much higher than your hull, first lifts your stern and then your bow as it passes, seeming at first to intend to swamp you, and on second thoughts only to sweep you onwards on your course.

We were about seventy days out of sight of land, between the Cape Verde Islands and Java Head, a thing not common anywhere with men-of-war nowadays.

Christmas Day is still the great yearly festival in a man-of-war, and it was then also a day of too much licence.

The morning after Christmas we were running before the south-east trade winds in the East Indian Ocean, with studding sails on one side. I was officer of the morning watch, and of the some

150 men, 'Watch and Idlers,' who should have answered their master round the quarter-deck capstan only about half could do so properly. I thought to myself, if a man falls overboard, now what should I do? and came to a decision; but happily the event did not occur.

The *Imperieuse* all her commission leaked badly, and on our way out it took a sub-division of the watch some quarter of an hour twice a day to pump her out with the hand pumps, when we were not under steam.

When between Anger Point and Singapore, and passing through the Straits of Rheo one morning a marine fell overboard. I was on the main deck at the time, and a young officer who saw it happen announced it in a very ordinary tone of voice. I got into a port and seeing the man going astern took it into my head to jump after him. But I was never able to reach him. There are many sharks there, but I do not think he was taken by one. He simply went down, and though I dived I could not see him.

At first I tried to encourage him by calling out, ' Do keep up if possible for a few seconds ' ; but I must confess I was reminded of Mr. Winkle and Mr. Pickwick at Pear Tree Green pond. By no means do I wish to joke about so sad a thing as a fellow creature's death, but only to relate a fact.

The life-buoy was at last let go, and failing all efforts to reach the unfortunate man, who was evidently lost, I disregarded the life-buoy and swam towards the boat which had been lowered, arguing to myself that a shark could get me on the buoy, but that if I met the boat I should be less time exposed to him.

I afterwards heard that the remark was made about me, ' Well he must be born to be hanged and not drowned.'

At Singapore we took in a deck-load of coal, to steam up the China Sea against the north-east monsoon, and so made a good run up to Hong-Kong.

We found the Commander-in-Chief, Sir James Hope, here in his flagship the *Chesapeake*, and a few days afterwards he had a blank commission for lieutenant sent him from the Admiralty, and in a very kind and complimentary way gave it to me, and took me into his flagship.

CHAPTER VIII

H.M.S. *CHESAPEAKE, COWPER,* AND *WATERMAN*

The *Chesapeake*—Tah-lien-wan Bay—Port Arthur—An Execution—Taku Forts taken—Tiensin—Nagasaki—The *Cowper* —The Yangtse River—Nankin—The *Waterman*—Canton River—Pagodas—The ' Cat '—Evacuation of Canton.

IN February 1860 I joined the *Chesapeake,* a frigate very similar to the *Imperieuse.* From now till May we remained at Hong-Kong very busy preparing for the expedition to the North, and the harbour filling with men-of-war and transports.

Lord Elgin arrived from England to act again as our plenipotentiary, and Sir Hope Grant as the General to command our troops.

In May we left Hong-Kong and went to Tah-lien-wan Bay, where all were to rendezvous before the campaign began. This place is an inlet of Korea Bay, but is now much better known as Dalny. In 1860 it had only some small Chinese villages on its shores, and the neighbouring coasts were most imperfectly known and hardly surveyed at all.

Our Admiral sent the gunboats to examine

the coasts near, and the *Algerine*, commanded by Lieutenant W. Arthur,[1] returned with the news that she had found a very good harbour ; which the Admiral named Port Arthur after its, so to speak, discoverer.

While we were here, a tragic event occurred on board the *Leven* gunboat. A marine of that ship called Dalhanty, having committed a theft and knowing he would be found out and punished (no doubt flogged), made up his mind to deserve still more. He was servant to the Lieutenant-Commander, and taking his master's revolver, he shot him from behind, in his cabin. Having done this he hid the revolver under his coat and went on deck. No one there had heard the shot fired. He approached the next officer in command—a ' second master '—and very respectfully said, ' The Captain wants you in his cabin.' The officer suspecting nothing went down the ladder, but as he reached the bottom of it Dalhanty fired at him and wounded him also. The marine was then secured.

Both officers recovered, but the crime was as bad as it could be. A court-martial was held, and Dalhanty was sentenced to death, and the day after the sentence was hanged at the yard-arm of the *Leven*.

For this the gunboat was anchored close to us, and as I happened to be doing duty as flag-lieutenant at the time, I was with the Admiral on our bridge.

[1] The late Admiral Arthur, C.B. The origin of the name of this now famous place is, I believe, little known.

The naval procedure in such cases is to place the prisoner on a platform under the fore yard-arm, the rope being rove through a block at the above, and manned by men from different ships. To do this every ship present sends a boat manned and armed to surround the execution ship, and the bow men of every boat are those sent on board to man the whip.

A gun is fired and the man is run up to the yardarm, where a stop is broken so that he falls about ten feet as a drop. In this case the body then swung for an hour at the yardarm, before being buried in the sea. This is at present the last execution on board one of our ships.

On 26th July the expedition left Tah-lien-wan Bay for the mouth of the Peh-tang River, a few miles north of the Peiho, and the transports of both nations, the French and ourselves, assembled there.

Landing the troops and preparing for the advance on the Peiho River to attack the Taku forts there, was a slow business. Allied operations are apt to be slow, and if slower than they should be, one nation can always throw the blame on the other ; which has often been done.

It was not till the 21st August that the first fort was taken on the north shore of the Peiho River. The fall of this led at once to the capture of the more important fort on that side. After that the Chinese felt the southern forts to be untenable, and so the allies became masters of the place.

Immediately afterwards our Admiral pushed

on up the river to Tiensin, and the advance there was followed by the armies.

In this campaign I took no part as a combatant, and so as to me it is only a matter then of what I heard, and now of history, I will not here relate it.

I was in charge of our working parties in the southern forts, which gave me a good opportunity of seeing them. They did credit to the Chinese and were in fact massive earthworks, raised on earth bastions, planted on the low and almost muddy shores of the river ; for those days heavily armed, and the guns well placed and mounted.

Outside the forts the approach of storming parties was rendered difficult, partly by the ground literally bristling with sharp stakes of different sizes, some one or two feet long out of the ground, some only a few inches, and here and there you found what are called crow's feet.

My work at the forts being over, I got leave to go up to Tiensin. I had hardly got there when orders came to explore the river above that place towards Pekin, and report if it would do for a flotilla to ascend it, carrying stores, ammunition, &c.

The senior officer at Tiensin happened to be my old Captain in the *Terrible,* and Commander Goodenough (late of the *Calcutta*), who was then in command of a ship there, was selected for this service. Between the two I was seized on to go also, and very glad of course I was. We started in two gigs, so called. The weather was hot and sleeping in the boats no hardship.

It was curious to see the Chinese. We had our small-arms of course, but could have offered no real defence if fired on from the banks. However, the Celestial showed no doubt his sense in not molesting us. Indeed at places they kow-towed to us, a thing always unpleasant to my feelings when performed to me.

I forget how far we went or for how many days, but the report of my senior officer, Commander Goodenough, on our return was in favour of a flotilla; whose proceedings and valuable services may be read of by those who choose, in the archives of the military expedition to Pekin.

I may just add that the Admiral meant me to go with this flotilla, which was commanded by Captain Roderick Dew, my former superior in the *Encounter*, but I could not be found, owing to the above expedition; and my place was taken by my good and valued messmate, Lieutenant Marcus Hare, afterwards lost in the *Eurydice*.

This prevented my seeing the Summer Palace, well looted and destroyed—so supposed—in revenge for the certainly inhuman treatment of our countrymen captured by the Chinese, of whom only two survived. But I must not digress into history. This last relates how the treaty was signed by the plenipotentiaries, Lord Elgin and Baron Gros.

The retention of the allied forces in the province of Chili was very well arranged, and it was a very nice question. It was not desirable to leave sooner than was necessary, but to have been caught by the freezing up of the river and its approaches would have been very serious. Enough to say that the happy mean was attained.

In the *Chesapeake* we stayed off the Peiho till late in the year and spent out Christmas at the Miatou Islands in the Gulf of Pechili ; the last two syllables of which name are very applicable there in the winter.

Pekin is about the same latitude as Lisbon, and the Peiho River is on an average frozen up for quite seventy days every winter, and the ice has been known to form for thirty miles off the land and even to fill the harbour of Chefoo by its drift.

In January we went to Nagasaki, then I think the only place in Japan where foreigners were allowed to land. All the Japanese were in native dress, and every yakonin, or gentleman, walked about with two swords, the long one to kill his enemies, and the short one to kill himself—if required to do so to avoid disgrace.[1]

From Nagasaki we went to Woosung and almost at once it was arranged to send an expedition up the Yangtse-kiang River to open its trade to Europe. A small squadron of light draft vessels was formed, and a paddle-wheel

---

[1] A Japanese midshipman committed suicide or ' Hara Kiri ' on board one of our ships, to avoid discredit for not learning as well as his Japanese brother officer.

steamer called the *Cowper*, which had been bought into the service, and drew only a few feet of water, was one of the above. Her Commander had been my superior as first-lieutenant in the *Cruizer*, and as she was to be manned from the *Chesapeake* I was selected to go as her executive officer.

This was pleasant for me. We fitted out at Shanghai, and the Admiral decided that as the *Cowper*, which was built for a passenger steamer on the Canton River, had much room we should take up several merchants representing the British firms at Shanghai, who were of course most anxious to go.

The squadron consisted of the *Coromandel* with the Admiral's flag and seven other vessels. We left Woosung on 12th February 1861 bound for Hankow.

The same day the *Cowper* and the *Centaur* ran aground, the river at that time being very little known, and its shoals frequently shifting. We were three days on the bank; it was freezing hard, and the keen north-east wind on our beam made things worse. The bulkheads were of the thinnest description. In the deck house where I and several more slept, we rigged up an iron oil cask as a stove, and used to go to sleep with it red hot, and wake up with the water in the place frozen.

At last we got afloat and arrived at Nankin. This place, formerly the seat of the Ming Dynasty government, should certainly be the

capital of China, chiefly because it is so central;
also because it stands on the bank of the Yangtse-
kiang, or ' Child of the Ocean.'

Nankin is said to have been the capital of
China since A.D. 420, when it was removed to
Pekin.

It covers an immense space and is not less
than seven miles across. It is walled round, the
walls in some places being over fifty feet high,
and their extent is twenty-two miles. This space
was never built all over, but contained gardens
and even cultivated fields.

Just outside the city wall at the south-west
side once stood the beautiful Porcelain Pagoda,
the only picture of which that I know of is in the
Admiralty Chart of the Opium War time. It was
probably over a hundred feet high, and the
outsides of all its bricks were covered with a
coating like china of various colours. I have one
perfect brick of it procured at our visit from the
mournful remains of the pagoda, which had been
blown up and so destroyed by the Taiping rebels,
who in 1853 captured the city, and held it till
1864.

When we were there the Tien Wang—or
' Heavenly King,' who was the head of the
Taiping rebels— lived in Nankin, and kept a sort
of court there.

He gave out that he was a Christian, no
doubt in hopes it would get him the countenance,
if not the actual support, of the western nations;
and had living in Nankin, under his protection
to give colour to the above, an English Protestant

missionary, the Rev. O. I. J. Roberts, who paid us a visit on board.

The latter wore Chinese dress, and no doubt tried to do good, but the really blasphemous doctrines enunciated by the Tien Wang forced him to give them all up as hopeless.

The Taiping rebellion began about 1850. Its object was not, like the Boxers in 1900, against the Outer Barbarians, but was anti-Dynastic, i.e. against the Manchu sovereigns. It was ended, as is well known, by Gordon's ever-victorious army about 1864. The rebels committed awful slaughter, and devastated many flourishing places. They cut off their pigtails, which are of Manchu origin, and wore their hair long all over the head in ancient Chinese fashion, and were often called 'Changmows,' meaning long hair, in consequence.

The towns we passed were mostly in the hands of the rebels. At Nankin the avenue to the Ming tombs from the city has on each side of it large stone figures of men and of various sorts of animals, now falling to pieces.

It is a common saying about a road in China, 'good for ten years and bad for a thousand.' This is of important roads paved at first with large smooth blocks of stone but never mended.

Our squadron was gradually diminished as we got up the river, ships being stationed at different places. On this occasion I went no higher than the Poyang Lake, where the *Atalante*, another merchant steamer bought into our service for a time, was temporarily stationed, and I was put *pro tem.* in command of her. The Admiral went on to Hankow, which is 676 statute miles from Shanghai.

We took up with us an expedition consisting of four persons, Colonel Sarel, Captain Blakiston, and two others. Their object was to explore the river as high up as possible, and probably then make their way through to India; which intention, having got about 1800 miles up the river, they had to give up, and returned.[1] Our Yangtse expedition was now over, and we returned to Shanghai.

On our return in the *Cowper* to Shanghai I found there the *Waterman*, whose late Lieutenant-Commander had just been promoted out of her. The *Chesapeake*, to which ship I really belonged, had gone down to Hong-Kong, and I was ordered to take the *Waterman* down there, the same vessel that in 1857 had been commanded by Lord Gilford at the Fatshan Creek action.

She was an old paddle-wheel steamer, built in India of teak, and had the old-fashioned flue boilers made of copper, both things long obsolete now.

Once she had been called the *Sir Charles Forbes*, so she was as used to aliases as a twice-deserted *Bounty* man. I had no officers for the voyage down except two engineers; however, we got there all right, and as the *Chesapeake* was going home, and the *Imperieuse*, to which ship

---

[1] See *The Yangtse*, 1862, by Captain Blakiston.

Sir James Hope shifted his flag, had no vacancy,
I was left in my new ship, and began a curious
commission.

The only further officers given me were a
second master, equal to acting navigating sub-
lieutenant, named Sherwin, who had just been
promoted from ordinary seaman in the flagship,
a most unusual proceeding ; and a boatswain
who had just got his warrant.

To man the vessel various captains were
told to send me a few men, so they naturally
selected their bad characters, no doubt feeling
sure they would all turn over a new leaf in new
surroundings. It was also, of course, a compliment to my moral example over men, at the
expense of their own personal influence !—but
these charitable hopes were not justified. I had
also a few Chinamen as part of my crew.

We were stationed for the summer up the
Canton River. I will not say it is the hottest naval
station in the world as I believe the Persian Gulf
is worse ; where I have been what is called
' credibly informed ' that in summer the starboard watch lie down on the upper deck and
sleep, while the port watch pump water over them
to cool them : and afterwards take turn about.

Canton was still held by us, so a few small
ships had to be kept in the river. I lay mostly
at Whampoa, and used to cruise about in a boat
I had specially rigged, making expeditions and
sleeping in her, by which I got to know the river
and its creeks pretty well. I also climbed up
three or four of the tall pagodas. Everyone

knows what a Chinese pagoda is like. If not let them go to Kew and see the one there. Their object has been much disputed, but I firmly believe they were erected at very various dates to propitiate the ' Fung Shui ' or spirit of wind and water.

There is no doubt, for example, that the one on the banks of the river below Hangchow, where is the highest Bore in the world, was built to control the Bore.

The legend is that a General, a native of Hangchow, was put to death unjustly by the Emperor, and that in revenge the Fung Shui made the Bore, which so terrified the inhabitants that the authorities built the pagoda as a peace-offering.

Marco Polo, who visited that region, does not mention the Bore, which he surely would have done had it existed then. I do not say this proves the above legend, but it seems to show that some change since his days has caused the Bore.

To climb a new pagoda—but I never saw one— you would ascend by stairs through the thickness of the wall, alternately from outside to inside, and the reverse, then when inside cross the floor to the next flight, or when outside walk round on a narrow ledge till you come to it.

My pagodas had usually lost their floors, and the ledges were often broken, but with ropes and planks we usually got up them, and took away a bell off the edge of the roof, or left a flag flying on the top.

One dark night when in mid-Canton River our boat was capsized by a sudden shift of wind, and in a moment was keel up. We could all swim, and by degrees unrigged the boat, uprighted her, baled her out, and re-rigged her.

Meanwhile I at one time swam away to get something floated off; I had in the boat two of my Chinamen, who missing me said: ' Oh Missa Sherwin I too muchee fear Captain have go bottom side.'

On one occasion I landed at night with men to get a tree I wanted as a spar—it proved a heavier job than expected, and it was broad daylight before finished ; also we had to get through a Chinese burial-ground, to, I fear, the detriment of some graves; which I regretted, as the Chinese greatly honour their dead.

In Canton is a mortuary where the bodies of the rich are often kept many weeks, or even months, in magnificent coffins, waiting till the Joss man finds out and indicates the fortunate spot to be buried in. This is, I believe, always on a hillside, where the interment then takes place, and a handsome stone covering is placed over the tomb, usually in a crescent, or half-circle, horizontally on the ground.

I have referred to my ship's company's characters. So bad a lot I have never had to deal with, and whatever may be thought of it in these humane days, I must confess that it was only by the wholesome deterrent influence of the ' cat ' that I kept order on board.

As regards this mode of punishment I have these few remarks to make. A hundred years ago it was administered both in the Navy and

FLOGGING IN THE NAVY

Army in a degree foolish, inhuman, and disgraceful to the services.

Forty years ago in the Navy it had got under such proper restrictions, the men were so protected from its hasty or ¦ill-judged use, and it was so seldom carried out, that only sentiment could condemn its existence. Ships often then ran a whole commission without the punishment, the knowledge of its possibility being sufficient. Like that I would have left it, practically a dead letter, but yet a deterrent.

Often since then I have seen a really good man ruined for life, and his family also, by a long term of imprisonment — sometimes five years' penal servitude — for an offence, not really disgraceful—insubordination perhaps—for which a few years before he would have had a moderate flogging, unknown outside the ship, and not there thought a disgrace, unrecorded on his certificate and forgotten; his family ignorant of it, and still having his money remitted to them, and nothing to prevent his rising to warrant rank.

Which of the two above pictures is the kinder? Would the parent of a public school boy rather have his son 'swished' or sent to prison? Once done away with I agree it cannot be restored, public feeling being what it is.

I dare say those—if any—who read the above will pronounce me a hard-hearted tyrant: still I do not think I am so; but anyhow I am not ashamed of my opinions, because they are based on long experience of sailors, and my only

H 2

object can be the real good of men and the service.

At the end of the year 1861 we evacuated Canton, having held it all but four years, and returned it to the Chinese Mandarin Government. This was done with more than one day's ceremonies at which I assisted.

I am sure that many, perhaps most, of the peace-loving, industrious, and trading Chinese were very sorry to lose us. I know a good many shopkeepers, who could, left for Hong-Kong to avoid being squeezed by the Mandarins.

This was my last job in the *Waterman*; ships were no longer wanted in the same way up the river, and we were paid off at Hong-Kong, and our ship was sold for about £6000.

CHAPTER IX

H.M.S. *SPHINX* AND *IMPERIEUSE*

Wreck of the *Norna*—Pelew Islands—Caroline Islands—Mariana Islands—Shanghai—Taiping Rebels—Ward's Contingent—Ship on Fire—Loss of a Gun—Naval Brigade—Singpoo—Kahding taken—Cholera—Gordon (Pacha).

On leaving the *Waterman* I went to the *Princess Charlotte*, the ship of the senior officer at Hong-Kong, to await passage to the flagship then at Shanghai, a vacancy having occurred on board her and the Admiral kindly appointing me to fill it.

While thus waiting I was employed running gunboats about on various errands, which I liked. One time I took out a gunboat, out of commission, with only a few of my men; she had no masts in, and so was dependent only on steam. At night on our way back to Hong-Kong the leading stoker rushed on deck and said, ' Oh sir, the engineer is drunk and has let all the water out of the boiler, which is getting red hot, and now he wants to let in lots of cold water to cool it.' What the result would soon have been all engineers know. The only thing to do was to draw fires, anchor, so as not to drift on shore, and let the boiler cool. The senior naval officer, to whom of course I reported it and who was the kindest of men, let the engineer off because he had a wife and family.

Let it not be supposed that I have a word to say against the engineers of the Navy. They have served us well, and the improvement in them in all respects since I joined the Navy is extraordinary. Now as a class they are abolished. The above is only a small episode.

Just at this time orders came from the Admiral to send the *Sphinx* on a cruise to the Caroline Islands to try and rescue a shipwrecked crew, whose history so far as then known was simply as follows.

An English barque called the *Norna* had sailed from Australia for Hong-Kong with a cargo of coals, and had run on shore on the St. Augustine reef,[1] latitude 6° North and longitude 158° East, and become a wreck. The captain, first mate, and some men had escaped in the long-boat and reached Manila, whence news came to China. The second mate and remainder of the crew were left on the reef.

On hearing of this our Admiral had sent a ship, the *Pioneer*, to look for the men left behind. She reached and searched the reef, but found no men there, only a record in a bottle saying what

---

[1] On the same reef a few years before the *Constance* of Antwerp was wrecked. Her crew got away in two boats, one of which reached the Philippine Islands, after great sufferings, and having killed and eaten two of their shipmates.

had happened and that they also had left the reef in a small boat. The *Pioneer* returned to Hong-Kong, but the Admiral was not satisfied and so sent the *Sphinx* for further search.

At this time that ship's Commander had just been invalided home, and her First-lieutenant was very ill. So the senior officer at Hong-Kong ordered me to go in her, against my wish, as I wanted to join the flagship, where fighting the rebels was going on. In the Navy one has to obey the last order, so I joined the *Sphinx*. She was a paddle-wheel sloop of six guns.

From Hong-Kong we went to Manila, and then searched the Eastern Philippine Islands for the missing men; thence going to the Pelew Islands, a most interesting group.

In 1783 the *Antelope*, an East India Company's ship, was wrecked here, and the King, Abbe Thule, let his son, called Prince Le Boo, be taken to England, where he died. In return for the kindness of the natives to the *Antelope's* crew, the company sent a present of cattle, pigs and fowls, which had greatly increased in numbers. The cattle were almost wild. The name of the islands is from Palos, the Spaniards giving it on account of the tall straight trees.

Arrived at Corror Island, where the King lives, we at once began friendly relations with him. He knew nothing of the men we looked for, but his quondam subjects at Babelthuap Island, the largest of the group, led by a Manila trader had revolted; and he knew not if our missing men were there or not.

When the King returned our Commander's visit, he came in a large war canoe, and dressed in a very gaudy uniform, looking like that of a Spanish Colonel.

Soon after the King landed, our Commander did so, and surprised his Majesty reclining, by the side of the road, in a state of nature, his uniform lying near, and trying to get cool. Still ' such divinity doth hedge a King ' that his courtiers stood respectfully round him.

So to Babelthuap we went in our boats, our acting-Commander, Ralph Brown by name, and myself. This was a few days' pleasant expedition. The natives at once began hostilities, which lasted two days, fighting in boats and up the creeks ; but the *Norna's* men were not there. On our return to Corror we were received with honour.

In Oceania city banquets and royal decorations exist not, but the extremes of tropical hospitality were extended to us ; till with much regret we had to leave these most friendly people. Our interpreter was a man called John Davey, who had been a seaman in a brig trading to the Matilotas Islands, not far off.

When leaving all hands except two got into a boat to tow the brig out. The natives saw their chance and boarded the vessel, leaving the boat's crew no option but to pull to sea for their lives. They reached the Pelew Islands, and afterwards all but Davey left in a passing trader, but he having a native wife, and still more being tattooed all over, decided to finish his life here. His case is nearly parallel with that of Gonzalo Guerrero, in Yucatan, related by Washington Irving.

Trade to the Pelew Islands was small, and chiefly for *beche de mer* and tortoiseshell. The former is a sea slug, about six inches long, found on the coral reefs. They are cut open and dried, and then taken to China, where they are esteemed a delicacy.

I am sorry to say that a few years after our visit a white man was killed in these islands, and a man-of-war was sent to investigate the matter. Her captain had no good interpreter, but was full of zeal. It was evident a white man had been killed, and as something had to be done, he had our dear old friend Abbe Thule (still the title) shot. I fancy this is not the first time zeal has outrun discretion !

From the Pelew Islands we started eastward, having an almost continuous easterly wind to contend with. Expecting this we had brought many axes. We now called at various islands, and when we did so landed our men and cut down trees, and brought off wood till we could only just move along the deck ; then went to sea, and burnt the wood mixed with coal, but it was soon expended, and after that we sailed only till next time.

In this cruise we did what is very interesting but equally rare now, viz. called at islands where there was no trace of their having had intercourse with Europeans. These islands were mostly roughly indicated on the chart, but that was all. Some were small atolls, with only twenty or thirty people on them. Their food was fish, fowls, cocoanuts, turtle in season, and some vegetables.

Sharks are very plentiful in the Caroline Islands. At one place we caught several, and one day I remember hauling one in, and on cutting him open we found three fins, and the tail of one of his relations inside him, and not yet digested. They belonged no doubt to some caught and cut up that morning.

At the same place I and the paymaster of the ship nearly came to grief. The wind was blowing off shore, and to leeward two or three miles off was a small island. We started in a skiff under sail to run down to it, which was no doubt rash of us.

The wind got worse, we could not return, but got through the fringing coral reef and landed. When we tried to return our boat began to fill, as soon as her nose was outside the reef. Thinking of the sharks we just succeeded in re-landing, wet through, which, however, in the tropics matters little. We took off our clothes to dry them, and as night came on went to sleep. Ultimately we were rescued by a large boat from the ship.

My companion, one of the best messmates I ever had, seemed fated. He was drowned in the Woosung River, below Shanghai, with others, their boat being swept by the current into a stake fishing-net.

At last we reached the Hogolu Islands, and as one morning we closed the land saw a boat running off to us under a canvas sail. Great excitement prevailed. She came alongside with two or three of the *Norna's* men, and this story. They had run westward before the wind, and at an island east of this had landed for water, and the natives had seized some of their crew, but these few had escaped and got on here. As the distance was not many miles, we made a boat expedition there, and rescued the few survivors of the capture, and taught their captors a lesson.

The kind natives of Hogolu were rewarded ; and having got all the *Norna's* crew who survived, we bore up for Hong-Kong, *via* Guam in the Mariana Islands.

Guam Isla Cara, I will never call these islands by their old Spanish name of ' Ladrones ' (*escepto del corazon*). Magellan discovered these islands in 1520. But the days are long past when Doctor Samuel Johnson could write of such :

> No secret island in the boundless main,
> No peaceful desert, yet unclaimed by Spain.

Guam now flies the Stars and Stripes, and America seems inclined to reciprocate the claims once made on her by Iberia.

In Guam few horses existed, and we often had to put up with oxen, not only to drive, but to ride. We spent but too few happy days there in the society of some charming Spanish ladies, with whom more than one of us fell in love, and a longer stay must have meant marriage.

I will say no more, except that we left Guam with the greatest regret, and finally reached

Hong - Kong nearly out of both coal and 'pro-visions. But our work had been well accom-plished, and our able acting - Commander was promoted.

On our return—we were four and a half months without any news of the world—we heard of the sad death of the Prince Consort, then four months past; of the beginning of the great Civil War in the then Dis-united States of America; and of how nearly the *Trent* affair had produced war between us and the Federal Government.

On leaving the *Sphinx* I went to Shanghai by P. & O. steamer and joined the *Imperieuse*, Admiral Hope's flagship, and my former vessel, as a mate. She was lying off the Settlement, and very exciting times were passing.

The Taiping rebels were devastating the pro-vince in the vicinity of Souchow and Shanghai, and even threatening the latter place. A very mixed contingent had been organised to resist them, and at this time it was commanded by a United States citizen called Ward, who I believe had been a filibuster previously in America. Ward's force consisted of pretty nearly any white man that he could get; and he had under him some deserters from our Navy, and probably Army too, enticed by the promise of good pay and occasional loot.

For a time our Admiral did not countenance him for the above reason, but the time seemed to show that it was best to make use of him, and so it came to pass that he was acting in conjunction with our naval and military forces.

I knew Ward a little. He was my idea of a typical modern western state soldier of fortune, energetic and quick, with a fine flow of strong language, and able to deal with the very mixed lot under his command.

Attacking Singpoo on one occasion he met an acquaintance, one of the opposite side, and fired at him, but missed. The other rejoined, 'What! Captain, can't you shoot straighter than that?' and put a revolver bullet into his mouth, from which, however, he recovered. Not long after he was killed in the neighbourhood of Ningpo, and he was succeeded in the command by a man of much the same type called Burgevine, whom I also remember.

To be a mercenary, or soldier of fortune, is very well if you can arrange to be either killed at once, or only slightly wounded, or better still not wounded at all ; but their position if maimed or badly hurt is a poor one.

Burgevine was wounded in the stomach, and I fancy suffered much pain which drove him to drink. Difficulties ensued, and if I remember aright he turned over to the rebels' side, but was taken by the Imperialists. The United States Consul made interest for him with the Taotai of Shanghai, but the only result was a report that he had unfortunately been drowned, or met with a fatal accident. Life counted for very little then and there.

About the time I got to Shanghai our Admiral

was wounded in action with the Changmows, and the French Admiral Protet was killed.

I commanded a company of small-arm men at his honorary funeral. I say honorary because the body was sent to France. At the above ceremony a custom I have not seen elsewhere was observed; viz. that the men, after the (temporary) interment in a sort of cave, all defiled past the coffin in single line, and as they did so each in turn discharged a blank charge from his rifle into the tomb.

One day about noon at Shanghai a large United States mail steamer about to sail for San Francisco caught fire. She was lying above us and the current was running strongly down the river. I went on board with men, fire engines, &c., to assist, as did others from the men-of-war of two or three nationalities. The ship soon became a sheet of flame forward, and evidently could not be saved. She broke from her moorings and began to drift helplessly down the river to the alarm of the many ships below.

The awkward part on board was that the seamen, both her own and those from the men-of-war, got at the wine stores and began to hastily sample the liquor. I saw men with a bottle in each hand of different brands, the necks of both bottles knocked off, alternately tasting each, and their lips bleeding from the sharp glass. Our anxiety of course was not to leave these votaries of Silenus to perish in a fiery furnace. The steamer was, of course, destroyed, but no other ship was damaged.

About this time an unlucky episode occurred. Our ship was almost denuded of officers and men. From the Admiral downwards, all who could be spared were away fighting the rebels. Only the two junior lieutenants remained on board, I being junior of all. News arrived that the town of Kahding held by the Imperialists, and distant some thirty miles, was fiercely beset by the enemy, and unless reinforced would probably fall.

The senior naval officer at Shanghai was the captain of a man-of-war troopship, and of course was referred to. He decided to send some hired boats, with stores and ammunition and what men could be scraped together; also a 12-pounder brass field-piece that remained in our ship, with its seamen crew, and a midshipman; but that his first-lieutenant should go in command.

Of course this made us very angry. The lieutenant, my senior, could not go, being in charge of the ship, but I could. So I went on board the senior officer's ship politely to remonstrate, until I was ordered to leave his ship at once.

The sequel was this: The expedition started, but when about half-way, going along a narrow creek came to a town, and saw a strong party of rebels entering it. They landed our gun to fight it and had to cross the creek by a narrow stone bridge, where it got jammed. The rebels won the day, the gun was lost, also the boats' stores, &c., and the sole survivors were those who hastily retired with only what they stood up in.

Our Admiral was, of course, very angry, and

the Flag-Captain said to me, ' Well, Seymour, of course they should have sent you, but you were perhaps well out of it as your choice might have been to be killed or to run away.'

Kahding fell into the hands of the rebels, and I was at the re-taking of it later on. Of course in all fighting with the Chinese, especially with the rebels, quarter by them is never given. It was the same with the Boxers in 1900.

During the summer of 1862 I was for a time away in command of a small-arm party of seamen, attached to the soldiers, and under the superior command of the Brigadier-General (Stavely). This of course we enjoyed, and not the less that we then got Indian pay and allowances. I was paid as a captain in the Army, the same rank as a lieutenant, R.N., which just doubled my pay. During the above we took Singpoo from the rebels, the place I referred to before.

The summer passed away in the above manner, but our ship's company from over-exposure to the heat, &c., became sickly, and we went to Chefoo at the entrance to the Gulf of Pechili to recruit our health.

In October we returned to Shanghai, and an expedition was arranged to retake Kahding, under the immediate command of our Admiral, and with some French allies. I had command of two small-arm companies. This part of China abounds in narrow creeks, and our way there was made mostly by water.

Society at Shanghai possesses many house-boats, commonly called ' chops,' for shooting, or other pleasure parties, to go away and live in. One of these seemed desirable for our accommodation and was accordingly 'requisitioned' by my enterprising midshipmen for our small family, consisting of ourselves and a commissariat officer, always a very good friend to have.

On our way back my young officers annexed some Chinese coolies employed by the French, and an interchange of hostilities in consequence was very narrowly avoided.

The attack on Kahding was well arranged, and the place soon stormed and taken, but misfortune attended our return in the shape of an epidemic of cholera. This was the first time I had been among it since the Black Sea, in 1854.

I suppose everything almost, except a broken bone, is now caused by a microbe ; but if so it is curious how at times in places a narrow line seems drawn for a disease. I have heard of it in ships, and on this occasion on shore at Shanghai, as regards neighbouring houses.

The above was our last active service against the rebels, and our Admiral, whose time on the station had already been extended, was relieved by Admiral Kuper.

It happened that at this moment the Imperial Contingent, which I have mentioned on p. 108, was without a leader owing to the disappearance of the unhappy Burgevine. It was a nice question who should succeed him. No one seemed specially prominent.

At this juncture Sir James Hope proposed that our Captain of Marines, who was a very good

officer, and had for a year on and off been employed against the Taipings, should have command of the local Imperial Army. This was
agreed to by the Taotai of Shanghai, and the
above officer took the command, with his subaltern
from our ship as his staff officer.

We now left Shanghai, but what followed
was that in a very few months the above
arrangement broke down. The post was without
precedent, and required perhaps a genius.

There happened to be at Shanghai a young
and then unknown officer of Royal Engineers,
named Charles George Gordon, to whom was
given the command of what then acquired the
name of the 'ever-victorious army.'

It has been said 'Happy is the nation that
has no history,' and perhaps the same applies to
a sea voyage, for an ordinary one is not interesting
to the general reader. From Hong-Kong we left
in November for England, of course round the
Cape of Good Hope, and nearly four months'
voyage took us to Portsmouth, where we paid off
in March 1863. The commission had been of
much interest, and the ship a united one, and had
changed her officers comparatively little.

CHAPTER X

FLAG-LIEUTENANT

Old Portsmouth—Channel Islands—Pirate Story—Anecdote of Nelson—Garibaldi—Lady Smith—Royal Yacht—French Fleet—Gale of Wind.

In March 1863 I was appointed Flag-lieutenant to my uncle, Admiral Sir Michael Seymour, the Commander-in-Chief at Portsmouth.

In those days most admirals' commands—except dockyards — entitled the Admiral on hauling down his flag to give a commander's commission to a lieutenant qualified by seniority and service for it. It was customary, and almost understood, that these promotions went to the flag-lieutenant. So the above appointment had much advantage for me, besides a three years' spell of agreeable service.

It was really my introduction to shore life and society in England, and though a naval officer's first requirement is to command a ship at sea, the higher he gets in the service the more he needs to be also something of a man of the world. At Portsmouth much could be picked up of one's profession, besides which I got the habit of reading, and learnt one or two things useful in society.

No old town that I know is nearly so much altered as Portsmouth and Portsea are since 1863. In those days both places were enclosed in their own fortifications, i.e. regular ramparts, with ditches, and narrow gates with drawbridges to them.

The idea was that each town should be independent of the other, and that one might be taken and the other hold out ; which possibly could once, for a short time, have been the case.

Between them was a large salt-water lake, now occupied by the recreation grounds and public gardens. This lake was, of course, fed from the harbour, and the block between it and the sea was called the ' Mill dam,' because a mill had stood there to grind corn for the garrison as required, and its position had contained the mill redoubt.

Just beyond the present Naval Club as you go towards Southsea were the southern lines of Portsmouth, and in them a gate and a drawbridge, at which it is said Lord Nelson as a captain was nearly killed by the horse he was riding bolting for the gate, a cart being in it and no room to pass ; but that Captain Nelson saved himself by jumping off the horse.

When I entered the service the dockyard ended at the Anchor gate, and Whale Island was no larger than a big ship's upper deck. As regards Portsmouth Harbour, it is really only a ditch after all, much increased and improved by dredging. But it can only be entered, or left, by large vessels at limited times of tide, and with tugs to help, and very skilful handling.

Part of the duty of the Portsmouth Port Admiral was to visit yearly the Channel Islands, to inspect the naval boys' training establishment at Gorey in Jersey. This he did in his official yacht the *Fire Queen,* a paddle-wheel steamer that had belonged to Mr. Assheton Smith, of fox-hunting renown.

My uncle always took a party, among them relations, and we much enjoyed it. Another vessel was required, and the old *Sprightly* went. My contemporaries will well remember her and her fine old ' Master Commander,' G. Allen, a regular specimen of the old British naval salt.

Allen has described to me when as a boy he saw the crowd run to see Nelson embark for the last time to pull off to the *Victory* at St. Helens in September 1805. Afterwards Allen served in the Walcheren expedition.

By Mr. Childers' retirement scheme Allen was retired and put on half-pay. The change of life soon unhappily killed him !

At Alderney one sees how absurdly the public money can be wasted, more than, perhaps, at any other place. I believe the history of it is, that when during the Napoleonic wars we were blockading Cherbourg it was thought a harbour at Alderney for our ships to run into for shelter would be useful.

The work was begun about the middle of last

century, and as ships increased in length, the first plan was altered by turning the breakwater outwards to give more room inside it. This made a ' re-entrant ' angle and a weak spot through which the sea made a breach.

The water deepened as they worked out, and I think about 1872 the authorities saw what an error had been made in doing anything at all there, and the matter was abandoned. The forts also, of which there were fifteen erected on the island, became practically valueless.

The interesting and surprising thing about it, to my mind, is the evidence of the extraordinary power of the sea ; I have been there as late as 1877, and seen pieces of rock equal in bulk to a cube three feet through, that after a heavy gale from seaward were found lying on the footway inside the breakwater.

Now the breakwater there was some twenty feet of perpendicular stone wall on its outer side, of which say half was above high-water mark ; this wall sprang from a slope of stone foundation that rose from a depth of quite ten fathoms there, so the above piece of rock must have been lifted by the sea and thrown over the wall. At least that is what the people there declared must be the case.

We went all three years to the Channel Islands and called at St. Malo and Cherbourg. This latter is a fine specimen of what art alone can do to create a naval port, but such a one can never be satisfactory against the modern long-range guns. The statue of the great Napoleon I admired with his ' J'ai resolu de renouveler à Cherbourg les merveilles de l'Egypte,' inscribed on it. Just the sort of way he would have put it I think.

I went to Mont St. Michel, which is indeed unique, and overshadows our St. Michael's Mount in Cornwall. While here we made acquaintance with a young priest of the Roman Church, who was anxious to point out to us the mark of the foot of the Archangel Michael when he descended and first alighted on a rock near Doll, a few miles inland of Mont St. Michel, and before the Archangel went there.

One day from Portsmouth I went with the Admiral to visit an old friend of his, by name Admiral Walcote ; in his dining-room was the picture of a fine brigantine lying in a tropical creek, of which the owner told us the following story.

He was First-lieutenant in the *Tyne* at the time in the West Indies, and they were in pursuit of this vessel called the *Zarngozanna*, which was a noted pirate. At last they came off the entrance to a narrow creek which they knew of in the Isle of Pines, and where the pirate ship was lying. Two other vessels were with the *Tyne*, but could not go up the creek; so the only thing to do was to send the boats in and attack with them. This they did, and after a good fight they carried the brigantine and defeated her crew.

The captain of her, Aragonez by name, a Spaniard, was not killed or very badly wounded. He was taken on board the *Tyne*, the Captain of which said to him, ' It is a sad thing, sir, to see a fine young man like 'you in this position'; to which the pirate replied, ' Don't worry yourself about me; if I had got you I'd have hanged you up to my yardarm.' There is the true pirate spirit !

The pirates were taken to Kingston, Jamaica, tried, and twenty of them hanged at ' Gallows' Point ' now Port Royal, when the pirate captain cheered his men up to the gallows.

Read ' Tom Cringle's Log,' that book whose descriptions of tropical scenery are unsurpassed, and in Chapters IX and XI you will see what might almost be these very episodes ; though I think the first is meant for another occasion also at the Isle of Pines, which is an island south of Havana, in Cuba. Here a lieutenant (Layton) went in in a gig to reconnoitre and was fired on ; a midshipman (Stroud) and some of the crew were killed, the lieutenant was taken prisoner by the pirates and murdered. Finally the pirates were destroyed and their schooner which they had sunk was got up again.

The position of flag-lieutenant at a home port has its advantages and pleasures, but provides no matters of professional interest.

I preferred hunting to any other sport, and carried it out as far as I could afford to. There were three other lieutenants stationed in the port, who were equally fond of it, and so we often made a party. We were nearly always with the Hambledon Hounds, because they were our nearest ; at that time their master was Earl Poulett, who spent a lot of money on them, though they were also a subscription pack. Four advertised meets a week were the regular thing, but they were often out more than that.

I have seen our M.F.H. amused and heard him make caustic remarks on young naval officers, when things were dull, 'larking' over anything promising that was near. But in many cases the mounts were 'hirelings,' and the Sea Nimrod was anxious to get his money's worth out of the animal.

I believe some people have wondered that sailors should be so fond, as they often are, of riding; but if you consider the classic legend of the naming of Athens, I think you will see we have a natural tendency—or right—to be fond of horses, considering that their origin is there said to be owed to our Father Neptune.

We used also to go with the H.H. and the Hursley Hounds, but that mostly required training out and home, which was an extra expense to be more rarely indulged in. I have also been with Mr. Neville's staghounds in the Basingstoke direction. The carted stag is not, of course, the real sport of hunting a wild animal, but it ensures a good gallop.

I remember once with these hounds we crossed the track of the Vine (fox) Hounds running a fox, and the stronger scent I suppose of our quarry attracted several of them from their own trail.

Admiral Sir George Westphal paid a visit to my uncle at Portsmouth and related to us an interesting story about Trafalgar. It was this:

He was a midshipman in the *Victory*, and soon after Nelson was wounded, he (Westphal) was hit in the head, carried below and put down near the Admiral, who noticed him and asking who it was, said, 'Put my coat under his head.' This was done, and as Westphal's head was bleeding his hair stuck to the bullion of the Admiral's epaulette, and to get the coat away they cut off some of the bullion, which he, of course, kept.

He said to me, 'If you look carefully at Nelson's coat in the Painted Hall at Greenwich you will see that some of the bullion has been cut off'; this I have done. I told this story to Admiral Mahan, who regretted he had not known it before he wrote the life of Nelson. I advise young people, if they have the opportunity of hearing from older ones interesting occurrences in which the latter were concerned long ago, to try and do so.

In April 1865 we had a visit at Portsmouth from Garibaldi, and the enthusiasm with which he was received in England was quite extraordinary. He came dressed, as he is usually represented, in a red flannel shirt, no coat, a soft light-coloured hat, and light-coloured trousers. He was a rather handsome and decidedly dignified man, with a grave, but pleasant expression.

He lunched with the Admiral, and I afterwards took him to Southsea to visit an old friend, a Mrs. White. It was not easy to find her; when we did it was up a narrow *cul de sac*, so we got out of the carriage and walked. I mention this because I was struck by the effrontery of an

Irishwoman who, amidst the cheers for Garibaldi
of the few spectators, put her head out of her
window, shook her fist and called out —— (not
a blessing) to the man that would! pull down the
Pope.

Among many guests staying in the Admiralty
House I remember Lady Smith, widow of the
General, Sir Harry Smith. Her name is immor-
talised by the famous Boer siege of the town
named after her, and defended by Sir George
White. Her meeting with her future husband
was romantic ; when Badajos was stormed and
about to be sacked, she, then a girl, found, and
threw herself by chance on the protection of,
Harry Smith, then a subaltern, who fell in love
with the charming young Spaniard, and afterwards married her.

She often wore an order given her for being
under fire in India. Even when I knew her she
spoke with a very Spanish accent.

We also had a visit from the great General
Todleben, the practical defender of Sevastopol.
He was a tall, strong-built, soldierly looking man,
with good high-class Russian manners. He spoke
French and German, but not English, which he
said he meant to learn.

In 1865 I was lent to the *Victoria and Albert*
for her cruise to Kingston to convey H.R.H. the
Prince of Wales (our late lamented King Edward
VII) to open the Exhibition at Dublin. The
Irish showed immense enthusiasm, and apparent
loyalty, which I believe most of them really feel
at such a time. It is, however, but fair to say

that the presence and patronage of Royalty in Ireland are not as encouraging to that country as they are to Scotland.

The Royal yacht was the most agreeable vessel I ever did duty on board. As regards discipline, it seemed natural to all in her, and not only were the men all of good character, but the idea of dismissal from 'the yacht' was sufficient deterrent from misconduct.

While at Holyhead we visited the South Stack lighthouse, where the sea-gulls are so tame that the sitting hen only just moves off her nest if required for a lighthouse-keeper to take an egg from under her; no barndoor fowl seems tamer.

In 1865 we had a grand official visit from the French Fleet. It was many years since the last one. Great preparations were made, and it all went off very well. The Admiralty gave a great ball in the Naval College in the dockyard. The enclosed stone-paved courtyard in the half H of the building was all floored over and made the ballroom, the windows all round were taken out and the rooms utilised as required. About 1640 people were counted into the place as guests, and the entertainment lasted till nearly 6 A.M., as I well remember.

But perhaps the most extensive fête of the occasion was that given by the Municipality of Portsmouth of the Governor's Green. It lasted in all about twelve hours. Beginning at 3 P.M. with a promenade concert and succeeded by a banquet, it then gracefully shaded off into a ball, towards the conclusion of which some of the society of Portsmouth, who had somehow not had invitations, graced the occasion with their presence, and did not detract from the conviviality !

Just before I left Portsmouth there came on one Sunday morning a gale of wind, more nearly approaching a hurricane in force than anything I remember in England. Next day the streets were strewn with tiles, chimney-pots, &c., and many trees both there and in the country near were blown down ; but what I want to mention is that in the afternoon the harbour could not be crossed.

A ship had gone ashore off Haslar and I was anxious to get over to the wreck, but no waterman would try it. I met the Commander of Coastguard, Frederick Robinson, who wanted to get there too, and had his service boat manned and offered me a passage. But the moment we were exposed to the wind blowing right into the harbour the seas began to sweep over our boat, and we only just succeeded in turning her round, and by baling hard getting back before she was quite swamped.

In March 1866 my uncle hauled down his flag at Portsmouth, and I was given what was called the ' haul-down promotion,' and so made a commander, and went on half-pay for the first time.

CHAPTER XI

THE *MAZINTHIEN*

Wolfrock — Peterhead — Young Surgeons — Sailing North — Whales—Seals—Walrus—Bears—Arctic Interests—Sir John Franklin—Festivity.

THE summer of 1866 was my first real freedom since I entered the Navy, and as such was greatly appreciated by me. But at that date there were comparatively few positions for commanders as second in command, and those were usually offered to officers who had been old first-lieutenants of ships, and commanders were frequently three years and over before they got separate commands. I had thus the prospect of long half-pay, and to consider how to occupy it.

During the summer being at Penzance I visited the Wolfrock off the Land's End, where a lighthouse was then being built by Mr. W. Douglas. Probably none more difficult to build exists.

The rock is of killas or green stone, which is very hard; it is oblong, the extreme size 110 by 140 feet at low water and then quite steep below. We landed with difficulty in cork jackets by order, as we might have to swim off. It took two years' work to prepare for laying the first stone of the Wolf, and three years to place the three first stones of the lowest course : while the present Eddystone Lighthouse was built in that time.

It took about eight years to complete the Wolfrock Lighthouse. The stones up to the twentieth course, where the entrance door is, are fastened together by cement, by metal bolts, about two feet long, half being in each course of stone, and by slate joggles, a foot long and six inches square, placed with half of them in each course. The Wolfrock light so far is a great success. I published an account of my visit in the *Nautical Magazine* for September 1866.

Towards the end of the year I soaked myself in Arctic literature, and felt anxious to see those regions, and if we had another Arctic expedition to join in it. So early in 1867 I arranged to go for a northern cruise in the whaling ship *Mazinthien* of Peterhead.

This vessel was about 400 tons, a full-rigged ship, but with an auxiliary screw able to drive her about seven knots. Her name is from an Indian chief, she having been built at Miramichi in New Brunswick. She was, of course, immensely strengthened to stand the ice. Her captain was Mr. John Gray, a first-rate seaman, and of a regular old whaling family, Peterhead being then, and for several years before, a great whaling port. Our total complement was fifty-five. She carried two mates, a spectioneer, four harpooners, two engineers, and various other odd ratings, besides a surgeon; but these latter in the whaling ships were usually young medical students from Edinburgh, who having ' outrun the constable ' felt safer at sea, and anxious not to revisit ' Auld Reekie ' till they had a few ' bawbees ' in their pockets.

One day when we were in the ice a man in another ship had his leg so smashed that it had to be amputated; the various young ' Galens ' near were invited to assemble and consult, but each was anxious that another should undertake the operation. I was assured that it was at last performed with a clasp knife and the carpenter's saw : what became of the patient I do not know.

The year before the surgeon of our ship (the same as in my year) took to his bed on going south ; the Captain visited him and, after inquiring for his symptoms and consulting the medical book he had, gave as his diagnosis that the patient had delirium tremens ; it was thought best to get him out of his bed, when the unhappy man was found to have been lying on a collection of empty bottles which he secreted there till the ship's southward route took her to dark nights, when the bottles could be consigned to the deep. The moral of this is, when in a whaler do not be ill or have an accident !

On 19th March 1867 we left Peterhead and began a very rough and most unpleasant voyage to the North. The ship was very lively, and a whaler is not built for comfort—the men's quarters are indeed bad. They sleep in bunks, often two men in one bunk; cleanliness is not thought of, nor perhaps what is said to be next to it. Our only religious observance, if such it be, was that every Friday we had salt fish for dinner.

The dirt of a whaler and her crew must almost be seen to be believed; as for the men, their faces become like niggers, and washing at all with many is relegated to a very dubious date.

Though the ship had steam power, it was kept mostly to move her when beset by ice. Wind binds the ice floes together, but when it is calm they are much more easily pushed apart, and channels made among them.

Our crew were not over-sober when we sailed, and even the first mate was so overcome by his feelings on discovering that his son and heir, fourteen years old, had stowed himself away on board that he required too much of the national liquid to steady his nerves.

By the end of March we were among the ice floes, and in the neighbourhood of Jan Mayen Island. Our destination was what is called 'Greenland,' i.e. the sea between it and Spitsbergen, in distinction from the course to the westward of Greenland, to Baffin Bay, and called 'Up the Straits.'

I may here remark that the whaling business altered much as time went on. Those who have read that most interesting book by Scoresby on whaling voyages know that a hundred years ago the right whale was far more plentiful than it is now, and vessels could then anchor in, say, Magdalena Bay in Spitsbergen, land their apparatus for boiling down the blubber, and with their boats catch many whales in the offing. This is now all over, and it seems possible that the right whale will become extinct before very long.

My readers may know that there are many kinds of whales, i.e. of sea warm-blooded mammals, somewhat fishlike in shape, and having no hinder limbs. These are divided into two general classes, viz. the Balœna species for those that have whale-bone instead of teeth, and the Delphinus species that have teeth and no whalebone; of the latter class the sperm whale or *Macrocephalus* is the largest, and most valuable, and best known.

Of the former, first in value is the *Balœna mysticetus*, called generally the 'right whale,' because it is the one most wanted by the Northern whalers. The Yankees call it the 'bowhead,' because of the shape of its profile. 'Whalebone,' I may be allowed to state, is a set of horny prongs or spikes attached to both jaws; when the mouth is shut they fit into each other, as the fingers of two hands might, and having a thick hairy coating to them, thus form a sort of sieve.

The right whales feed on medusæ, which are about the size of a grain of rice. Having found a part of the sea where these abound, the whale swims with his mouth open, and when he feels there are many medusæ inside it, he closes his mouth ; and the above sieve, when he then squirts the water out, retains the medusæ, which he swallows and thus feeds himself.

When the above so-called 'whalebone' is six feet long in the upper jaw, the whale is called 'sized.' The oil is, of course, got from the blubber, which may be considered the creature's

great coat, as it keeps him warm. When I was
in the whaler, the oil was worth about £45 a ton,
and with the value of the whalebone[1] a very large
whale would be worth about £2000 in all. A
whale is, of course, not a fish, but the whalers
always call it so, and indeed to them 'a fish'
is nothing else.

The object of our voyage was to get both seals
and whales if possible. Many other ships were
bent on the same errand. In the Arctic regions
there are four species of sea seal, viz. the *Phoca
hispida*, or, as it is called, 'bladder nose,' from
a sort of appendage over the nose in the male only
which is inflatable ; these are the largest seals
there and grow to ten feet long. Next the
Phoca greenlandica or 'saddle-back,' so called
from the marking like a saddle on its back: they
grow to about seven or eight feet long. Next the
'floerat,' as called by the sealers ; these grow
to about three and a half feet long. Also a
ground or shallow water seal only found near the
land.

The saddle-back is by far the most numerous
there ; and I have been in the 'crow's nest' at
the masthead with ice all round, and thickly
covered with the 'saddle-back' seals. Thousands and thousands of them—such a sight of
warm-blooded animal life as I think can be seen
nowhere else. These are the seals sought in the
Arctic regions; they are not fur seals at all, but
their skins make fine soft leather, and their
blubber yields oil worth about £40 a ton.

[1] Used principally, I believe, for ladies' corsets.

Birds are of various types; the mallemuck is by far the most numerous, but rarely seen south of 62° N. There are the lordly Burgomaster gull, the graceful snow bird, the placid puffin, the greedy mallemuck and the lively kittywake, besides others.

In April the young seals are born on the ice, and they and their mothers are killed and skinned. It is a most pathetic scene, and painful to witness. In about a month the young can take to the water and shift for themselves; the mothers then leave them and go away with the males who are waiting for them. The first is called the ' young sealing '; now comes the other, or ' old sealing,' when you hunt the seals up and shoot them as you can. About this there is often real sport.

I have frequently noticed that if you approach a seal right in front of him, he does not seem to make you out nearly as quickly as if you are on one side of him. Paley, in his ' Natural Theology,' at p. 16, says he believes that the seal has not the ability to see an object with both eyes as if it were only one object—is this true ?

Also I have noticed, when stalking sleeping seals over the ice, if one scents you and raises his head, the others do so too ; but if, when you have lain down quietly, the first alarmed again reposes himself, the others do the same.

A seal in motion is not very easy to kill. On the ice it bobs up and down as it goes on, and unless you hit it right through the head or heart, it will probably escape. In the water you must, of course, wait till it shows its head, and then if you kill it at once the head sinks under the water, the air does not at once escape, and it may float till picked up.

One day we saw a large walrus on the side of an ice floe and a boat went after it. I was in her with the second mate. In the bow was a harpoon gun; I was anxious to fire it, but the second mate said that he was more used to them, and therefore the best hand at it. I was just behind him with my rifle. The walrus was asleep on ice some eight feet high, the lovely snow bird and greedy mallemuck walking about close to and fro, now and then arousing him with their cries. At last he woke and reared up his ponderous form. The second mate fired the gun and both he and I at once disappeared in the bottom of the boat. What had happened? Is the walrus on top of us? Happily no; but the swivel of the gun has broken, and the second mate, with a terrible gash on his face, and the gun, are on top of me. I shake myself clear and with my rifle finish off the walrus, who is trying to capsize our boat. I have his head now.

Sometimes we saw polar bears, and chased them over the ice; it is wonderful how well, heavy as they are, they can get over ice barely strong enough for a man's weight. We got a few at which I assisted. The polar bear *Ursus maritimus* is so called because he is almost amphibious.

The Rev. J. G. Wood, in his book, ' Homes without Hands,' Chapter I, says that the female polar bear, when expecting to have cubs, first eats enormously, and then towards December scrapes a hole in the snow near a rock, lies down and lets the snow cover her; this forms a cell in which she stays during her accouchement, and suckles her cubs till March, when she emerges with them. She usually has twins. Her breath keeps open a hole in the snow which provides her with air to breathe.

It was irresistible to wander over the ice floes with a gun or rifle, but one should not go alone as the ice is apt to be treacherous. Twice when alone I nearly came to grief. The ice, newly frozen, gave way and let me in, but I at once threw myself forward and spread out my arms, thus covering as much ice as possible. In this way I struggled on to firm ice, and eventually regained the ship, with both gun or rifle, but with frozen clothes.

On one occasion when with others I regularly fell in, and was hardly consoled by being told I was now a 'Freeman of Greenland.' This occurred owing to the ice having got rotten in the late spring. At the 'old sealing' I usually went away in a boat for several hours, regardless of time, as the sun was always above the horizon. It was a fine healthy life, and the fresh air of the best.

Accidents of course occur, through careless shooting and nips of the ice, but one only wonders the first are not more common.

The air is wonderfully clear. I have seen Mount Beerenberg, 6700 feet high, quite clearly eighty miles off.

Life in a whaling ship has many phases foreign

to the shore, and very different from a man-of-war. I remember one afternoon, when we had been unlucky in getting anything, the mate came into the cabin to take off his sea boots and warm his feet before the stove, on top of which, in a boiler, was always kept a decoction of tea, well boiled, and calculated to ruin the stomach and nerves of anyone but a Caledonian sailor.

Enter the steward, by name Alexander, and of course called ' Sandy,' in a great state of excitement, because the captain had just well abused him.

The mate said, ' Ah weel, Sandy, do ye ken there was a man called Napoleon Bonaparte ? '

Sandy replied, ' Ah ken it.'

The mate rejoined, ' He was at St. Helena, and one day going down the hill by a narrow path overtook two ladies also descending, and met an old man coming up and carrying a heavy load. The ladies kept to the path ; but Napoleon stepped on one side and said, " Ladies, if you do not respect the man, respect the burden."'

It is curious how many whalers take up a dog or two. We had three large ones. Of these one named ' Teazer ' one day had a fit. I was below when they called out to me, ' Teazer has gone mad.' I ran on deck and saw he was in a fit. The scene was amusing. Many of the men had taken to the rigging, but the more courageous were getting rifles to shoot the dog. I dragged him right aft, and tied him up there, this being the only condition on which they would spare his life. In time he recovered.

During the cruise I had various occupations: kept the log, took sights for the reckoning, went aloft, often to the crow's nest (a cask secured to the main-top-gallant mast) ; sometimes I conned the ship, or took a trick at the helm and helped in various jobs for many hours together. And I was frequently away in the boats, working as one of the crew, and shooting seals, a most healthy outdoor life. When tacking the ship it was often curious to see at the order ' Mainsail haul ' how a heavy shower of ice frozen on to the rigging aloft came down on us on deck.

The tragic story of the expedition under Sir John Franklin has always to me possessed great interest. I only refer to it here because of what the mate of the *Mazinthien* told me, which I will preface by one or two remarks.

Arctic exploration has in my opinion ten times the interest of Antarctic, for the following reasons. When the first attempts were made at the beginning of the sixteenth century, great hopes were entertained that a practical short passage for ships from Europe to China would be found. Arctic voyagers, though they failed to find that, found human beings (the Esquimaux) and animals of many kinds and in profusion, besides an intricacy of bays, creeks, and islands to examine and chart.

In the Antarctic nothing comparable to the above may be said to exist. Since Sir James Ross in 1841 with H.M.S. *Erebus* and *Terror* discovered Victoria Land and the mountains named after his ships, it has been pretty apparent that a lofty and large island, in fact a continent, covered the area about the South Pole, and further researches have shown that continent to be bare of life, except as to some birds.

That the interests and attractions of the North are not to be found in the South only, if anything, adds to the heroic efforts that have been, and are being, made to reach the South Pole ; but the North to my mind must always have the greatest interest.

I need hardly remind my readers that Sir John Franklin in 1845 left England in the *Erebus* and *Terror* to discover, and if possible pass through, a north-west passage. In 1846 his ships were permanently beset by ice about 20 miles N.N.W. of King William's Land, and all their crews perished in endeavouring to escape by Back's fish river.

I know no more pathetic document than the 'record' found by Lieutenant Hobson in 1859 at Point Victory in King William's Land, when all that it conveys is well considered. Few words seldom indicated more.

A quaint old whaling captain, by name Martin, who was up in a whaler when I was, had in 1845 commanded a ship called the *Enterprise*, and our mate, by name Aitkin, was then a boy on board her. She met Sir John Franklin's ships in Melville Bay, and all three vessels made fast to the same iceberg to get fresh water from it.

Several of Sir John's officers came on board the *Enterprise* to ask Captain Martin to dine with Sir John that day and to take their mail for England. Martin asked the officers down into his cabin, and, leaving his mate there to entertain them, retreated to the crow's nest in order to avoid society. And two hours before the dinner time he suddenly cast off from the berg, made sail, and stood away without giving the members of Sir John Franklin's expedition their—as it proved—last chance, of sending letters home.

In April we had one really bad night; a gale of wind from the south-east caught us just to windward of the pack. In such a case there are two options: one to burrow well into the pack if you can, and get shelter from it, but you must go a good way in ; the other to get away from the ice altogether.

The first we could not do, so had to try the second, which resulted in many collisions with bits of ice, the loss of a boat, our figure-head, cut water and head knee, and very nearly of the bow-sprit. Nothing but a specially fortified ship could have stood the ice blows that our poor vessel got through that night.

A propos of Caledonian Sabbatarianism I see in my journal that on Easter Day the crew worked specially hard from 5 A.M. to 10 P.M.

Indeed we may be said to have acted like the West Coast of Africa palm-oil trader, who when he got abreast of Cape Palmas, outward bound, called the crew aft, produced a piece of board, wrote 'Sunday' on it, then threw it overboard, and said to his men: 'No more Sundays, boys, till we pass here going North.'

Of course we never anchored, being in very

deep wazer, but when we found ourselves fast to ice near another ship we sometimes exchanged hospitality, which generally meant a long evening of drinking, smoking, and yarning.

I remember specially one such symposium in our ship—three or four whaling captains came ; one was an elderly man, much given to drink, and if the adage *in vino veritas* is true, not a pleasant master for his men. In a few hours he got tipsy, abusive and quarrelsome, threw the inkstand at me, and tried to follow it up with the coal-scuttle.

Finally his spectioneer, who knew how to manage him, was sent for, and having been got back to his ship, he ascended to the crow's nest, a first-rate place in which to cool his head.

On this occasion I was much struck with the calm conduct of our captain (John Gray). It is a very awkward position for one of your guests to get riotously drunk at your table, and in these days happily it rarely occurs.

But if it does, or did, you have to remember the duties of hospitality, and that the inebriated one is your guest. This our host did, and behaved in a way worthy of anyone in rank from a prince downwards.

Very few whales were got in ' Greenland ' that season ; we saw some, and went away in the boats after them, but had not the luck to get fast to one at all. We neared in turn both Greenland and Spitsbergen and went up to about 80° North.

I should like to tell various stories that I

heard, but I will refrain. By the way, why is the word ' story ' of such ambiguous meaning, and doubtfully veracious reputation ?

Finally we returned to our port, Peterhead, and I took leave of as fine a set of honest, hardy seamen as one would find. Our voyage, owing to the large quantity of seals that we had got, paid the owners very well.

CHAPTER XII

THE COASTGUARD

Queenstown—Coastguard Cutters—Plymouth.

ONE morning to my surprise I got an official letter from the Admiralty appointing me additional to H.M.S. *Frederick William* at Foynes in Ireland, for service in H.M. Coastguard.

As the Fenians were then in full swing and I was a loyal subject—now called a 'Unionist'—I hoped and thought it was to try and exterminate James Stephens and his followers. However, I found it was not so high an office, but simply an ordinary berth as inspecting commander of the Queenstown Division of Coastguard.

Nowadays lieutenants and commanders going into the Coastguard are expected only to retire from such appointments which end their careers, but then it was different, and many young commanders were put into it, till they could get to sea.

I proceeded to Queenstown and took a cottage on the other side of the harbour at a place called Aghada near Rostellan Castle. A large Atlantic steamer was wrecked on the coast in my division just as I went there, and my wits were much exercised to arrange the business, get through the voluminous correspondence, and compound with the hungry natives. But the saying that ' the mountains of the future become the molehills of the past ' is often true.

The duties of an inspecting commander are, or were, not too onerous. If he does his duty they are sufficient to interest him, and fill up enough of his time to make him the more enjoy the remainder of it.

In those days many of the officers of stations, and many of the men, were civilians who had never been in the Navy, and some even had not been to sea. The divisional officers were generally commanders or lieutenants, but there were some civilians. The station officers were a very mixed lot, some lieutenants, or masters Royal Navy, some civilians, who were gentlemen, and some warrant officers of the Navy. Station appointments then lasted till the officer was superannuated.

The duties, or work, differed very much at different stations. In some it was all patrolling the coast by day and night ; in others boarding duty by boat was included, and was in fact the chief work.

The houses varied immensely; the divisional officer practically always had to find his own house, but all others had service accommodation. When the houses had been built for the Coastguard they were always good, but of the rest, hired as they could be got, some were almost disgraceful. This has now been long ago remedied and the Admiralty Coastguard houses are a credit to the service.

The Coastguard afloat consisted chiefly of cutters of about 80 tons, and very good sea boats. I had one, the *Scout*, attached to my division. Her commander was of chief warrant officer's rank.

He had on one occasion taken his wife to sea; they fell into a heavy gale of wind, and were battened down for thirty-six hours. His wife was more than half dead with sea-sickness and fear; however, she survived it, but in his account of the affair he added, as a curious fact, that she had never forgotten it.

Talking of sea-sickness, it has often occurred that young seamen, drafted to serve for a time in the Coastguard cutters, have been so sea-sick that they have begged to be sent back to the regular man-of-war. Of course most people know that the quicker the motion of a vessel the more apt people are to be ill, also that pitching is worse than rolling, as regards the above malady; because owing to the greater metacentric height for fore and aft stability, the motion of pitching is more violent and jerky than that of rolling.

Private life where I lived was very agreeable : everyone knows the hospitality of the Irish. In summer we played cricket and other games, and in winter hunted to a moderate degree, and shot.

The forts about Queenstown Harbour were at that time garrisoned by the Royal Marines in the winter : because as that corps are only recruited in England, and are supposed to have no

Irishmen in them, their loyalty, as regards any tinge of Fenianism, could be better trusted than that of a regiment of the line.

My object and wish in the Navy has always been to serve actually at sea, in preference to anything else, and indeed I cannot understand anyone who voluntarily becomes a sailor doing otherwise.

I must allow I enjoyed my time in Ireland, but when I had been there rather over a year I was moved to the Plymouth Division of Coastguard, the reason being curious, as follows.

At that time the leading feature in our Government's service was rigid economy, in which the Admiralty set an example—noble or otherwise. An officer I knew intimately, who was very well off and anxious to get command of a ship as soon as he could, he being a commander, was appointed to a ship on a distant station before his turn, because he offered to pay all his passage money out there by mail steamer.

My case was a minor one ; it was desired to reduce some of the Irish Divisions of Coastguard from commander to lieutenants for economy, and the offer of the Plymouth Division was made to two officers in Ireland whose divisions they wished to reduce. Both refused to go unless ordered, but if ordered the Admiralty would have to bear certain expenses. They then thought of me, though mine was not wished to be a reduced division, and the matter was so put to my friends that I said I would go voluntarily, and went.

The pay of commanders in the Coastguard I

considered quite enough : besides the pay of this rank, they had lodging allowance ; what was called 'moving duty' allowance ; and an allowance to keep two horses, concerning which they were only obliged to keep actually one. The idea of this, of course, was that at any moment they could have the horse saddled and rush off to any part of their coast in case of emergency.

The horses were, of course, very convenient for hunting also ! In the Plymouth Division I lived in Durnford Street, nearly opposite the Royal Marine Barracks ; I had also a 15-ton cutter provided by the service as my yacht ; and what may seem more strange still, a mounted orderly provided by the service to escort me as I pleased. My man had been a trooper in a Dragoon regiment. It was, of course, a relic of the days when fights with smugglers occurred, and the officer had some one to help protect him.

I was not long at Plymouth, when I was appointed to commission the *Growler* at that port for the West Coast of Africa.

CHAPTER XIII

H.M.S. *GROWLER*

'Bugtrap'—Sierra Leone—Kroomen—A Wreck—Bight of Benin
—Dogs—Fernando Po—African Kings—Rivers—Slavers—
Fight with Congo Pirates—Ascension Island.

THE *Growler* was a new ship, one of a strange
class, inasmuch as they were built to use up a
large stock of gunboat engines. To do this
two sizes of ships were designed, all to have twin
screws, the first so fitted in the Navy, I believe.

The larger class had two sets of 80 horse-power
engines, the smaller class two of 60 horse-power.
My ship was one of the smaller, the sort of vessel
dignified by the name of a ' bugtrap.' However,
I was very glad to get her and go to sea, even to
the hated West Coast of Africa, whose dry and
thirst-promoting climate has proved a snare to
too many sailors, and justified Virgil's 'At nos
hinc alli SITIENTES ibimus Afros.'

The *Growler* was barque rigged; her good
points were that she was extremely handy under
steam, not a bad sea boat, and good for rivers,
drawing only nine feet of water. But though
you could tack and wear her, as I often did,
Neptune himself could not have made her work
decently to windward, under sail only.

We fitted out at Devonport and left in the month of July for our station. We called at Sierra Leone to embark our Kroomen. I should explain that these are negroes from the Kroo country, who enter on board our ships on the West Coast of Africa, only for service in them on that station. In the *Growler* we had about ten, of fine physique, impervious to the rays of the sun, or the bite of the lady mosquito, who, however, had not then been diagnosed as the conveyer of fever. They slept and lived on the upper deck.

I may here remark that in the *Growler*, as was often the case in small craft, we had no mess tables for the men, which gave more room on the small lower decks.

While at Sierra Leone a man came on board to say his ship had gone ashore some twenty miles south of the port and would he feared become a total wreck, but would I see if I could salve her?

My orders did not admit of much delay, and after hearing his description I quite discouraged all hopes. However, I sailed one evening and thought I would have a look at her. By the light of a fine moon we found her, but saw she was a hopeless wreck, and only likely to be pillaged entirely by the natives.

When one is young one acts a good deal on impulse, and I allowed my First-lieutenant and warrant officer to ' salve ' some very useful spars, canvas and other things. You should never neglect the gifts that Providence places before you, but ' take the goods the gods provide thee,' unless, of course, actually prevented by your conscience, or the policeman, but neither in this case interfered.

A man-of-war, at the time I speak of, had perhaps all that was necessary to carry out her intended service, but the official establishment often left a good deal to be desired, and every sailor loves to see his ship look well.

I had painted the *Growler* yellow with a red streak, boats to match; in those days all common men-of-war were black, never white or grey. I now gave her a long mizzen topmast, and jib and flying jibboom, and immensely improved her appearance.

I must say I felt a little anxious lest our salvage operations should be misconstrued by some narrow-minded people; but it was not so.

We now began our coast service mostly in the Bight of Benin, where ' Tom Cringle ' says that ' one comes out where a dozen go in '; but this happily is far too pessimistic a statement.

' THE COAST,' as *par excellence* it used to be called, was of course hot, but its worst fault almost was its dreariness, and that bred many rows and serious troubles. I entered the rivers whenever I could, and my ship's shallow draft permitted it. Besides the service reasons for doing so, it was very interesting, and I thought it better to get the African fever than to die of monotony off the coast. It is no use disguising the fact that intemperance has been the bane of West Africa Coast service in the Navy, and many officers, who elsewhere might have done well, have been ruined by drink; the craving for it is much induced by the monotony and tediousness of the life, lying, or quietly cruising, off that coast.

My ship carried very few officers, of whom only two executive ones were reliable. One was my First-lieutenant, whom I lost in a curious way. We were at great-gun target practice, and as it went on I noticed that he seemed to have more difficulty in hearing my orders to him.

An hour or two after the firing was over, the Surgeon reported that the First-lieutenant was perfectly deaf. He remained so for several weeks, stone deaf, and had to be invalided home.

Running into the Channel in the winter the captain of the mail steamer had occasion to fire a pistol. This the deaf patient heard, and his hearing came back by degrees; but he was advised to retire lest the same thing should recur, and he did so.

I had a retriever on board who presented us with puppies—one was named after the ship, and should have been a cat, so charmed did his life appear. Lying in the Brass River one night, with the stream running four knots, 'Growler' fell overboard; it was quite dark and nothing could be done. We gave him up, but next day I heard much excitement going on, and they reported that 'Growler' had come on board. What almost must have happened was that the dog had been carried down towards the sea, but swimming in one direction had landed on the last point inside the bar, crawled to a native village, been taken in, and brought up to the settlement. I could relate at least two other of his wonderful escapes, but will forbear.

I was often at Fernando Po in the Bight of Biafra; it is one of the most beautiful and luxuriant islands in the world. On account of the first it was at one time called by the Spaniards 'Formosa.' As to the latter nearly any tropical thing will grow there. I have carefully measured cotton trees quite 200 feet high. The native inhabitants are called 'Boobies,' and are I think about the lowest race I personally know. The females used often to be without any clothing, a thing most rare with any savages.

The peak is 10,093 feet high; it rose so steeply from the sea near the anchorage that it is almost like looking at Nelson's column from the Union Club. The island is very unhealthy for Europeans; the Spanish, nine years before my visit, sent out a volunteer colony, to have free grants of land, but soon the survivors begged to be taken back, to starve in Spain for preference.

The British Consul when I was there was Charles Livingstone, brother of the great doctor, with whom he had often been in Africa and of whom he talked much. He said that when his brother was seized by a lion, though really much hurt, an extraordinary fascination of the beast seemed to possess him, and to deaden the pain.

Consul Livingstone made several official trips in my ship, living of course with me, and we had interesting visits to rivers, and 'palavers,' so called, with the native kings. The Consul had the African fever engrained in his constitution, and when with me was often down with it, and thoroughly sick and wretched in my tiny cabin. Africa's toll of the white man is heavy !

The African 'Kings' are often amusing. I remember one, 'King Dido' by name, who after freely partaking of refreshment in my cabin, could hardly be got to leave till he understood that I would write to Queen Victoria—who he thought used to drink rum and water in my cabin too—to send him out a breech-loading rifle just like mine.

When the Consul remonstrated with the King of Brass, which is just to the eastward of the Niger, on his people pillaging a British merchant vessel which had run ashore there, instead of helping her to get off, and told him that in England, on the contrary, we were always most kind to shipwrecked people and tried to save stranded ships, and when this had been conveyed to H.M. by the interpreter, the King after a little time replied: 'That be good law for you, but mine be best law for me here,' and no doubt from his point of view it was so.

The title King may serve to designate these noble potentates as well as any other, but it is usually ridiculous when the monarch himself appears. Often previous to a visit to you by the King, he sends in advance a messenger with his stick of state, a highly carved staff, which is, of course, taken away after the visit. I have received on board a 'King' dressed only in the full-dress tailcoat of a naval officer, a red hand-kerchief round his middle, a tall black hat on his head and nothing else—all these worn with an air of perfect gravity. A few of these kings send their sons to England for education, but the return to their native surroundings can hardly be satisfactory.

The traders up the rivers often live afloat in hulks, or if on shore their goods are often kept in hulks for safety. A fire-ship can hardly be more inflammable than these vessels are.

Imagine an old wooden ship well baked by the tropical sun, her cargo, rum, palm-oil, and gunpowder, and when she catches fire, as occurs at times, the only thing to do is to desert her.

I entered all the rivers I could find excuse to, and was surprised to find how ill surveyed some of them were. The Old Calabar was the worst I found. Having the Admiralty chart, I did not take a pilot—it is about ninety miles from the bar up to the settlement. When we had got about thirty miles the chart became quite useless.

I afterwards made a running survey of the river. The chart was as if one man had begun at the settlement, and another at the bar, each had worked about thirty miles on different scales, and an inventive genius had then inserted the middle part from his inner consciousness. The result may be imagined !

At Old Calabar meat was sold with some of the animals' hair on to show it had had four legs, and not only two !

The Bonny River, when I was on the coast, was the scene of much disturbance. Two kings, named respectively Ja-Ja and George Peppel, quarrelled; the latter was helped by a powerful trader, called Oko Jumbo, and a fight was arranged. They collected cannon of various calibre and date, and placed them in positions some quarter of a mile apart, with houses dotted here and there between, and opened fire; how many were killed I do not know, but on arrival soon after the action I found Peppel and Oko Jumbo triumphant, and Ja-Ja defeated and fled.

Subsequently, after I had left the station, Ja-Ja was made prisoner by us and deported to the West Indies. The sequel I happen to know. Being at Grenada some years after I saw the captive, who soon after that was released by our Government, and put on board a corvette for passage back to his country. The vessel, however, went no farther than Teneriffe, and landed him there.

Our Consul at Santa Cruz—Captain Harford— one of the kindest of men, did all he could to console Ja-Ja, and assure him he would be sent on to Bonny. But in vain, the ex-King gave himself up to despair, 'turned his face to the wall' and died. I think our Government felt all had not been as it should, and they ordered that the body should be taken up, embalmed and sent to Bonny. It was not a pleasant job, but some Spanish doctors were got to do it, and sent in a very long bill which our Treasury at first demurred to paying; the doctors pointed out the grand points in the matter, one that it was the body of a monarch, and the other that the party to pay was the British nation, who eventually cashed up. All this the Consul at Santa Cruz told me.

Sometimes we went up the rivers to shoot crocodiles; the niggers always called them alligators, but the latter I believe only exist in the Americas.

A crocodile asleep on the bank looks just like a tree covered with mud. So much so that the first I saw deceived both me and my companion, though warned beforehand, till the niggers saw it and cried out 'Hi ha, alligator.' They are very hard to kill, unless hit in the eye, or one or two other places.

I have no doubt cannibalism still goes on near the West African Coast in places; it certainly did when I was there. I was told by an English trader, that up the New Calabar River he came on some natives just after a fight cooking some of their vanquished foes for dinner.

As regards slave ships, they were all but over when I was there, but the middle passage was still a possibility. Of course we all had 'slave papers,' i.e. authority to act; without which interference was illegal.

At that time the French only half agreed to give us powers over their ships; you might board them, and ask to see their papers, but if the 'Congé' and 'Acte de Francisation' were produced, and seemed bonâ fide, you had no authority to do any more, whatever your ground for suspicion.

On one occasion, ' from information received,' as the police say, which seemed trustworthy, that a certain French ship was about to take in slaves at a place named, I went there and found the vessel, boarded her, and saw her papers, which seemed right. However, I told them my suspicions, and said I should watch her, unless they let me search the ship, which they did, and I let her go.

A vessel about to take slaves would have her decks, water tanks, or casks, and probably slave-irons, in readiness.

Everyone knows how badly off Africa is for harbours. I visited St. Paul de Loando, which is about the best on that coast. In its neighbourhood were the best specimens I had ever seen of the Baobab tree, or *Anansonia digitata*, so named from its shape—a gigantic carrot, but protruding more from the ground in proportion, with immense spreading boughs may be taken as a rough resemblance.

Consul Livingstone told me he had seen some that could shelter a whole regiment. In the Canary Islands I have seen trees much like them; they are often of very great age, but have no actual beauty. The Consul used to praise very much the inner and higher parts of Africa where he had been with his brother.

We went to Lobito or Benguela in 12° 30′ S,. where you can pick oysters off the mangrove trees!—off the roots of course.

Soon after I proceeded to the River Congo, where numbers of pirates were about, and it was much desired, if possible, to recapture a negro chief called Manoel Vacca, who had been our prisoner formerly, but was now released.

To catch him was not easy; the Portuguese are great traders there and own slaves. One Portuguese merchant said to me, 'I think I know how you could catch Manoel Vacca. Ask him to come and see you, and promise you will let him go free. I think he will believe it and come, and then of course you can keep him.' It shows a very curious morality and sense of honour. Perverted diplomacy shall we call it?

My time on the coast was shortened by the following affair. Arrived at the River Congo I heard that an English merchant vessel in that river had just been seized by Congo pirates.

On my anchoring off Banana creek one morning five men of the schooner *Loango* came on board to say that she had been boarded by pirates the day before higher up the river. It appeared that they had escaped, leaving the captain and a boy on board. At once I was off and in a couple of hours sighted the schooner, manned and armed boats and boarded her; the pirates who could escaped up the creeks near, but I got one and kept him as a guide. The vessel had a regular West African cargo, viz. rum, gunpowder, and sundries. It was extraordinary how much they had cleared her out in twenty hours.

The job now was to find the captain and boy, if alive. From my prisoner, with threats and an interpreter, I got some hints where to go, to surprise in his lair King Mpinge Nebacca (pronounced by Jack 'pinch of tobacco'), who was the chief pirate known there then.

From Señor Oleviera, a Portuguese merchant

slave dealer and owner, I borrowed a slave as guide. Next morning we were off before daylight in three boats, and landed in a mangrove swamp at low-water ; here owing to difficulty of language mistakes were made, but finally we got to shore. If anyone wants to know what it is like to be really muddy, induce them to land in a mangrove swamp at low-water. I find this description of it in a letter of mine: 'You writhe like a snake among the roots, then climb over them like a monkey, or again wade deeply through the mud like a man shrimping.'

Speed was now necessary to try and surprise the natives; we ran as hard as we could along the narrow paths, and through pools of water often three feet deep, about three miles, arriving at last at the village of Mpinge Nebacca. The niggers did not stay to fight, but fled into the bush and opened a very desultory fire from there with small-arms. This town was so hidden in the forest that without a guide I should never have found it, and probably no white man was ever there before. Like rabbits the inhabitants jumped up and fled; had they only stockaded and defended the path we came by, we should have had much trouble.

I wanted, of course, prisoners for information, so I ran on till I got hold of a young negro about nineteen years old, secured him, and handed him over to one of my men who then came up, and I went on into the bush after the others.

The chase was amusing; it was through grass and reeds some eight feet high in places. Their

advantage was custom and want of clothing, mine a path partly cleared by them. I had my sword in my hand, and could at times have run one of them through; but to kill was not my object, and besides, you cannot kill a person from behind—at least not usually.

At last one of the fugitives fell down, so near me that I was able to fling myself on top of him. We rolled over in the grass, my captive's only garment came off, and I found in my arms a young woman !

I was of course all the more glad I had not at all hurt my ' chase,' but a woman can talk as well as a man. Some say better, or faster. So I gave her in charge to my coxswain, and took her on board. Meanwhile one of my officers found the captain of the schooner alive but badly wounded, and too stupefied to be any use. The town was full of plunder from the *Loango*, so their guilt was clear; they had several hundred kegs of gunpowder, which I blew up, and many other things. The town was burnt, and with difficulty we carried off the captain, and took my two prisoners.

How many men were killed I cannot say ; but it is a well-known fact that the British sailor or marine, and I believe soldier, is not very squeamish about taking life when once he is thoroughly excited.

The day was one of temptation to the thirsty ' Tar ' or ' Jolly,' as it was very hot and much trade rum was about in the village. As we were returning I heard a marine artillery gunner say, ' I've killed two and murdered two more,' and had I not been commanding officer I should have liked to ask where he drew the line.

I have often been amused by people saying, or pretending, that the gentle Britisher is far more humane than the other European warriors. In my opinion and experience, under similar circumstances, there is not very much to choose between them. This I know is heresy! But they are the 'proper fighting beast,' as Barry Lyndon says—when excited.

Our day's work was not over, and we went in the boats to another very narrow creek, which with difficulty we got up, landed, and found another village and more gunpowder. But the natives were prepared, and having retreated to the bush, kept up a loose sort of fire, and no prisoners could be got.

My slave amused me—he would not land here, but lay down in the bottom of the boat to avoid the shot, so Exeter Hall may rejoice to think that even a slave feels his life well worth preserving.

Having destroyed this village we returned to the boats, as no more could then be done. As we descended the creek I was shot through the leg, and was glad it did not happen sooner. I may say that the wound at the moment felt exactly as if some one had hit me very hard there with a big stick. I believe this is frequently, if not generally, the case. And I have been told that a sword cut is like a very severe slash with a whip, but that I have not had the pleasure of feeling.

We returned to the ship. I kept my slave for several days—he was most useful to me—but at last, in spite of Exeter Hall and his being in British territory, viz. a man-of-war, I felt I must in common honesty return him to his Portuguese master.

Had I been a rich man I might have offered to buy him and bring him to England, but I have no doubt he was really much happier in Señor Oleviera's plantation, and under his native skies. He used to sit up all night with me if required, and often his cool grasp of my hot and aching foot was a great comfort. A negro's 'skin is naturally cool, and though you may say, then it is like a snake,' yet it has its advantages in fervent climes.

The boy still remained to be recovered. I found out about where he was and sent word that all the villages there would be destroyed if he was not at once brought back. This succeeded and we got him, but he had been very badly wounded.

My lady prisoner cried and howled near me all night, but when I had got the boy back I returned her. My other prisoner proved to be the son of the noted pirate chief—Manoel Vacca—mentioned above, and named Movica, so he was a great catch, as hostage for his father.

I now had a dreary time of it. My wound proved serious; my surgeon was an able and kind man, but took to drink and was unable to come and dress my wound or attend properly to others wanting him. No other doctor existed within more than a hundred miles at least. However, our medical officer's career was not much prolonged in the service afterwards.

I have little more coast work to relate ; though quite laid up, and in much discomfort or pain, with the above drawback, and short of officers, I did not like to leave my station.

After several weeks the Commodore[1] arrived in the *Rattlesnake,* and was most kind, and ordered my ship to Ascension Island. Never was I more glad to arrive anywhere; to quit a small, hot cabin, to be free of the responsibility of the ship, under the existing circumstances, and to have good medical attendance, was indeed a delightful change, and I have always blessed Ascension.

I have previously mentioned the island when here in the *Pique*; it is about the size of St. Helena. Everyone did all they could for me. A commander—Kirby—governed the island ; with a lieutenant under him, two medical officers for the hospital, a Captain of Marines, and some accountant and warrant officers.

A curious sea phenomenon here is 'the rollers,' i.e. the sea suddenly and for no apparent cause rising in a sort of ground swell, and its waves violently breaking on the shore, and coming higher than usual as they do so. I believe the cause is thought to be volcanic submarine action. Concerning this a very tragic event had just occurred there. The Captain of Marines and his wife had two young children; their nurse took them one day to the beach, when the elder waded in a little way, as children often do. Suddenly the rollers set in, and carried the child off its feet, the nurse dropped the younger

---

[1] Now Admiral Sir William Dowell, G.C.B.

one which was in her arms, and rushed in to try and save the first one. She was washed away, and the baby also. The sea, and the sharks which abound there, completed the catastrophe.

I used to see at Ascension my captive Movica, ' the quivered Chief of Congo,' as Campbell sings ; he was fond of coming up to me, and I felt compassion for him in his exile, but what became of him I do not know : as I was but hobbling on crutches I was at his advantage when we met.

While I was at Ascension a mishap occurred to the *Flora* which might have been most serious. She was a frigate like the *Pique*, but unrigged, and so helpless. She lay always as depôt ship here. One night late, the watch on board her luckily looked and thought that the lights of the garrison got fainter, and soon decided that they were becoming more distant.

The Lieutenant of the island happened to be on board her that night; he was called, ran on deck, and gave the order to let go the anchor.

This was done, and brought the ship up, but only just in time before she got off the bank, into deep water.

Had THAT occurred, the ship with many invalids on board, but short of provisions and water, would have been blown away by the south-east trade wind, helpless, and there was no seaworthy craft to send to look for her.

What had happened was that the ship's bow long rising and falling with the swell had caused the ring connecting the cable from her to the moorings below to hammer constantly on a rock, till it became disconnected. Had the *Flora's* being adrift been discovered, say, half an hour later, the results to those on board would have been most serious.

I cannot pretend that I left the West Coast of Africa with any regret. It was our most unhealthy and most monotonous station. This latter has, through inducing officers to drink, ruined more careers than any other station has done.

This is all over now, but was well known when I was young, and 'the coast' was looked on nearly as 'black list.' There I had seen the worst phase of our Navy, and not in my case redeemed by a good set of officers.

In a very few weeks the Commodore arrived, a medical survey was ordered on me, and they resolved I must be invalided home, whether I liked it or not. The *Roman*, a Cape mail steamer, called in, and I was ordered passage in her. She was an old vessel, with a single screw, of course ; at sea we broke one of our cranks, but at last crawled into Madeira, repaired damages and finally reached Southampton. She brought home the headquarters of the Cape Mounted Rifles, which had just then been disbanded.

I went to London, and was officially medically surveyed and pronounced unfit for service for a year on account of my wound. At this moment the war broke out between the French and Prussians in 1870, and, of course, absorbed all our attention.

CHAPTER XIV

COMMANDER—H.M.S. *LIVELY*—CAPTAIN

Lausanne—H.M.S. *Vigilant*—H.M.S. *Lively*—North of Spain
Channel Fleet—Story of H.M.S. *Amazon*—Promotion—
Long Half Pay—Officers' Lists—Greenwich R.N. College—
France—Italy.

NEXT spring, though I could not serve, I went to Lausanne in Switzerland to improve my French, and lodged with a M. Borel and his family. Among the few *pensionnaires* were a Prussian named Von Arnim and a German from another province, both also learning French. We there used to row on the lake together and the war produced many arguments.

In the pension was also a beautiful young Danish girl, who matched Sir Walter Scott's description of the 'Danish maid,' with form as fair as Denmark's pine, &c. Von Arnim fell a victim to her charms, and I chaffed him about Denmark's revenge over Prussia.

An interned French soldier was being questioned about the war, and his interlocutor said to him : 'Mais vous avez manqué de tout n'est pas, même des tentes.' The soldier replied : 'Ce

164

n'etait pas une question de tente (tante), mais nous avons manqué de l'oncle.'

I was suddenly called home by a severe domestic affliction. In spite of efforts to be certified as fit to serve, I could not advance the period; but at length I was appointed to the command of H.M.S. *Vigilant*.

This vessel was at Devonport; she was quite new and was a paddle-wheel despatch vessel. Her armament was quite insignificant. Soon after she had been fitted out I broke my right arm out hunting, and had to go to the naval hospital at Stonehouse: this was my third sojourn as patient in a naval hospital, and, as far as I am concerned, my personal experience is all in their favour.

While I was in the hospital my ship had a bad accident, and it was decided to pay her off and turn us over to the *Lively*. This vessel was also new, and nearly a sister to the *Vigilant*, but she had better engines, viz. Penn's oscillating cylinders, than which none in the Navy were better for paddle-wheel ships. She could steam 15 knots, a speed then extraordinary in the Navy.

We went to the north-east of Spain to protect British interests in the Carlist disturbances— hardly a war—then going on. I got into the River Nervion and as near as I could to Bilbao, where are the famous Somorostro iron mines. The country is very varied and picturesque.

At San Sebastian we lay in the harbour called 'La Concha,' and while there I visited the famous monastery in Aspeitia founded by the Jesuits and built of black marble, but never completed. It was curious to see so grand a building in so secluded a spot.

San Sebastian is pleasant as a place, and interesting from its history, its capture by us in 1813 not being its only attraction. I visited the graves of some of our countrymen killed in the Carlist War in 1836, under Sir de Lacy Evans, and remember one with this inscription:

' To the memory of poor Court who fell under his colours at the battle of Aeta. Beauty and friendship truly mourn him.'

From Santander I paid my first visit to Madrid, and things having quieted down, and complete *indulto* proclaimed, I was ordered to join the Channel Fleet under Admiral Sir Geoffrey Hornby.

We have had few, if any, better handlers of a squadron at sea than the above officer, and though he had not had the good fortune to see war service, I am sure that during the latter years of his active service life, the Navy generally, had we become engaged in a serious naval war, would have wished to see him in command of our principal fleet.

A sailor's life so frequently calls for sudden action in emergency, for coolness and decision at critical times, and for the evident power both to command and to lead men, that the good officer can be judged quite well without the mere going under fire.

Our first service was a popular visit to the home ports, of Ireland, and the West of England and Scotland, Liverpool and the Clyde, &c.

These cruises do not improve efficiency, but are no doubt of much value in helping to popularise the Navy; besides which it is only fair that the public should have a chance of seeing what they pay for. The hospitality shown us was unbounded, indeed you required to be young to keep up with the luncheons, dinners, and dances, besides your own work.

At Devonport I always (by order) went in and out of the Hamoaze without either pilot or harbour master. One summer morning I arrived very early at Portsmouth and went straight in, but could see no buoy, wharf, or berth, to take up. A signal of inquiry to the flagship only got the answer, 'Anchor as convenient,' no authority being out of bed. Seeing only the Royal Yacht's buoy vacant, I thought it good enough for me, but to my surprise on steering for it ran on shore. However, no harm was done.

This may sound odd, but charts of Portsmouth Harbour were not allowed to us.

In the autumn I had a collision outside the Needles, on my way to Portsmouth. It was a very dark night, and I was going fast; suddenly a schooner loomed out on my starboard bow, crossing my track. She could not be avoided, though we, of course, tried; her jib-boom passed close over our heads on the bridge as we ducked down, and the smash then came.

Her figurehead was found lying on our quarter-deck—it was that of a woman—and the First-lieutenant rushing on deck in the dark mistook it at first for a dead body. I was told afterwards it was an effigy of the owner's daughter, who was married that day. A very odd chance, and an ill omen.

For the winter the Channel Fleet was abroad, which is in all service views the best thing to do with them; and no officer who has the service at heart would wish, unless necessary for the protection of the country, to remain in England between the months of October and May.

All exercises, drills, &c., are better carried out farther south with longer days and milder weather, besides the question of having your men on board; also it is best for health.

Before I entered the service Lisbon was a frequent haunt for our Channel Fleet, but for many years now it has been much less so. The strong current in the Tagus is the great drawback to it as an anchorage, and even when moored ships have been known to drag.

When I was in the *Lively* we were there at various times. There were then regular roulette tables at which the public could play, known by the name of ' Pero Grande.' It was supposed to be ' taboo,' and was so officially, but such restrictions are hard to enforce. The opera was, of course, a great attraction to us.

Talking of the opera at Lisbon I will venture to relate a story in which it is just mentioned because my great-uncle Richard Seymour, then First-lieutenant of the *Amazon*, figures in it. The *Amazon* was with Nelson's Fleet off Toulon, when the Admiral in order to get his despatches to England sent that ship with them to Lisbon, choosing her partly to give her a chance of prize-money. Sir John Orde was blockading Cadiz ; he was no friend of Nelson's, but his senior officer ; and Nelson told Parker in a private note to avoid Sir John's Fleet if he could. This Parker tried to do, going through the Straits of Gibraltar in the night and hugging the African shore. However, he was caught by Captain Blackwood in the *Euryalus*, one of Orde's cruisers. Blackwood came on board and gave Parker orders from Orde to join his Flag. Parker showed Nelson's note, and said : ' I believe you are under obligations to his Lordship, do you not think it would have been better if you had not seen me to-night ? ' Blackwood said ' Yes, ' and acted accordingly.

The *Amazon* arrived at Lisbon and gave the despatches to the packet for England. Parker's First-lieutenant then said to him : ' It would be a great treat to the officers who have not been at a civilised place for a long time to have a run on shore and go to the opera.' But Parker said : ' No, our best chance of prize-money is to go to sea at once and cruise for a day or two off this coast.' They went out, and next day at daylight sighted a vessel which proved to be a Spaniard with treasure on board, and a prize.

Parker's share was £20,000. When he rejoined Nelson, the latter asked what he had done, and hearing the above, remarked : ' Well, I'm glad you've got some prize-money, but I wish it had been only £10,000, because now I suppose you will get lazy and only want to be on shore and spend it.' My great-uncle was killed on board the *Amazon* when she captured the *Belle Poule*.

We were at Gibraltar in February 1873, when we heard that King Amadeus was driven from his throne in Madrid, and had retired to Lisbon. Recently the opposite might have occurred. 'Hodie mihi cras tibi.' In consequence a few ships, mine for one, were ordered to Lisbon to offer the ex-King conduct to Italy, which he declined ; and it only gave us a reception and banquet by the King of Portugal in his palace.

While at Gibraltar I was at times over at Tangier, where was Sir John Drummond Hay, then Consul-General in Morocco, and soon to be Minister there. He almost ruled over the immediate neighbourhood. He was equally able and agreeable, and used to take us out wild-boar shooting. The position had been a ' family living,' and he showed me the mark on the wall in his drawing-room, where a round shot came through when the French under the Prince de Joinville bombarded Tangier in 1844. His mother was in the room at the time.

Some of us used to make short trips of two or three days to see places of interest as the service permitted, and I was thus staying at Cintra when I got a telegram to say I was promoted to the rank of captain. Captain Dowell (mentioned before) was one of our party, and justly remarked that I had now entered on quite a different phase of the service, having got on to a purely seniority list.

In some foreign navies they have seniority to the rank of captain and then selection to the flag list. I have always thought this quite wrong, and ours much the best plan. We select, and thus eliminate, officers, till they get to the very important rank of captain; which rank has then a stability and added grandeur that it could not have were it still a struggle for the next step.

This I say; but always, of course, bearing in mind that no officer can force the Admiralty to employ him; and that besides age, periods of non-employment condemn an officer to retirement. I could say much more about this, but will not here.

In a few weeks my successor arrived, and I left my ship and the Channel Fleet with real regret, hardly effaced by promotion. The Coast of Africa had disgusted me with the service, but the Channel Fleet restored my love for it.

In the year 1873, when I was made a captain, and for several years before and afterwards, officers of that rank were almost always on half-pay for five years before they got a ship, unless they happened to go as flag-captains, and flag-captains were usually men who had been commanders of large ships.

It is no doubt bad for the service to have officers five years unemployed, but it mattered less then than it would now when things change rapidly, and ships get out of fashion nearly as quickly as ladies' hats.

I am all for officers of the rank of captain, and higher ranks, being at times on half-pay and thus able to travel, mix with the world and general society, get their minds enlarged, and learn that the quarter-deck is not the world.

At present officers are in my opinion too short a time in the rank of captain, and therefore unable even to get enough of the very valuable experience to be learned in that most important rank. Indeed it has lately happened that officers had to be promoted to rear-admiral without having served the regulation time at sea. This is all wrong, but not easy at once to remedy, unless by enlarging the captains' list, which would mean reducing for a time the lists below it; and these lists also are no larger than is required for the large Fleet we feel necessary to keep in commission.

The lieutenants' list is now some 1900 in number, whereas forty years ago it was only 660; it is, however, none too numerous, partly because we must have more large ships and swarms of small craft in commission, and partly because the battle-ships' quarters are so distributed and divided off, that many more officers than formerly are required to command them.

In 1847, when of course no retired list existed, there were 2448 lieutenants on the so-called 'active list,' but the commission of the senior one was of December 1796 (over fifty years), and nearly 1600 were of about twenty years' seniority. A frigate seventy years ago had usually only three lieutenants and a master—just enough in fact to keep the watches; and I believe that till thirty years ago only three-deckers ever carried eight lieutenants, a number often both borne and wanted in ships now.

Mr. Childers, when First Lord, had brought

in the age retirement scheme, and done much to clear the lists. In 1873 Mr. Goschen, then First Lord, completed the above by a temporary offer of retirement on a very liberal scale. So much so that I felt I could never in future complain of my pay, because I had not taken that retirement.

But all this is a digression, and to return to my humble self, I had probably five years' half-pay to look forward to. The Royal Naval College at Greenwich had been opened the previous summer, so I applied to go there as a student.

Its first President was the late Admiral Sir Cooper Key, than whom no better could have been selected. His abilities, scientific knowledge, judgment, and encouraging manner with those under him, showed him to be the very man for the appointment. I joined the Greenwich College in the autumn of 1873, when the first real ' session, ' so called, began, and remained there till its end the next autumn. All students above the rank of lieutenant were on half-pay, and we all, I think, felt it was a great privilege to us to be allowed there on such terms ; though the further boon of full pay has since been granted.

The winter of 1874 I spent at Cannes with my father and sisters, and I certainly prefer the Riviera as it was then to what it is now, when over-building and crowds of motors have quite changed the place, and the dust of the latter nearly chokes you and obscures the view.

In the spring we travelled in Italy, but as I do not presume to think my private movements and doings will interest anyone who may honour me by reading my memoirs, I shall as a rule touch but casually on them.

In 1875 it was decided to send out an Arctic expedition to try and reach the North Pole, and Captain George Nares was appointed to command it. My secondary object in 1867 in going to the Arctic regions in a whaler was to be qualified for a Government expedition if one were sent. I therefore, of course, offered my services on this occasion, and should have got command of the second ship (*The Discovery*) were it not that the naval medical authorities were the same men who had surveyed me after my wound in Africa, and would not now pass me for the expedition. As is well known the command of the second ship was then given to my friend Captain Henry Stephenson.[1]

Some months after I happened to visit Birkenhead to stay with my friend Captain Meyer, R.N., and seeing there H.M.S. *Orontes*, a troopship, preparing for re-commission, the idea occurred to me that, though I could not yet get a corvette, the Admiralty might be induced to give me command of the above ship. I therefore made the request, and as their Lordships, especially Admiral Sir Alexander Milne, then First Sea Lord, were very kind to me, on account of the above Arctic business, they made an exception in my favour and appointed me to the ship.

The trooping service had long been at times

[1] Now Admiral Sir Henry Stephenson, Gentleman Usher of the Black Rod.

conducted by the Navy. Everyone remembers the loss of the *Birkenhead* in 1852. Under the master hand of Admiral Sir William Mends the Troop Service was reformed, and became worthy of its very important duties.

It might, and I hope did, help to make our two sister services allied, and pleasantly known to each other, but after all it is not the proper duty of the Navy. It has been quite rightly given up by them, and I think its dissolution is regretted by neither sailor nor soldier.

For a naval officer it was a curious experience. It greatly enlarged my knowledge of that seemingly volatile, yet really constant, element called ' Human Nature,' and in the knowledge of which I should think a man who has spent his life as officer and captain of a mail steamer must be a past master.

The *Orontes* had just been lengthened by fifty feet amidships, and was a very efficient vessel. She was built of iron, and had just been fitted with compound engines, then only first coming into the Navy.

CHAPTER XV

H.M.S. *ORONTES*

Lord Lytton—Bombay—Irish Militia—Ceylon—Singapore—
Mauritius—Natal—The Cape—South African Ports—Bad
Harbours—Wreck of *Eurydice*—Occupation of Cyprus—
A Derelict — Bermuda — Halifax — Barbados — Trinidad —
Jamaica—*Thunderer* Explosion.

AT Portsmouth in March 1876 I commissioned the
above ship, as what was called 'an Imperial troopship'—in distinction from the four Indian troopships, which were exclusively for that work;
while our sort were for service everywhere as
required.

Our first job was to go to Bombay, taking out
odds and ends, and conveying Lord Lytton, who
was going to be Governor-General of India, accompanied by his wife, family, and suite. In the
above society our voyage out was very pleasant.

The Lyttons crossed the isthmus by train, *viâ*
Cairo, and while my ship was detained at Ismailia
I made acquaintance with the great Ferdinand de
Lesseps, who asked me to breakfast. He was
then to me the courteous hospitable French gentle-
man, very different from what he was to us when

I was there in 1882. But he had very much to try him then.

At Suez, by arrangement, we met H.R.H. the Prince of Wales (our late King) on his way home in the *Serapis*. At Aden Lord Lytton landed in state, it being the first point reached of his new dominions. Everyone turned out to see the procession through the town, such as it is. Aden is to my mind like a cross between Gibraltar and Ascension Island. It is hot, healthy and dull, and Europeans often get fat there; yet I have known people who liked it.

On 7th April we reached Bombay, and Lord Lytton landed with great ceremony.

I think the ' towers of silence ' the most curious things at Bombay. They are of stone, round in shape, about 25 feet high and 160 in diameter, with one small door about 4 feet square for entrance. Inside is a flat stone floor marked in four circles. The outer is for the men, the next for the women, inside that for the children, and in the centre is a deep well into which the bones are thrown after they have been well picked and cleaned by the numerous vultures that are kept to devour the corpses. It is a gruesome sight, and the vultures look worthy of their ghastly occupation. In readiness for the vultures the corpses are placed on their backs in their respective circles, and divested of their clothes.

While at Bombay I dined with a Parsee gentleman; no ladies appeared till after dinner, when we were taken into a room where we found them with bowls of scented water, and garlands of flowers, with which last we were copiously adorned, and we then left for our boats to go off. But we endeavoured to hide our floral decorations from the anxious gaze of our boats' crews. The Parsees are a much respected sect; they worship, I believe, both the sun and the moon. In their temples a sacred flame is always kept alight.

On 18th April we left for England with about a thousand troops on board, and arrived at Portsmouth on 22nd May. My homeward journey showed me that Indian life is apt to be demoralising both physically and morally to the English of both sexes. This statement will no doubt meet with contradiction, but, be it as it may, I have no doubt that modern times are an improvement on former ones.

I was told by Major P—— of the 92nd Regiment that the widows of privates married 'on the strength' are often engaged to a would-be husband, while the first is only very ill.

Military married officers were not allowed to bring their wives for passage if an addition to the family was likely to occur *en voyage*. When off the Ashrafi lighthouse on our way home, the wife of an officer of the Bengal Staff Corps presented him with a daughter. He came to apologise to me for this escapade, excusing it on the plea of its being the first child. I accepted the excuse, and only suggested that Ashrafi would be a pretty and appropriate name for the little girl.

During the summer we were employed on what was called 'coastwise service,' i.e. about the British Isles.

In July we brought two Irish Militia regiments, viz. the Armagh and the Monaghan, over to England for the manœuvres. The Armagh Militia own a very interesting trophy of which they are very proud, viz. a French regimental colour of the 2nd Battalion of the 70th Regiment of the line, taken by the Armagh Militia in 1798 at the Battle of Ballinbrack, when the French invaded Ireland. The flag is white, with a gold border; in the centre is a red cap of liberty, and inscribed on the colours is 'Discipline et soumission aux lois militaires.' Colonel W. Cross of the Armagh regiment told me that this flag is always kept by the Colonel for the time being in his private house, and that one day being in Paris and at the Invalides, a Frenchman pointed out to him a British flag there that had been captured from us. The Colonel put his eyeglass up and regarding the flag with great interest said, 'Yes, I see it, and I keep one of yours captured by us in my own house.'

On 8th August while off the coast of Wales, with troops on board, and steaming at our best speed, the low-pressure piston suddenly smashed, and having only one screw we were helpless as to steam. However we were barque rigged, so I handled the ship under sail till next day, when we got into Holyhead, landed our troops and were towed to Birkenhead for repairs, by Messrs. Laird & Co., who had both built and lengthened the ship. The West float of Birkenhead was then rather a sad sight, being crammed with vessels, chiefly steamers, unable to find employment. The old *Great Britain* was there.

Our repairs were completed about the end of October, when we went to Portsmouth. While there the Arctic expedition under Captain Nares returned ; they had done what they could by that route, and Commander Albert Markham had attained the then highest latitude.

Our next trip was to Singapore with the 74th Highlanders. On 12th November we went to Portsmouth, and calling at Belfast reached Malta on the 29th. On the 30th, St. Andrew's Day, I dined with the 42nd Highlanders, the ' Black Watch,' at Florian barracks, a good old-fashioned Scotch festival dinner, such a sight as is, I fancy, quite obsolete now, to the detriment of wine merchants.

I have known nearly every Scotch regiment in the Army, some very well. I am not at all prejudiced in their favour, having I believe no Scotch blood in my body, but I have always liked the Scotch regiments, and never known one with a bad tone in it.

We passed the Suez Canal in 53 hours and 20 minutes, say $2\frac{1}{4}$ days, being about eighteen hours under way at an average speed of 4·8 knots. I only mention this for comparison with the present faster time. At that date the British shipping passing the canal was seven-tenths of the whole world's traffic through it ; the charges on tonnage dues (for which every ship was given a special certificate in England or her own country) were 10 francs a ton, Suez Canal measurement ; and pilotage dues were 20 francs per decimetre of draft of water. Passenger dues were 10 francs each for all over twelve years old, and 5 francs for those under it, but above three years old. The total for the *Orontes* passage on this occasion was about £1416.

The bitter lakes between Lake Timsah and Suez were evidently the sea once, and on drying up such a deposit of salt was left behind that they have become salter and denser than the ocean, to such an extent that our Indian troopships while passing through them drew four inches less water than they did in ordinary sea water.

Our next port was Trincomalee in Ceylon, than which perhaps no tropical island is more beautiful, and more than that cannot be said of any place. The above port is our naval station in the island, but now much discarded.

The Admiral's house here is, or was, a most delightful one. While in the harbour a military officer got a sunstroke in an odd way; he went to sleep one afternoon in the saloon, quite shaded; the ship swung and the sun shone on him with the above result.

Sober Island in the harbour is a grand place for picnics, that not seldom made the name a satire; and it has a charming bathing place, thought safe till a few years ago when an officer was there seized by a shark.

Our next port was Penang, the word meaning 'betel nut,' of which many trees abound. From here we went to the Dinding Islands in the Straits of Malacca. These islands are rarely visited by troopships, but the close of the Para war took us there, and from thence we went to Singapore *viâ* Malacca. The Governor here, Captain E. Shaw, R.N., had been one of my first shipmates, and with his advice I got several Malacca canes. They grow like ivy twisted round trees and are straightened artificially. The less ' rib ' the better the cane and more valued; when cut and dry they are naturally a light colour, but are darkened for the market by smoking them over a fire into which tobacco juice is put. Captain Shaw told me he took some first-rate canes to a man in London to mount, who tried to make him admire others with large ribs, which were of really much less value.

At Singapore I visited our Government Prison. It contained about 600 prisoners, 30 being European and the rest Asiatics, of whom five-sixths were Chinese. Corporal punishment for offences in the prison is given—I happened to see it done—with a rattan about half an inch thick on the bare skin —a most severe punishment, marking men for life. Flogging in our Navy, of which I have seen much, is child's play in comparison.

We embarked the 1st Battalion of the 10th Regiment for England, having other drafts also, making 1030 troops.

I paid a visit to the (now late) Maharajah of Johore, who was a perfect specimen of the high-bred Asiatic. Here I ate my first durian, a fruit equally praised and abused. Wallace calls it ' the king of fruits,' but it is no doubt an acquired taste. Its smell is unpleasant, its inside pulp, which is what you eat, and has been rather fitly compared by its lovers to a mixture of sherry, custard, and onions.

From Singapore we went to Mauritius, but as

measles broke out on the way we were kept in quarantine and could not land—a great disappointment. I arrived off the harbour Port Louis early one morning, and seeing no sign of a pilot went in. On hearing we had the measles the horror expressed by the health authorities was amusing; several newspapers—in French—were sent to me calling me long bad words which I had to look out in the dictionary !

It is, of course, a cyclone region, but they are now so well understood that steamers in the open ocean should be able to keep pretty clear of them. I felt sure I was following one, as proved to be the case. A man assured me that stone that was in a cemetery on a pedestal six feet high was blown in a cyclone a distance of seventy yards in all, crossing a ditch at least two feet wide.

We next went to Natal, anchoring off Durban to land some of the 80th Regiment in quarantine under a high cliff. This is a real bad anchorage, both because it is unsheltered and because the bottom is rocky. No end of lost anchors and cables are there. From Natal we went to East London, where there is no pretence of shelter, and then to Simon's Bay. Here, for the first time since Singapore and the only time till we got home, we had pratique.

We called next at St. Helena, which island like several others was discovered by the Portuguese, taken from them by the Dutch, and from the latter by us. Here we were in quarantine, and a Captain of Artillery, bringing off some passengers for England, himself insisted on coming up the ship's side to the gangway, with the result that the island would not have him back, so he came to England.

We then called at Ascension, and from there came home, and landed our regiment, which had been on board the ship for three and a half months, a most unusual and unheard-of thing in these days.

In June 1877 I had another South African trip. We embarked the 88th Connaught Rangers at Kingston, and lying there was Lord Clanmorris's yacht with H.R.H. the Duke of Connaught on board.

I dined there on a Saturday night, and the Duke said he would come to church on board the next day and see the troops. The Colonel, when I told him, said: 'Oh, they are nearly all Roman Catholics, and cannot be forced to come, and are supposed not to by their Church, but I 'll tell them the Duke is coming.' He did, and they all came as if they had been zealous Protestants, and they were none the worse for it.

The Connaught Rangers had with them a curious trophy ; it was called ' Jingling Johnny ' and was made of brass. It is a pyramid in shape, but round, not square, all open work ; about six feet high and covered with bells that rang as it was moved. It was carried at the head of the regiment with the band. The 88th had captured it in the Peninsular War from a French regiment that had taken it in Egypt where it originated.

On our way to the Cape we called at St. Vincent in the Cape Verde Islands for coal, also at Ascension and St. Helena. At this last were two tortoises about $2\frac{1}{2}$ feet long which are known to be over 100 years, and some say 200 years, old.

On one occasion here I was coming down Ladder Hill, which was a flight of 708 broad wooden steps; the effect on one's legs of running as fast as possible down it was said to be curious, so I tried it with two other officers, and afterwards for two or three days our knees gave way whenever we tried to go down any stairs, though we were all right walking on the level.

At Cape Town I stayed with that charming, and able, and ill-used man, Sir Bartle Frere, and with him made a short trip up country. We now had a very rough experience trooping to East London and Durban in the winter months down there. I lost two of my three anchors and had to put to sea when bad weather came on to save the other one. At East London the troops were landed and embarked in large decked lighters, the passengers all below, battened down and in the dark ; the crew on deck to warp her over the bar, with seas sometimes sweeping over her.

Imagine the experience to a young married woman, wife of either officer or private, put into the hold of a lighter, and battened down in the dark. Soon she rolls and pitches violently and the passengers play at nine-pins with each other as they tumble about. At last comes quietude, then a bump against the jetty ; off hatches, and there bursts on their astonished gaze the truculent Zulu, or the hardy Kafir, or quaintly formed

Hottentot, alike guiltless of much drapery, and forming a picture startling to the fair exile.

I went in on deck to see it, and came out in the lifeboat as no ordinary boat could look at it. But all is now, I am told, changed by the building of breakwaters. A rocky bottom is the worst for anchoring; one of my anchors was broken in half in its shank on weighing, because it was (unknown to us of course) jammed under a rock.

I spent twenty-four hours in a strong north-west gale off Cape Agulhas on this voyage, which quite resembled the gale I was also in there in 1858 in H.M.S. *Pique*, and it was curious to see how much less serious such a thing was to the modern ship, both larger and a steamer, than to the old sailing frigate.

In an excellent little book on seamanship by Captain Liardet, written more than half a century ago, he tells you not to disbelieve old sailors' stories of fearful storms seemingly much worse than anything known now, and that in fact it only means they seemed so, because ships were smaller and in many ways more helpless.

We took home the 32nd Regiment, commanded by Col. Hon. R. de Montmorency, a pleasant companion, and a keen soldier, with his regiment in very good order. At Ascension Island I visited what is called 'Wide-awake fair,' it then being its season, which is when myriads of sea birds called 'Wide-awakes' come for their nesting season; their noise is surprising, and thousands of eggs are taken and preserved for eating. Ascension turtle are some of the best in the world. The females only land for a few weeks ending in June, to lay their eggs, and then re-enter the sea. They lay from 230 to 250 eggs at a time, and bury them in the sand ; in about five weeks the sun hatches them, when they at once take to the sea, and the males, I believe, never land again. It is supposed that they take seven years to grow up, and live probably for half a century or more.

After arriving in England, my ship was employed on home service till June 1878, when we went to Malta to join in the occupation of Cyprus.

This memoir is not meant to describe my life and doings on shore in England, as however interesting to me I cannot suppose they are so to the public, and my life was probably like most others of my age and position.

While at Portsmouth I used when able to visit the wreck of the *Eurydice*[1] off Dunnose, where the operation of raising the ship was going on. Her Captain, Marcus Hare, was an old messmate of mine in the *Chesapeake* in China, a good sailor, and a careful officer, one of the last I should have expected such a mishap to befall.

It occurred about four o'clock on a Sunday afternoon ; she was a 26-gun sailing frigate converted into a training ship for young seamen, and was on her way home from the West Indies.

Some years after when on half-pay I took a passage home in a New Zealand frozen-meat ship, and her captain told me he was mate of a sailing ship running up Channel with the *Eurydice* in

---

[1] Lost on the 24th March 1878, and only two seamen saved.

company. That off St. Catherine Point the latter ship hauled her wind for Spithead and thus closed the land. That his ship running for the Thames was off shore and saw the fatal squall coming down over the high cliffs near Dunnose, and shortened sail as quickly as possible, while the *Eurydice* not seeing the squall so soon on account of the land carried on her sail. My informant said the squall soon hid the frigate and they wondered what became of her.

What happened we know: the squall struck her and she did not capsize, but sailed to the bottom! Her main deck ports were open, she heeled over a good deal and water came in, especially at the lee bridle port, her bow depressed more and more and she dived to the bottom—one proof of this is that her fore foot was knocked off by the force with which it struck the ground, and her top-gallant masts remained out of water.

To the modern eye she would have looked too heavily rigged, but her spars were the same size as when she was a new ship; but what was changed was, that much of her standing rigging was of wire instead of hemp. This perhaps greatly caused the mischief—the wire held on and the upper masts did not give way, as has often in former times happened on such occasions.

The so-called ' salving ' of the *Eurydice*, that is raising her wreck, took many months and cost much money: To have blown her hull to pieces where she lay would, of course, have been the practical thing to do; but probably sentiment, on account of the great number of human bodies

THE ISLAND OF CYPRUS

inside her, forbade this. Finally she was raised, and beached in St. Helens Roads near Bembridge, and afterwards put into dock at Portsmouth, and broken up. As the Master-attendant of that yard said to me: 'We have learnt one thing by the above, and that is that it does not pay to raise a ship.' 'A sea change,' indeed, but not 'into something rich and strange.' I think Ariel cannot have visited the 'half-regained' *Eurydice* at St. Helens.

I visited her at St. Helens, a gruesome sight below, and better not described. It was curious how, though she lay in what seemed clear water, the insides of her most tightly closed drawers and lockers had much black mud in them.

About this time our Government decided to occupy the Island of Cyprus, with what special object I cannot say ; perhaps in memory of its long departed importance. But whenever I consider the matter I am reminded of the delightful picture of 'The Dog in the Manger,' by Mr. Walter Hunt, in the Tate Gallery, as it seems to me easier to guess what other nation might like to possess the island than to see what actual great value it is to us. I am, however, far from condemning the policy that induced us to occupy it even for reasons germane to the above, and indeed I know personally another island smaller than Cyprus and nearer to England which I think might well have remained ours for not unlike reasons.

We next went to the Mediterranean ; on 11th July arrived at Malta and began embarking Indian troops and horses for Cyprus. This bringing of our

Indian troops to European waters gave rise to the music-hall ditty,

> We don't want to fight, and by jingo if we do
> We won't go ourselves but we'll send the mild Hindoo.

Sir Garnet Wolseley came out to command the Army, and Lord John Hay, Admiral of the Channel Fleet, commanded the squadron at Cyprus.

The general ignorance in England about Cyprus was I believe great, as *Punch* said there was a general idea that from the reign of Venus it passed to the Venetians, when Othello as Governor smothered Desdemona, and that was about all. Indeed the great Lord Beaconsfield, in spite of Admiralty surveys, I believe said that they hoped a good harbour in Cyprus might yet be found, much as they might hope to dig up a statue of Venus.

As Macaulay says, every schoolboy knows that in Cyprus Richard Cœur de Lion married the Princess Berengaria of Navarre. No doubt many Crusaders have been there, and at our occupation many pieces of old armour were found, which had probably been worn in the Holy Land. Some young men from England in search of El Dorado arrived at Larnaka soon after we did, but I fear regained their native land richer only in experience.

In fact a good harbour is the chief want in Cyprus. The best natural anchorage is perhaps Larnaka, where the ships anchored, and the troops were landed. The old port is Farmagousta, which possessed a shelter for Venetian galleys and like craft, but to make real shelter there for modern ships would be a costly business.

On 22nd July Sir Garnet Wolseley was sworn in as Lord High Commissioner of the island, with addresses in Greek, English, and Turkish, and a salute of 21 guns to our flag. The landing was excellently arranged, conducted, and completed, and it was rather curious that this, the most permanent and important result of the war between Russia and Turkey, as regards the Mediterranean, was conducted as to the Navy by Lord John Hay, then commanding the Channel Fleet; the Mediterranean Admiral, Sir Geoffrey Hornby, being up the Sea of Marmora, and near Constantinople.

I would back Cyprus for dry thirsty heat against most places, and within a few weeks of our landing it proved unhealthy to many soldiers. When we were there the thermometer ranged from about 117° in a tent by day to 60° at night. A cool night's rest is, of course, a great thing, but the above changes in camp life under canvas often produce severe chills and illness.

The island generally lacks trees, which I believe were far more plentiful till the Turks cut too many down. The sea water well off shore was 83° and so clear you could see your anchor and cable in 13 fathoms.

On 28th July we left for Malta and thence to England. I had orders to find and tow home a refractory transport called the *Maraval*. She was a sailing ship, no more wanted, but in pay till she got to her home port. The surface current in the Straits of Gibraltar runs always into the

Mediterranean, and to get out with westerly winds is rather difficult. Twice the above ship had been towed out by tugs, and twice returned to eastward of the Rock, apparently quite happy thus to ' do time.' I found her, put men on board, and towed her as required.

In September I again went out to Cyprus, arriving in October. I rode up to Nicosia, the capital, and stayed with Sir Garnet Wolseley at his headquarters near there, about twenty-six miles in all. Sir Garnet and his staff formed a most agreeable society and one at once felt at home with them. I think no one who has ever really known the present Viscount Wolseley will differ from me in my opinion of his charm of manner.

A Cyprus mule, however, is a beast indeed to ride on, no paces, and the saddle a veritable 'little ease'; the animal has an armour belt round it and is further protected with cloths, rendering it impervious either to whip or spur, of which fact it seems by its paces to be perfectly cognisant.

After being roasted all day, one cannot heap too many blankets on oneself at night in a tent.

Lord Gifford of the staff kindly lent me his horse, a very good one, to ride back on, a favour I have never forgotten. The two great curses of Cyprus have been drought and swarms of locusts. It is curious to see a cloud of these insects in the air before they decide to alight, as they do in a numerous compact army. Some say the island's name is from *kupros*—copper—which was got here. The importance of Cyprus in olden days seems hard to realise now. A Turkish prisoner from the battle of Lepanto (1571) comparing the loss of Cyprus to the Venetians, and the above defeat as concerned the Sultan, said, ' The latter is to the Sultan but as the loss of his beard which will grow again, the former is to Venice as the loss of an arm which can never be recovered.' However, Bacon was right when he said that ' Lepanto arrested the greatness of the Turk.'

At Larnaka in October we embarked the 101st Regiment for passage to Halifax. This regiment since their arrival in Cyprus had become very sickly, and it was advisable to move them to a more healthy place. They were commanded by Colonel de la Fosse, who was one of the only three survivors of the massacre of Cawnpore. I became very good friends with him, but as his officers told me, he would never talk about Cawnpore, so painful was the impression of it left on his mind.

On our way across the Atlantic we sighted a deserted water-logged vessel, which I closed and boarded. She proved to be the *Fix*, a brigantine loaded with paraffin oil. No boats left, and no record was to be found on board. I never heard what became of her crew. I took her in tow with much trouble, but bad weather coming on next day had to abandon her. It was my only experience of towing a water-logged ship, with the sea at times washing over her, and no means of steering her. These derelict vessels are, of course, dangers to others on dark nights, and had I been in an ordinary man-of-war I might have stayed and tried to destroy her. Her cargo, of course, kept her afloat.

We called at Bermuda, or rather the Bermudas, for there are said to be three hundred of them; there are nine chief ones, most of the rest being mere rocks. The anchorage is good, well sheltered and safe, except in hurricanes which come at times and of which they say : 'August prepare, September beware, October all over.'

The islands are very fertile ; the natural rock is so porous that a strong dock cannot be made of it. This is why we had to send out a floating dock to take our ships for repairs ; when I was there they were repairing and cleaning the dock, and in doing so took 170 tons of iron rust out of it. A new one has since gone out there. There are caves with the sea water so clear—though there was good light—that you did not notice water was there, and I have been deceived and walked right into it.

It is said that a solid space of 6 miles by 4 would contain all the Bermudas, equalling about 15,000 acres in extent. There is a small island or rock off Ireland Island (which has the dock-yard on it), and on this small rock is a cross cut, one arm of which is supposed to point to a treasure hidden by the Spanish in 1620, but no one knows which arm it is !

The Bermudas must always possess a charm as the islands 'where Ariel has warbled and Waller has strayed,' and their soft climate certainly lends itself to such roaming 'along that wild and lonely shore,' as the poet warns 'sweet

Nea' not to indulge in. The channel to enter by is long and winding and is thus a great defence, but the long-range modern guns would deal havoc from outside.

At Halifax we landed the 101st Regiment and embarked the 1st Battalion of the 20th Regiment, for Cyprus. On my way I passed through the Azores Islands—the name means Isle of Hawks. They are mostly volcanic, and are said to have had no animal life on them when discovered in the fifteenth century. Eruptions and earth-quakes still sometimes occur.

At Cyprus we landed the 20th, and embarked the 71st Highland Light Infantry, a regiment I had long known and much liked. I landed them at Gibraltar, and we lay there some days.

I have hunted at various times with the Calpe hounds—in those days always managed by military officers quartered at the Rock. It is said those hounds were first instituted by naval men. The country is so hilly and covered with rocks, cistus and other bushes that it looks at first unrideable at high speed.

We embarked the 1st Battalion of the 4th Regiment for the West Indies, and went first to Barbados. This is probably the healthiest of the West India Islands, but by no means the most beautiful—far from it. The rainfall of the year is usually sixty inches, but I am assured that twenty inches have fallen in twenty-four hours.

We went next to Trinidad off the mouth of the Orinoco River. The Governor's house at Port of Spain is in the most beautiful tropical garden;

coffee, tea, and cocoa grow in it. Here one thinks of Columbus the Discoverer, and of Raleigh's last sad expedition to the Orinoco. The pitch lake of Trinidad is much noted; it covers ninety-nine acres.

From Trinidad we went to Port Royal, Jamaica, and landed the headquarters of the regiment, detachments being left at the other islands. The great earthquake that sank old Port Royal under the sea was in 1692. In many cases the earth then opened and people were swallowed in the crevices of it.

Jamaica is nearly all hills and valleys. When Queen Isabella asked Columbus what the island was like, he is said to have crumpled up a bit of paper in his hand, put the paper on the table and said, ' Your Majesty, Jamaica is like that.' The chief military quarters are at Up Park Camp, near Port Royal; but there are barracks in the Blue Mountains which are healthy and have a splendid view.

From Jamaica I went to Malta with troops, and from thence to England. From Malta I brought home the main part of the ship's company of H.M.S. *Thunderer*, on board which ship the terrible explosion of the 38-ton muzzle-loading gun had lately occurred in her foremost turret. Both turret guns were being fired simultaneously, but evidently one did not go off. It may seem hard to believe such a thing could happen and not be noticed, but from my own experience I understand it. The men in the turret often stopped their ears, and perhaps shut their eyes, at the moment of firing, and then instantly worked the run-in levers, and did not notice how much the guns had recoiled. This no doubt occurred. Both guns were then at once reloaded, and the rammer's indicator, working by machinery, set fast and failed to show how far home the new charge had gone. This, too, may seem unlikely, but no doubt it happened; and the gun on being then fired burst, killing two officers and several men, and wrecking the turret. Experiments made with a similar gun double-loaded burst it in exactly the same way.

On 25th March 1879 I was relieved in command of the *Orontes*, having been in her over three years. During that time the ship had run about 98,000 miles, and carried of troops—849 military officers, over 30,000 N.C.O.'s and privates, and with wives and children nearly 38,000 persons in all.

It is most important to our nation above all others that good fellowship, and a sort of brotherhood feeling, should exist between our two services, and if the Troop Service contributed at all to that it was an extra reason for it; trooping is not proper naval work, but it gave me very valuable experience in handling a ship under many circumstances, showed me many ports and coasts, and added enormously to my knowledge of human nature.

I will only add that invariably the military officers embarked treated me with the greatest consideration, and I had practically no trouble with the fair sex entrusted to my care.

CHAPTER XVI

CAPTAIN

Torpedo Course—Law Courts—Touraine—Winter in France.

I WAS now on half-pay again, so applied to join the torpedo course at Portsmouth, which was granted. In these liberal days I believe officers are put on full pay for College, gunnery, torpedo, or other courses, but formerly our zeal was considered to be enough inducement. We had a ' cabin ' in the old Naval College in the dockyard (if there was room) and could join the mess there. The course lasted over two months.

I then went abroad for a short time, but mostly spent the summer in England, where it was about the wettest one I ever knew.

Sometimes I attended the assizes of the Oxford Circuit at Worcester, the Judge being kind and giving me a seat by him. I valued this experience to help me to deal with offenders at courts-martial, and otherwise to hear how trials are conducted on shore.

A Barrister in Court and an M.P. in Parliament are, I believe, privileged and say what they like about other people. If so, I think it wrong; but however that may be, I remember on one occasion, Mr. Huddleston, who could be very bitter when he liked, took the line of abusing the solicitor on the other side ; which I am told is the regular thing to do when you feel your case a bad one. At all events he did so in no measured terms ; till at last the abused attorney, a Mr. O—— of Stratford-on-Avon, having got very red and angry, at last got on his legs and said to the Judge : 'My Lord, I must demand your protection from these libels on me.' The Judge very calmly replied : ' Sit down, Mr. O——, sit down ; no one thinks at all the worse of you for what the learned counsel says ! '

I fear I formed a generally low impression of the jury's intelligence, and felt that if I were guilty I should like to be tried with a jury, if innocent only with a judge.

I remember one case of two men tried for highway robbery with violence ; the jury found a verdict of guilty of one charge without the other. The Judge told them it must be guilty, or not guilty, of both. The jury consulted a very short time, and then said 'NOT GUILTY,' and this verdict was about to be recorded when it became evident that all the twelve did not agree, one only holding out for Guilty.

The Judge remarked that he would have them locked up as required to debate, but after some sharp arguments in the jury-box for a very few minutes they unanimously gave a verdict of 'GUILTY.'

The opinion of England generally is no doubt for a jury, and I suppose on the whole it is right. I have also heard it argued in favour of a jury that especially in cases involving the capital sentence, a single man (the Judge) might well hesitate to convict, especially on only circumstantial evidence —though he believed the prisoner guilty—when a combination of men not singly responsible would not mind doing so.

I heard another case that was singular, and a proof to me of the great power an English judge has. It was Lord Brampton (then Hawkins) on the Bench. The case that of a young man who, having had a natural child sworn against him by his sweetheart (the mother) in a fit of anger tried to cut her throat. For this he was tried and found guilty. The Judge then said : ' I shall reserve my sentence till to-morrow.'

Next day the Court was crowded. The prisoner was put in the dock and the young woman in the witness-box, when the Judge said to the prisoner : ' Would you marry that young woman if you could ? ' The reply was : ' Yes, my Lord.' The Judge then asked the young woman if she was ready to marry the man, and was not afraid of him. She said, Yes, she was quite ready to. The Judge then said : ' Prisoner at the bar, you are for the time discharged, if you promise to marry your sweetheart to-morrow morning, and do so ; but if within a year your conduct to her is improper you will be arrested, and sentenced, for the crime of which you have been convicted.' The audience were delighted as may be supposed, and their loud cheers had to be suppressed.

As I have said, I do not mean to inflict on my readers (if I have any) long details of my life on shore, but shall only occasionally refer to them. In the early autumn I stayed some time in Ireland. The contrast between it and England is certainly great. I have often been there, and to many parts of it, and believe I should, if a landed proprietor, delight in the people, till they boycotted or shot me. But as for governing the country satisfactorily, I believe it is impossible.

Had Cromwell reigned as long as George III, Ireland would have been reduced to quietude, but not by kindness.

That autumn I spent at Azay-sur-Cher near Tours. At the Château de Nitray, a François Premier house near us, was a family whose ancestor was one of Napoleon's generals and thus became enriched; they were of course strong Bonapartists, and arguments with the young ladies on the cruel way in which we treated the great ex-Emperor were good practice for my French.

My experience of real French ladies and gentlemen has been that they are usually either Royalists or Bonapartists, and very rarely Republican in their sentiments and wishes. The then owner of Nitray was grandson to the above-mentioned General, and told me his grandfather was Governor of Stettin for eight years, during which he made his fortune.

Living with a curé to improve my French, I have several times since stayed in Touraine, and can recommend it strongly. Its natural beauties, numerous very fine old historical châteaux, and good roads and railways for locomotion, make it a most desirable place for a sojourn.

In summer it is often hot, and in winter it can be very cold. When I was there in 1879 the thermometer in December went down to 15 degrees below zero of Fahrenheit, i.e. 47 degrees of frost, the River Cher, about the size of the Thames at Windsor, was not only frozen, but owing to its current the blocks of ice were heaped one on top of the other, like ice floes in the Arctic regions, and the river was frozen nearly to the bottom.

The French began by saying, ' It is as cold as the year of our unhappy war ' (1870) ; next, ' It is as cold as 1812 '; then, ' It is as cold as in 1789 '; and finally, ' We don't know when it was so cold before.' In my bedroom I had to wash as soon as the water was poured out or else it became ice. This is no doubt exceptional for the middle of France.

I am a strong advocate for naval officers knowing some foreign languages. Tardily—but at last—the Admiralty have awoke to the necessity. But I should make a rule that no boy might become a naval cadet unless he could hold an ordinary conversation in at least one foreign tongue.

I consider the worst linguists, as naval officers, are those of the United States Navy, and after them it is a toss-up between us and the French, but they at least have the excuse that their language is that of diplomacy. On the other hand I consider the Austrians to be the best naval linguists I know.

Foreign languages are really more necessary to a sailor than to a soldier, because the latter is seldom or never officially brought into contact with foreign troops—unless it be in a war alliance on actual service in the field.

But men of war constantly meet others of many nations in peace time, and occasions of combined operations on shore to meet sudden and unexpected emergencies have at various times arisen.

On my way home I stayed in Paris and walked over the Seine there on the ice, which is rarely possible. The snow was very plentiful, and I was told a million francs had been spent in clearing it away. Sleighs were plentiful in the streets. It was said in the *Times* of 29th December 1879, that in Paris on the 9th 40 degrees of frost by Fahrenheit, i.e. 8 degrees below zero, were registered, and that it certainly was the coldest on record then.

In the spring of 1880 I served on a combined naval and military committee to review the troopship instructions, which had become out of date. In truth a good deal of arrangement and mutual consideration was necessary to provide for all the complications attending misconduct of soldiers when embarked in a man-of-war, i.e. a ship flying the actual naval pennant.

CHAPTER XVII

H.M.S. *IRIS*

Loss of *Atalanta* — Trial Cruise — Palermo — Russian Torpedo
Boat — Messina — Adriatic — Ionian Islands — Olympia —
Paestum—Egypt—Trieste—Tunis—French Ships—Syria—
Roustem Pasha and the Bear—1882 War in Egypt.

IN April 1880 I commissioned the *Iris* at Portsmouth. She was the first ship in the Navy built of steel, also the first ship of war that could steam 18 knots, and her hull and lines were beautiful. Not a straight line about her ! Her lines were decided by experiments made by Professor Froude with paraffin models in a tank ; and below water in shape she much resembled a fish, carrying her beam well forward, and tapering off to the stern. She carried fourteen 8-inch guns, all on pivot carriages, had Whitehead torpedo-tubes, and was designed to carry torpedo-boats.

In the spring of 1880 the *Atalanta*, a 26-gun sailing frigate, almost sister ship to the late *Eurydice*, was lost—no one knows how—in the Atlantic on her way home from Bermuda. Her Captain, F. Stirling, was a charming man and first-rate officer. He and his wife were great friends of mine. She would not believe the ship was lost, and asked me to come and see her, and made me promise to try to get the Admiralty to send my ship to look for her husband. It was a very sad episode, and very curious its following on the *Eurydice*.

We went out for a trial cruise in the Channel, and one day under sail only carried away our foremast—the first time I ever saw such a thing happen. The truth is the mast was a single spar of wood, and had a flaw in it; a steel mast was substituted.

In July we left for the Mediterranean to join our Fleet, then under the command of Vice-Admiral Sir Beauchamp Seymour, afterwards Lord Alcester. We reached Malta at the height of summer, and found the ship very hot, and no wonder ; for comfort, of course, give me a wooden ship. Steel vessels are like tin kettles, the heat or the cold is through them at once, unless they are very thickly lined with wood.

From Malta we joined the Commander-in-Chief and squadron at Palermo. The ships were not numerous, but all were quite different in design, armament, and size. The French in those days had much more uniformity in ships than we had. Our flagship was the *Alexandra* and was the finest ship in the Fleet.

Even in 1880 brigandage was prevalent in Sicily, especially near Palermo ; so much so that when the *Bacchante* with the two sons of our then Prince of Wales were at the port, and the Princes were going for a picnic in the country, the authorities insisted on sending a regiment of soldiers to guard them, and begged that no one should go outside a cordon of sentries drawn round their party.

From Palermo I went to Messina, then most flourishing, with some 118,000 inhabitants. The harbour is an extinct, submerged volcano.

In 1859, owing to the war between France and Italy, we commissioned a great many ships, and some could not get bands in England.

The *London*, a two-decker, went out with none, and being at Messina a man came aboard and asked if they wanted a band. On hearing they did he said: 'I am bandmaster of an Italian regiment, and we have all deserted with our instruments, and should like to join'; which they did, fiddles and all. The Prefet here told me he was imprisoned by Bomba for ten years for political matters and occupied himself in translating Milton and Byron. Many of us would like at times to see SOME of our politicians thus harmlessly employed!

While on this coast I visited Catania and from there ascended Mount Etna with some of my officers. We slept at the Casa Inglese, 9652 feet up, and went to the summit (10,870 feet) next morning. It was in August and there was no snow, except a few patches. It was odd to sit on the side of the cone with a cloud below you, look over the cloud at the sea, no land being visible, and feel as if, should you slip on the side of the cone, which seemed quite possible, you would go into the sea!

While I was at Messina the Russian torpedo-boat *Batoum* arrived from England on her way to the Black Sea. She was commanded by Captain-Lieutenant Zatzarenny, who told me that in their late war with Turkey he, then a lieutenant having charge of a 28-foot steam cutter, fixed a Whitehead torpedo fore and aft under her keel, went into Batoum, and discharged the torpedo there at a Turkish man-of-war, which then sunk in five minutes, and for this service he was promoted and given command of this boat, named accordingly. All the details he described, and drew a plan of it. At the same time I had before me on a shelf the book written by Lieutenant C. Sleeman, late R.N., then in the Turkish Navy, who described the above attempt, but said it utterly failed. The two accounts amused me, and one felt inclined to ask, ' What is truth ? '

When I was at Sevastopol some years later I heard that poor Zatzarenny had there met with a very tragic end.

We visited several places—one was Ragusa in Dalmatia. Here is a very small island called Lacroma, where it is said our King Richard I was imprisoned by the Austrians; but as other places have been so cited, it is probably doubtful which is right. The Cathedral at Lacroma is said to have been endowed by King Richard to fulfil a vow, perhaps on gaining his freedom ! We went to Brindisi, which then had massive walls and fortifications, now destroyed. The canal into the port had four fathoms of water, but the Consul said that fourteen years before there was not one fathom, till they set to work to make it the important harbour it became. The classical remains of ancient Brindisi are interesting, and the spot is shown where Pompey is said to have defended himself when besieged by Julius Cæsar.

We were, of course, often at Malta, which island, in the middle of the Mediterranean, with its first-rate harbour, seems situated on purpose to shelter the ships of the Power meant to be predominant in that sea.

The siege of Malta by the Turks in 1565 is, of course, the most important event regarding it as concerns the world at large, and I consider the two or three embrasures low down between the dockyard and French creeks with much respect, as the guns from them are said greatly to have prevented the Turks taking that position, which would probably have meant the fall of Valetta, and Malta becoming a Turkish stronghold. But Malta is far too well known for me to attempt any description of it.

In October we formed one of the Allied Squadron in the Bocce de Cattaro to determine the question of Dulcino. The ships of six different nationalities were assembled and our Commander-in-Chief — Sir Beauchamp Seymour — was the doyen, and acknowledged as the chief. It was an interesting occasion, and I think not at all without diplomatic difficulties, which our Admiral, so far as his part went, was well fitted to contend with.

The Gulf of Cattaro consists of more than one spacious anchorage surrounded by lofty hills, and a series of havens leading to the town of Cattaro, sheltering under a lofty and precipitous hill— almost a mountain.

Captain George Tryon [1] and I rode up to Cettinge, the capital of Montenegro, to call on the reigning Prince—now King Nicholas. The road is mostly up and down hill and it took us seven good hours in torrents of rain ; one pass was 3500 feet above the sea. Our uniforms, slung on other horses, got so wet that we stood as near as we could to the Palace fires that evening to dry them.

Montenegro then was, perhaps still is, a fascinating country, the people being a very fine race physically, and giving you the impression of honesty and open-heartedness.

The Royal family—as is known—are worthy to govern such a people. Montenegro was under the protection of Austria, but the predilection of Prince Nicholas was evidently for Russia, partly no doubt because his religion and that of most of his people is the Orthodox Greek Church. The Prince talked much to me of his visit to St. Petersburg, and the Czar, who had a great military review for him ; but what seemed to have most impressed the Prince was the collection of stuffed bears in the Winter Palace, which had been shot by the Emperor. Four Montenegrin Princesses were then at school in Russia.

Cettinge is 2800 feet above the sea ; the Palace is by no means grand, a gentleman's house, no more—at least when I was there. Near the town is a building, interesting to visit, containing very various weapons, and a collection of flags taken in war, some from the Turks. I was told that thousands of Montenegrins carried out the custom

---

[1] Afterwards Admiral Sir George Tryon.

of making each other blood relations by mutually drinking some drops of the other's blood.

The Admiral now sent me as senior officer in the Ionian Islands, and a more pleasant duty I never had. When Mr. Gladstone decided to give up our occupation of them, the British Army lost one of their most agreeable stations. Of the seven islands I prefer Corfu, though each one has its advantages.

The climate is never really trying, and the Isles of Greece almost deserve the praise that 'Eternal summer gilds them yet.' When I was there in 1880 war was thought to be imminent between Greece and Turkey. In consequence of this the Greeks were mounting troops and drilling them in Corfu, a thing contrary to treaty, as had to be pointed out. That island and Paxo were then, and now are, under protection of the Great Powers, on condition of their not being military stations. When I visited Zante, they sent me an invitation to attend next day, officially, at a religious ceremony. Having found out it was not connected with the Turkish imbroglio, but an annual ceremony done to record the emancipation of Greece, I accepted.

We landed in uniform, cocked hat, &c., and I walked through a mass of people, some on their knees, all most polite, bowing, waving handkerchiefs, and saying something. The Consul who was with me said: 'Do you know what they are saying?' I said: 'No, I can't understand Greek.' He replied: 'They are blessing you, and saying they hope the English are about to retake the Islands under their protection.' I said: 'Do you think if a plebiscite was now taken votes would be mostly for us to come back?' and he said: 'They would tear in pieces anyone voting against it.' Such apparently was public feeling in the islands just then, in view of a possible war with Turkey.

The old saying of 'When Greek meets Greek, then comes the tug of war' hardly seemed to apply to the Ionian Islanders. At Santa Maura I resolved to satisfy myself about the so-called 'Sappho's Leap.' The legend, of course, is that the poetess for despairing love of Phaon threw herself into the sea. At Santa Maura it is supposed to have occurred; and in such a prosaic thing as the Admiralty Chart you may see 'Sappho's Leap' marked, but it is an impossible place, as it slopes back from the sea. We found the, perhaps, real one about 200 feet high, sheer down to the water, and near it are the remains of what was probably the Temple of Apollo.

Cephalonia has the curious feature of the sea running into the land by a very narrow water course and disappearing down a natural hole. It was used to turn a mill wheel; I have never heard any scientific explanation of it.

The roads in that island are good, said to be greatly due to the energy of its once Governor, that splendid soldier, General Sir Charles Napier. Of him while there the story is told that there lived near him an Ionian nobleman who was in the habit of beating his wife. One afternoon in summer, all windows and doors being open, our General heard the cries of the unhappy lady and unable to endure such treatment of a woman, Sir Charles rushed into the other house, and himself began to beat the husband. On being persuaded by his A.D.C. to retire to his own dwelling, and there gradually calming down, the Governor saw the enormity he had been guilty of towards a foreign noble, so sent his A.D.C. over to say he was ready to give satisfaction by a duel. The nobleman however replied : ' What does he want ? He enters my house, stops me beating my wife, beats me, and now wishes to kill me. No, tell him I never want to see him again.'

From the top of the Black Mountain (5218 feet high) in Cephalonia you can see the sites of two of the most important sea fights of the world, viz. Actium and Lepanto, their positions only a few miles apart.

We visited Olympia—it is most interesting ; the Germans were at work excavating, but allowed only to make casts, &c., not to carry any antiquities off. Olympia was first ruined by an earthquake, and then flooded by the River Alpheus, and gradually buried. The inscriptions on the bases for the statues are mostly as plain as when cut, but the few statues that remain, except one of Hermes, are not very impressive.

On the Isthmus of Corinth I visited the works of Nero's canal, begun but never finished; it was to have been about 200 feet wide nearly on the same line that the present canal has now been made.

I visited Schliemann's Troy, which I believe is the real one : it also fulfils Virgil's ' Est in conspectu Tenedos,' &c. There are seemingly the remains of four towns one over the other, of which I understand the second from the bottom to be Priam's city, and you can see marks of fire in it, and make out the Scæan Gate.

I must resist mentioning most of the places I visited, but the Mediterranean is to my mind the most interesting part of the world historically, and one is much inclined to enlarge about it.

If you want to get exercise quickly, run down the cone of Vesuvius; we did so, and in five minutes got so much violent motion of arms and legs that we were stiff for two or three days.

I visited Paestum, anchoring off it, and landed to see the three ruined temples there, which are magnificent. The name of the place was Poseidonia, from its principal temple which was dedicated to Neptune. The place, once no doubt prosperous, is now quite deserted. We nearly came to grief in embarking. The ship was at anchor as near the shore as safe, but there was no shelter. It came on to blow from seaward. Most of the officers who landed got off in a semi-lifeboat we had. I was in my private skiff with one officer, my coxswain, and dog. We ran her out through the surf and jumped in, but found that the dog had jumped out, not liking the sea, and swum back to shore. To save him, we returned, but the sea had got up so much, that our only plan was for a ship's boat to anchor outside the breakers and a man to swim in with a grass line. This we made fast to the boat and, lashing the gear, were towed out through the breakers. Happily no one was drowned, though one officer very nearly was, and my coxswain had to invalid home in consequence of his ducking.

I was swimming about with a photograph of Neptune's Temple in my pocket, and said I would never again have believed in the great Sea God if any of us had 'lost the number of our mess,' as the sea expression is.

I then went to Alexandria, a harbour which my ship could easily enter. Certainly Africa, generally, is worse off for good harbours than any other country of half its size.

I visited Cairo and the Pyramids, and corrected some errors in Murray about them. Their fascination must be confessed, and the fact that the area covered by ' Cheops ' about equals Lincoln's Inn Fields impresses one with its massive contents ; now everything there is both over well known and quite overrun with tourists, so I will say no more on that subject. In Cairo already Campbell's line—and ' coming events cast their shadows before '—was being foreshadowed, and was justified the next year.

The *Iris* was, as I have said, the first steel ship in the Navy; she was coated with Simms's composition. I had been trying her powers of tacking under sail only, and in doing so noticed the cement coming off in flakes owing to the ' bloom ' on the steel ; a thing not expected, so we were again docked at Malta.

From there we went up the Adriatic, visiting many ports and staying at Trieste. · While there, we visited the famous Grotto of Adelsberg with its subterranean river in Carniola ; its stalactites and stalagmites are probably unrivalled elsewhere. We got a specimen of the *Proteus* or *Hyporthon anguinus*, the very curious water lizard or saurian whose eyes are there, but undeveloped and covered with a sort of skin.

While at Trieste I used to see much of that extraordinary man, the late Sir Richard Burton, and his wife. They were both most industrious in writing pamphlets about various subjects. One pamphlet of his was a plan to dispose of Constantinople, by making it a free city guaranteed by the Great Powers. Lady Burton was devoted to her husband, and he to her in his way. She started at Trieste a society to prevent cruelty to animals. A cart used to go round every morning to catch any stray dogs, which were put into it, confined there by bars and nets, and left for the day, unless claimed, and often in the sun, so as to leave no excuse for their not going mad.

The Austrian Admiral at Trieste was most friendly and genial, and a great linguist ; he told me he talked Italian to his wife, German to his daughter, Slav to his servants, and English to the governess, also French when required. He gave us a ball and acted master of the ceremonies as if he had been a dancing-master.

The squadron joined us at Trieste, and general leave was given, with more riotous results than I have ever seen elsewhere. We next went to Tunis, to watch British interests, in company with the *Monarch* and *Falcon*, during the French operations on that coast, and especially at Sphax.

The French squadron was in good order and commanded by a vice-admiral who, though just civil to us, evidently hated our presence here. He was a martinet of the old sort.

The site of Carthage can be clearly made out, i.e. no observant person can go over it without seeing there was a city there. The immense ancient water reservoirs are the most evident remains. It can never have been the least like Turner's famous picture, but that does not matter !

Mr. Reade, our Consul-General at Tunis, remembered the loss of our *Avenger* on the Sorelli rocks in 1847, and her four survivors being put up in his father's house, and said the Arabs behaved well to the shipwrecked men. At Tunis is the grave of Colonel Howard Payne, who died in 1852, and is stated to be the author of ' Home, Sweet Home.' Is this so ?

Mr. Reade said that when Lord A—— P—— came here in his yacht he (Mr. Reade) accompanied Lord A—— to pay his respects to the Bey. The audience chamber at the Palace is a very long narrow room, with the door at one end and the throne at the other. On the left hand as you go in are at least six windows and opposite each window is a large mirror. Between all the windows and the mirrors are tables, and on every table is a clock. After presentation Mr. Reade asked if Lord A—— wished to say anything to his Highness, on which his Lordship, with that assured complacency well known to his family, put up his eyeglass, looked round and said :

' Oh yes, ask the old cock why he has so many clocks, and all keeping different time ! '

The Fast of Ramadan was on when I was at Tunis ; it changes its season each year, according to the moon, and as no food or liquid may be swallowed by the faithful during it between sunrise and sunset, it is, of course, much the most trying ordeal when in the summer. All persons over twelve years old ought to keep it.

On board the French ship *Marengo*, her Captain—Layrle—asked if I was related to Sir Michael Seymour, who commanded the *Amethyst* in 1808 and captured the French frigate *Thétis*. When I said ' Yes,' he said, ' My grandfather was taken prisoner in the *Thétis*.'

We lay off Tunis over a month of very hot weather, then visited Sphax and several other places. The French had bombarded and taken Sphax, and their troops were dying fast of typhoid, &c. In the country near here are old Roman remains, showing it was once civilised and very populous.

I rejoined the Admiral at Palma in Majorca, and we went to Gibraltar *viâ* Cartagena, which is a good anchorage ; and an aphorism of Admiral Doria's was that the three best harbours in the Mediterranean were June, July, and Cartagena.

We visited Port Mahon in Minorca, which only wants to be larger inside to be a first-class steamers' man-of-war port. Everyone knows we have held it three times ; it is too much out of the road between Gibraltar and Egypt to be quite what we want. In the sailing days getting in and out with a foul wind could only be done by warping, or towing with boats. I believe Lord Collingwood's flagship, leaving with him in his last illness, took twenty-four hours to get out.

'As lazy as a Port Mahon soldier' is an old naval expression ; and I was amused, on visiting the fortifications, to see the Spanish sentry justifying the above, by leaning his rifle against a wall and sitting down near it. The Spaniards have now fortified the port, by a fort in the right place, to the eastward of the entrance.

I visited Barcelona, which I call the Liverpool of Spain. But it is far more prosperous than loyal.

Next winter, among other places, we were on the coast of Syria, and rode up to Jerusalem, which I am glad to have seen before desecrated by a railway. We landed, of course, at Jaffa, where Jonah embarked, and where Perseus liberated Andromeda, but the Holy Land is too well known for me to describe it. When leaving Jerusalem one of our party was disappointed in not getting the bottle of Jordan water he had been promised. In vain the waiter tried to pacify him, so after swearing there were no more he hurriedly retreated, and presently returned saying that extraordinary to relate one more had been found ; and no doubt it did very well.

At Beyrut I called on Roustem Pasha, the Governor-General of Syria, afterwards well known in London. In the room where he received me there was an immense stuffed brown bear, of which he told me the following story : He was going out to a bear-shooting drive between Peters-burg and Moscow in the winter. The man who usually carried his second rifle was wanted for a special job, so he took another man. The shooters were posted as usual, deep snow was on the ground. At last a bear appeared in front of him, but seeing him turned to try and break back. He said: 'I had not a good chance and should not have fired; but I did, and only wounded the bear, which at once rushed at me. I fired my second barrel without effect, and called for my other rifle, but my man had fled. The bear came on, throwing the snow up in the air in a shower as he came. I fired all barrels of my revolver, and the bullets were found to have hit him, but on he came. I saw a huge thing in the air and found myself on my back in the snow. The bear made one claw at my face, leaving the scars you see, but his claws luckily missed my eyes. I put up my left hand to protect my face, he took my hand in his mouth, and I could hear the bones being crushed; I tried with my right hand to run my hunting knife into him, but could not. Fortunately other shooters heard the shots, came up, killed the bear, and saved me.'

At Tripoli I was on shore with my black poodle and old Jose, our interpreter; in the market the natives gathered round the dog, and curiously felt him. I asked Jose what they said, and he replied: 'He say he think he sheep.'

Much sponge-diving goes on off here; state-ments as to divers' depths and times under water differ from 25 fathoms and 2 minutes to 31 fathoms and 4¼ minutes—I believe the former, if either.

We went to the Gulf of Iskanderun and Alexandretta, founded after the battle of Issus. Near here we were shooting at Jonah's Pillar, where he landed from the whale (or fish). Instead of going to Aleppo I camped out, with some of my officers, on the ancient Pyramus River to shoot a very varied bag—francolin, swan, ducks of kinds, cock, teal, &c. They say twelve varieties of game in all.

Aleppo reminds one of its ' button,' so called— a very bad boil—the water is said to cause it. Natives usually have it on the face; few residents, I believe, escape it.

From here I went to Cyprus, and at ancient Salamis, near Farmagousta, where excavations of the tombs were going on, were found some small vases two thousand years old, and just like what aie made now.

In the spring of 1882 we went to Greece, and had a very pleasant cruise in company with H.M.S. *Bacchante*, commanded by Captain Lord Charles Scott, with our two Princes, Albert and George—the sons of our late King—on board her as naval cadets; Prince George being our present Gracious Sovereign. They, of course, visited the King and Queen of the Hellenes, who kindly took me also out to Patoy, their home in the mountains, a beautiful spot.

In June we went to Alexandria. The famous riots there took place on the 11th and were the prelude to the occurrences that summer, but this is not history and only a general narrative of events. Until just before the bombardment (on 11th July) my ship was very actively employed examining the coast, and going to Malta and back. The only two battleships, then called ironclads, that could get into Alexandria harbour were the *Monarch* and *Invincible*, and in the latter ship our Admiral (Sir Beauchamp Seymour) flew his flag during the bombardment. The rest of our large ships had to remain outside and attack from there.

Till just before the crisis we expected the French to join us, and I think from this point of view the French President made a great mistake in withdrawing their ships, though for us ever since it has no doubt been an immense advantage, and simplified our position in Egypt.

I had hoped to join in the bombardment, and the Admiral would have kept me for it, but the Admiralty fearing what might happen at Port Said, and to the Suez Canal in case of warlike operations, I was sent there, to our great disappointment.

On 7th July I arrived at Port Said and moored ship abreast of the Egyptian corvette *Sakaa*. I prepared for action, and sent a lieutenant on board her to say that if she moved or took any active part I should fire into her. She at once beat to quarters, loaded and trained her guns on us—but unfortunately did not fire.

I had all planned out to land such men as I could spare in case of a fight, to do certain things on shore, and it might have turned out very interesting.

Meanwhile great alarm grew in Port Said, so much so that I chartered a large merchant steamer and put the British and other European residents who wished on board her for safety, with one of my lieutenants in charge of the ship. About 360 refugees lived in the vessel.

On 11th July the bombardment of Alexandria took place, and the same day there arrived from thence the French ironclad *La Gallissonière*, with the flag of Rear-Admiral Conrad, a charming man, whom I knew before and have often seen since.

To the westward of Port Said is a large shallow lake called Lake Menzaleh, communicating with the sea by a narrow channel defended by a fort called Ghemil. It seemed to me suitable that this fort should be put out of action, but our position was that we were friends with the Khedive and Egyptian Government and could do no violence unless they began. I went out in one of my ship's torpedo-boats to reconnoitre the fort, on which they turned their men out, loaded and pointed their rifles at us, but to my surprise did not fire and so give me an excuse to attack the fort, which I should have done with my ship.

The Suez Canal Company under the direction of M. de Lesseps from the first showed an animus towards us; for this there were excuses, and certainly the condition we reduced the beautiful garden of Ismalia, the creation of Lesseps, to later on must have been maddening to him. But worse still was the fact that he had assured Arabi

Pacha that he might be sure the English should not be allowed to use the canal for any warlike operations, and that therefore there was no occasion to block or injure the canal. This was a promise that we, of course, could not give, or if we did, must keep. Given by a man known not to be our friend it was believed by Arabi, but did not bind us at all. The last straw was that we seized the Canal Company's premises at Port Said and took our men-of-war and transports up ourselves; we paid for their canal passage dues, but refused to pay for their long detention in Lake Timsah on the ground that it was original water.

I was employed with Captain Gill, R.E.,[1] to find out things connected with the canal. Lesseps' head man at Port Said—a French gentleman— said to us in the plainest French: 'I refuse absolutely to give you any information.' Such was their feeling towards us.

Captain Lomen of the *Zabiaka*, a Russian cruiser lying at Port Said, told me he was a small boy at their Government school for the sons of distinguished officers, when the late Czar Nicholas I visited it. He called the boys—all under ten years old—out to the playground and said: 'Now, boys, I'm a fort, come and storm me,' he being in uniform. At first they feared to, but encouraged by the Emperor, who laughed heartily, they climbed up him and even tore his clothes and epaulettes.

---

[1] A few weeks after this, poor Gill, a very valuable officer, perished at the hands of the Arabs with Professor Palmer and Lieutenant Charrington, R.N.

I visited the battlefields, and was never more thirsty than in some long rides over the sandy desert, but all camps and posts provided cold tea on arrival, and nothing is better to quench the thirst.

I had the job of dismantling the Rosetta mouth of the Nile forts, and destroyed an immense store of ammunition. The Rosetta Stone, which was so useful to assist translations from the ancient Egyptian characters, was found here in 1799 by M. Bouchard, a Captain of Engineers in Napoleon's army.

The mirage plays such odd tricks with the vision that I remember one day they reported to me that a large number of men, probably troops, were seen near. They proved to be only traps, for quail, about eighteen inches high, magnified. I am inclined to relate other things, but must not digress.

Late in October I took Sir Garnet Wolseley and his staff to Trieste on his way home, and found him a very agreeable companion.

In November I returned to Malta with our Admiral and his flag on board my ship. We entered the grand harbour with much excitement, Sir Beauchamp Seymour being received with great enthusiasm ; and the Egyptian campaign was now over. Two days after the Admiral told me to take command of the *Inflexible*, and I said good-bye to my beautiful *Iris*, and was sorry to leave both ship and officers.

CHAPTER XVIII

H.M.S. *INFLEXIBLE*

Effect of a Shell—Torpedoes—Strike a Rock—Lord Alcester—
Ball's Monument — Summer Cruise — Exercises — Austrian
Horses—Venice — Loretto — Navarino—Delphi—Salonica—
Thasos—Mount Athos—Odd After-glow—Candia—Cyprus
—Nelson Island—Ephesus.

THE *Inflexible* was five things, viz. the largest
ship in our Navy, being the only one then of 10,000
tons ; she was also considered our most powerful
fighting ship, and she was the only one that had
cost a million pounds ; she was also certainly
the most complicated vessel, and was the first
man-of-war illuminated by electric light.

She had been commissioned about a year before
at Portsmouth by Captain J. A. Fisher,[1] whose
talents and knowledge made him a very proper
person to start such a ship. But illness acquired
during his active service in Egypt had forced him
to invalid home.

At the bombardment of Alexandria a Palliser's
shell had hit the ship on her starboard quarter,
turned over, and then base forwards had struck

---

[1] Now Lord Fisher, Admiral of the Fleet.

the iron stern cable bitts, they having afterwards been landed at Malta. Some United States officers were being shown over the ship, and on the First-lieutenant telling this story and seeing a look of incredulity on the shrewd Yankee face he added, 'If I had not seen it myself I should not have believed it.' The American replied: 'Then, sir, you will allow me the same privilege.'

We went at once to the Ionian Islands, Patras, &c. In cold winters there are at times plenty of woodcock to be got about there, and hiring a small cutter for a day or two's cruise and shooting on the opposite coast to Corfu was a favourite form of sport.

The *Inflexible* was the only regular sea-going man-of-war with submerged torpedo-tubes that were not fixed, but trained, through an angle of 37 degrees—viz. 27 degrees before the beam and 10 degrees abaft it. This plan was a mistake; the different deflections to be allowed for training and speed of ship were very difficult of settlement and certain tabulation, and one might add as an objection the possibility of a mistake as to how the torpedo-tube was trained. However, all this has long been given up.

The ship had six different torpedo-discharges —viz. the two already mentioned, two ordinary above-water ones, a peculiar bow scoop, or frame, down which the torpedo when relieved ran, and a pair of sheers aft to throw one out by. These two last were more toys than of serious value; but all taken together gave us endless torpedo practice. In spite of which we lost only one torpedo finally, though many gave long hunts for them. The one lost was off Port Said, and I am not sure our surmise was not correct, that a crust had formed on the ancient layer of mud once deposited by the Nile when it had a mouth there—since the river changed its course—and that our torpedo dived through, and remained under that crust.

When a torpedo had sunk to the bottom, we used to send several boats to watch for its air bubbles coming up, whenever it was calm, and in this way we have found and recovered torpedoes more than two days after they had gone down.

In February my last ship, the *Iris*, grounded at Port Augusta, and we were sent to help her off, but on arrival found she had happily got off without us. The entrance marks there are not easy to make out ; much sea experience has shown me that no one can guarantee they will never have a mishap by grounding or collision ; the great thing is whenever such has occurred to any ship to find out the how and why, and so avoid perhaps anything like a repetition.

In the *Inflexible* we had a very narrow shave of loss—it was also in Port Augusta ; we were running torpedoes and steaming round the harbour at full speed, when suddenly the ship heeled slightly over, but continued her way. The chart marked deep enough water there, and no rocks near. I sent boats away at once to sound, but nothing could be found. The ship made no water, and though opinions were divided it seemed as if she could not have struck anything. However, soon after, in examining the double bottom, some bolts and nuts were found displaced, and it was evident we had touched something. The rock was eventually found. Good fortune had befriended us in that it was not a foot or two higher. The ship had scores of times passed close to it, but the fact is that in shallow water only a ' sweeping ' survey can be said to make the chart perfectly sure.

About seventy of us naval officers entertained our Commander-in-Chief, Lord Alcester, at the United Service Club of Malta on his being about to be relieved in the command.

In his speech he advised officers when in doubt always to fight. This is good general advice, for when any real ground to do so exists our country will, I believe, always back up anyone who has fought well, even if not actually successful. I say this in spite of the sad Minorca episode of 1756.

In February Lord John Hay arrived from England, and relieved Lord Alcester in command of the station.

About this time I took it into my head to get the monument to Admiral Sir Alexander Ball on the lower Barraca of Valetta restored. He was Captain of the *Alexander* at the Nile, and presented Nelson with the coffin made out of the *Orient's* mainmast. After that he commanded on shore the operations which ended in our taking Valetta, and he was the first British Governor of Malta, the only naval one, and much liked by the Maltese. The monument was erected by the public at Malta, on Ball's death, but was now much dilapidated. I got a committee formed, and after much trouble the work was satisfactorily carried out.

The only other restoration I undertook at Malta was to repaint and do up the public house in Bermola called ' Charley Moore the fair thing.' I did this on account of the story of a marine being flogged, who, when his Captain found fault with the flogger for not doing his duty, said : ' This man 's a-flogging me properly, and I think I knows best ; I believe you knows Malta, and '' Charley Moore the fair thing,'' that 's all I wants.'

We were much in Malta in the spring of 1883. In those days it was very fairly healthy, and its climate, except between June and October, is very pleasant. September is the worst month owing to the Sirocco wind, and next to that August.

Although I often wished to be less at Malta it yet had many social charms. In winter I much enjoyed riding picnics to various places ; and in summer to dine on the housetop at Mellea's at night was very pleasant, especially when you could be sure of driving home with the right person !

That summer we cruised much with the Fleet under our Commander-in-Chief, Lord John Hay. I have been amused by shore people thinking fleet summer cruises must be delightful. As a matter of fact they hardly can be so. The weather is too hot, and the intention of them is to drill and exercise as much as is practicable, and make the fleet efficient. The short stays in port must be much occupied by official visits and harbour drills; but for these and not for amusements the ships are intended, and should then thus be occupied.

But the summer cruises, and all proper squadron cruises, are of great value. Competition is the soul of energy; in England we are nearly mad about our games on shore, but from cricket, which I consider the first of them, downwards, can you imagine a game of any sort without competition? Thus is it on board ship, and thus was it especially with rigged ships. Before the invention of steam no one questioned the use of masts and sails because they were the legs, the life, of ships and a fleet.

Steam came; for many years they were kept on as faithful old friends, as stand-bys, and perhaps for economy. But they had beyond this a special value, viz. exercise aloft was a competitive one that no other can compare to now, or probably ever will. Why? Why because every man could see how his ship was getting on compared to the others. And this made him, if worth his salt, throw his heart into it.

The isolated ship, rigged ship or brig, in like way competed mast against mast.

As that first-rate seaman, Captain McNiel Boyd, who wrote the 'Naval Cadets' Manual,' and nobly perished trying to save life in a gale of wind at Kingston harbour, said, 'The romance of the sea is buried in the coal bunkers.'

I quite understood his feeling, and 'sic parvis componere magna,' it is the case as regards competitive exercises; none other as regards the individual sailor will ever come up to exercise aloft, for the reason given above.

We cannot help it, times change, and we must go with what should bring in the war indemnity. As concerns mere physical development I consider masts and sails have been much overrated, and are not to be compared in those respects to the ships' companies generally with the Sandow's, Swedish and other exercises, now well known and practised.

But I believe no modern naval officer can conceive the excitement and emulation evoked generally in all ships that pretended to be ' smart ' by general exercise aloft. Fatal accidents by falls, of course, occurred at times, but the only wonder was that they were not more frequent.

We went up the Adriatic to Trieste and visited many places ; among them Pola, the American Portsmouth. Nothing could exceed the kindness and courtesy of the Austrian ladies and officers and others. It was only in 1856 that they began Pola as a naval arsenal, but any account of it in 1883 would be out of date now.

I also visited Livitya, the great breeding establishment for the riding and carriage horses of the Emperor. This was first established in 1580, with many horses from Spain. Now Arab blood is often brought in. The horses are seldom over 15.2, but mostly powerful animals, and often with the very arched necks shown in pictures by Van Dyck and Velasquez. White seems the general colour ; I was told they are frequently born dark, but change to white as they grow up. At about three years old they are sent to Vienna to be trained. I have seen them there in the Imperial establishment, called the Spanish riding school, and their performances are very remarkable. One is to rear up with a rider on the back, and remain for many seconds immovable, then balance on the hind legs. I have seen pictures by Velasquez at Madrid showing it. Another performance is for the horse, with a rider, to spring up into the air, and when there with body horizontal to kick out with both fore and hind legs.

We went to Venice, the squadron, of course, lying at Malomocco outside, but I will not venture any account of the 'Spouse of the Adriatic,' as she is too well known.

While in the Doge's Palace I met the carpenter of my ship, a very zealous warrant officer, and said to him, ' Well, what do you think of this place ? ' He replied, ' I tell you what, sir, I wish we could get the dockyard to put gilt like that on our ship.' We visited Fiume and Mr. Whitehead's famous torpedo factory ; here we are in Hungary, and at a public dinner you must toast the King and not the Emperor. The Hungarians are as clannish as the Scotch, and as unmalleable politically as the Irish.

We also went to Ancona, the port for Loretto, and saw the Santa Casa, or holy house, that we are assured was miraculously transported here from Palestine. It is built of thin bricks and of stones.

We visited the Bay of Navarino, replete with its memories of 1827—that 'untoward event,' as it was phrased in the King's speech. It is often (if not always) easy to be wise after an event; however, as things seemed then, and now, I do not see that we were far wrong.

The Turk has some great qualities: courage, sobriety, and enthusiasm for his religion, for instance; but, say what you may for him, Mahomed II took Constantinople in 1453, but in four and a half centuries they have never added to the arts or sciences of the world, or joined the European family. A Turk is, in my experience, usually a gentleman, but seems best suited to the days of the Arabian nights.

I went to Delphi; it was long ago quite altered by an earthquake, but the memory and interest of such a place cannot fade. One can picture the Priestess of Apollo seated on her tripod, and her eager and credulous listeners. 'Tempora mutantur,' but fortune-tellers, though less classical and romantic, still exist.

Boat regattas, both sailing and rowing, were much looked forward to and enjoyed by the squadron; the principal one was in the autumn, but at that season the wind was often too light for sailing and better for oars. Cheering boats by the ships' companies was forbidden, but at times they seemed irrepressible, and earned some signals and remarks, of a mixed character!

In 1883 we had our pulling regatta in the Gulf of Volo, and as a final summary were much pleased to come out first as bracketed with the *Temeraire*.

We visited Salonika, scripturally interesting as having been the Thessalonica to whose people St. Paul's Epistles were written. When we were there half the population was said to be Jewish, descended from Spanish Jews who fled from Spain and came here early in the sixteenth century, and even now they talk Spanish much among themselves.

Near here brigands still abounded, so much so that the authorities were afraid of our officers going out a few miles to shoot. We went to Thasos Island, and there had our squadron sailing regatta. Thasos is in the north of the Ægean Sea, and is a most attractive island. It was the dowry of the Khedive's wife at that time. It is beautiful and fertile, partly formed of fine white marble, and once had both gold and silver mines. Ruins of fortifications and other buildings proved the importance and great prosperity it once possessed.

I visited Mount Athos and went over the monastery of Batopedion, the second in size of the twenty large ones at Athos. Besides these there are many smaller places of retirement there, as well as actual hermitages, the whole number of monks lay and clerical being put at about three thousand. Batopedion was founded in the fourth century by Constantine the Great. From the sea it looks like a fortified town, and is only two or three hundred yards from the beach. It was necessary to be protected against the raids of pirates. The monks speak Greek among themselves, but a few knew English, and some other European languages. The library has many books, mostly in Greek. The monks were dignified and courteous.

Next winter was mostly spent at Malta. The sunsets in December were quite unusual, due, it was supposed, to the tremendous volcanic eruption at Krakatoa, in the straits of Sunda between Java and Sumatra in the previous August. The astronomer's opinion was that the immense quantity of dust then thrown up into the air took months to settle down again, and meanwhile that it reflected the sun's rays in a remarkable manner.

Whether or not this was the case I cannot say, but I well remember the bright afterglows often visible, and specially that one evening on 5th July when a party of us were riding back to Valetta from the west end of Malta, our horses' heads turned to the eastward, with the full moon risen in our faces, our shadows were plainly thrown towards the moon, though the sun had set more than half an hour—the idea being that the reflection from the above dust particles caused this.

In the 'Capua of Malta,' in winter, much entertainment and gaiety goes on, but of that I will only chronicle that we gave a ball in the *Inflexible* lying in the grand harbour ; we think it would have been a success, but hardly was everyone on board and dancing well begun than at about 10.30 it came on to blow and rain in torrents, and went on nearly all night. Ships' awnings cannot stand that, and the moral seems to be 'Do not give balls in a ship.'

We were often at Corfu, and never sorry to be there. A Greek friend there gave me a peacock and peahen, which used to roost aloft at night, the only case I ever knew of such pets in a man-of-war. I had a clever black poodle dog, called Toby, and the Vice-Consul's wife, who was fond of animals, was very kind to him, so he was often at their house. One morning we arrived very early, and the above lady's maid, who was French, coming in to call her mistress exclaimed, ' Oh Madame, Madame, le bâtiment de Toby est arrivé.' Different people view things differently ; that was her view of what we thought the most powerful ship in our Navy.

In 1884 we again visited many places already mentioned. We lay a short time in Suda Bay in Candia ; it is the crater of an extinct volcano. The Minotaur's labyrinth in Candia (or Crete) is, or was, laid down in the Admiralty charts. Who the hydrographer at that time was, or what the Minotaur thought of it, history does not relate.

In August we were in Egypt, and sent our two 48-foot steam pinnaces up the Nile to assist in the intended operations there, with two of my lieutenants in command; boats and crews were alike most useful.

We again visited Cyprus, and stayed in tents on top of Oros Troados, which is 6500 feet high, and the nights very cool in the middle of summer. The natives still, I was told, have a form of worship of the Virgin, which seems certainly to be a continuance or relic of the cult of Astarte (Venus), who is by classical legend supposed to have landed at Paphos, the west end of the island, after her birth from the foam of the sea.

Some ceremonies relating to divine maternity here are more curious than describable.

From Nicosia we visited the mountains along the north coast of Cyprus. Hilarion Castle was most interesting ; it was very large, and solidly built, covering much ground ; on the slope, but with precipitous sides to its site, and it must have been almost impregnable. Its history is little known, but it seems certain that it surrendered to our King Richard I after a siege.

The ancient Cathedral in Nicosia has long been used by the Turks as a mosque, and it is curious to see how the arrangements inside it have so far as possible been turned from facing east, to south-east in order to point towards Mecca.

Our kind hosts at Nicosia were the High Commissioner, Sir Robert Biddulph, and his wife, who did all that was possible to show us the many interesting things about the island.

In October I was again in Egypt, and on one occasion anchored in Aboukir Bay, on the site of the Battle of the Nile. While there one morning early I landed with one of my lieutenants on Nelson Island to shoot quail, which were expected in their autumn flight southwards. However, they had not arrived, so we set to work to explore the island, and found an underground passage, evidently very ancient. There were inscriptions cut on the sides of the passage, which were a sort of hard white cement.

The passage is horizontal, running in from the cliff about sixty feet long, terminating in what was, I suppose, a sepulchre. It was probably an Egyptian one, and closed up for centuries, till the cliff falling away disclosed the passage. One inscription was in Greek dated 1559, some were in Latin. The more modern ones were 1798, first some names of French ships and sailors, evidently Admiral Bruey's men employed making a battery on the island to protect his fleet; and then others of Nelson's ships and men, no doubt landed there to carry off the French guns after the battle.

Attempts have been made to recover treasure taken from Malta by the French from the wreck of the *Orient*, but I believe there is little doubt it had been removed from her before the action, in which she was blown up.

We visited Smyrna, which might be made a good naval port, as forts could protect it from the fire of ships outside. I went to Ephesus, where the ruins of the Temple of Diana justify Byron's lines, ' Its ruins strew the wilderness and dwell the hyena and the jackal in its shade'; but I cannot grant that the noble bard ' beheld the Ephesian miracle,' which had then long since ceased to stand, and its very site when discovered in 1870 was more than fifteen feet under ground.

Smyrna is a great place to buy Turkish and Persian carpets, the stores of them are immense; but you hardly ever see a new one—at least they are rare. I am told the Americans are great purchasers of the very old ones.

I should like to enlarge much more on my Mediterranean experiences, but must not do so, in consideration for my kind readers. We returned to Malta the end of 1884, and early in 1885 were ordered home.

The *Inflexible* had an unusual fitting called a 'rolling chamber.' This was a strong water-tight compartment running across the ship from side to side. It was to be about a third to a half filled with water, the theory being that as the ship rolled, the water trying to keep its level, of course, moved also, but was not quick enough to keep pace with the motion of the ship, and thus resisted the return roll and so reduced it. The operation made a great noise, and was somewhat of a strain on the ship, but it did check the rolling a little.

Since armoured vessels were first invented, say in 1860, by the building of the French ship *La Gloire*, their variations have been endless. The *Inflexible* was our first echelon turret-ship, the idea, of course, being to fire all the heavy guns, either ahead or astern; in her case this proved a complete failure.

It was never tried in her till we were coming home, when I got leave from the Admiralty to do so. The results were surprising, and alarming. I will not enter into details, but merely say that only one gun of the after—starboard—turret, fired with a reduced charge 75° before the beam, rendered the port turret and armoured conning place untenable, and shook the foremast funnel so that had I continued the experiments, as permitted at my discretion, it would probably have come down.

It is curious that a ship should have been designed to do what she so evidently could not.

All modern ships soon fall out of date ; the old *Victory* was forty-one years old at Trafalgar and then considered the finest ship in the Fleet ; the *Inflexible* when she left Portsmouth for the Mediterranean had cost about a million pounds, and twenty-five years afterwards she was sold for £25,000.

I left the Mediterranean with real regret, very sorry to leave the station, and to part from my Admiral, Lord John Hay, and many friends all round the ' Midland Ocean ' ; also to pay off my grand ship, and leave an excellent set of officers and a good ship's company.

We were paid off at Portsmouth, I having myself been nearly five years on actual sea service, and four and a half years from England.

I think the present rule of the Admiralty to limit commissions to only two years is a great mistake ; there is a happy medium in all things, and that is about three years for a ship's commission. It takes some months for officers and men to shake down and really know the ship and each other.

On the other hand I allow that four or five years are too long, and for more than one reason : first that people get tired of each other, as I myself have seen ; and, second, that it is hard on married men, either officers or ship's company, to keep them so long from their wives and families. I am for the three years' commission.

By me foreign service has always been much preferred to that at home ; abroad your ship *is* your home, and everyone feels that. In England, too many are only wondering when they can get away on leave.

When I entered the service I believe only a quarter, certainly not more than one-third, of the service afloat in the sea-going ships were on the home station—the rest were on foreign service; now it is the opposite. This is for reasons which I need not state, as they are evident, and just now it must be so.

CHAPTER XIX

CAPTAIN—H.M.S. *OREGON*—CAPTAIN

Trial of the *Oregon*—Manœuvres—Admiralty Committee.

I WENT to live in London, which then for many years became my home, when not employed by service away from it, and London is, perhaps, the best residence for an officer anxious for success in his career, as he is in the centre of intelligence, and can if he likes benefit in many ways thereby.

In April I went to stay for a time in Paris, but came home suddenly, because war between us and Russia seemed to be imminent and I knew I should get a ship. On leaving Paris I took leave of my friend Admiral Conrad at the French Admiralty, who talked disinterestedly of the prospect, the French and Russian Alliance not then existing.

The war 'scare' soon passed off; but while it lasted the Admiralty had decided to commission as a man-of-war the *Oregon*, a Cunard Atlantic liner, and at that time the largest one. My cousin, Admiral Sir Michael Culme Seymour, was to have hoisted his flag in her, to command a special fast squadron in case of the war.

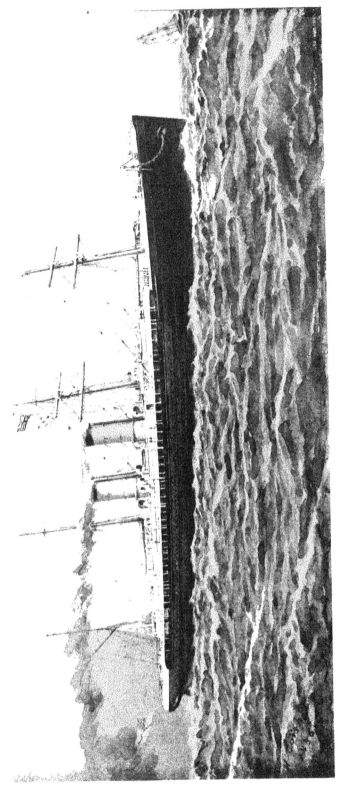

H.M.S. OREGON

The first Atlantic liner commissioned as a Man-of-War
1885

My cousin had had the *Oregon's* mizzen-mast-head fitted with a semaphore, the first thing of the kind aloft on a mast, and very useful it proved. To fit her as a cruiser over a hundred cabins had been destroyed to provide coal armour for the engines. The decks had been strengthened as required to mount the guns, and magazines, and shell rooms were fitted below and lighted by electricity. An attempt was made to protect her steering gear, and other details were attended to. But you cannot make a good fighting ship of a fast modern passenger mail steamer; it is not possible.

Now as the *Oregon* had been got ready they wished her tried, and selected me to do it.

I arranged about officers and men, and went to Liverpool and commissioned her. She looked to me a monster, and she was so then, being nearly considered what the *Olympic* is thought now. Everything in this world is comparative, and no one can guess what ships will be like half a century hence, of course supposing that flying machines, &c., have not superseded them.

I kept the first and second officers and all of the engineers, having a naval one as my staff officer. The rest of the officers and men were all naval except the stokers. These I entered at Liverpool, and a queer lot they were. I put them to live in the third-class passenger saloon, which from their usual quarters was much like removing a dog from its kennel to the drawing-room. They were also clothed with two suits of sailor's clothes, and really at times they *were* clean, for the first time probably. They had not been twenty-four hours in the ship when I was told they all insisted on leaving her. But on being made to fall in on deck and confronted with Marines with fixed bayonets and ball cartridge, order was restored.

I read the Articles of War—with much unction—and with subsequent good result. One of their own engineers was told off to look after them; he had to see their hammocks up in the morning. One day a stoker would not turn out, and the engineer lowered his hammock down. Fearful language ensued, but no report would have been made had not the stoker remembered that profane oaths, &c., were contrary to the articles of war, and said he would report the engineer for using them; the engineer then remembered that 'to strike or offer to strike' your superior officer was a dire offence, the stoker having shaken his fist in his face; so both repaired to the quarter-deck, and I fear both my Commander and myself were amused at the proceedings, though I hope we did not show it.

The *Oregon* was 520 feet long between perpendiculars, with a single screw and a very small rudder. Her displacement was about 12,500 tons; the largest in the Navy then being the *Inflexible* (about 10,000). I measured her circles very carefully at sea in calm weather: her 'tactical diameter' was 2000 yards, i.e. about a sea mile.

Perhaps I should explain to lay readers that this means, that if she was steering north, and you put her helm hard over—either way—the distance from the ship's beam at the moment of putting the helm over, to her beam when her head became south, i.e. when she had turned a half circle, would if measured east and west be 2000 yards. Ordinary men-of-war's tactical diameters are usually about one-third of that, some much less ; though there have been great exceptions, and I have been told on good authority that the tactical diameters of the *Warrior* and *Black Prince*, two of our earliest ironclad ships, were about 1400 yards.

Of course this turning question is now all quite modified and improved by having twin screws to use for it, if necessary. This extreme unhandiness matters comparatively little to an Atlantic liner, because she only runs on a rail, as it were, from Liverpool to New York and back ; and if required to make any sharp turns in or out of harbour, can get a tug to help her. Whereas a man-of-war never knows what may be required, and with no help.

I used when weighing in narrow waters, with the *Oregon's* head the wrong way, to snub her bow round with the cable before lifting the anchor, but it is ticklish work not to snap the cable.

We went first to Portland, and from there to Plymouth, and Gibraltar, and to join the flag of Admiral Sir Geoffrey Hornby at Berehaven. This was a large squadron assembled for the first regular summer manœuvres.

Admiral Hornby was at the time Commander-in-Chief at Portsmouth, so this employment of him was very exceptional.

At Berehaven the squadron made two booms of a vast number of spars lashed together, one across the eastern entrance to the anchorage, and one across the western one. Steel wire hawsers were also employed.

Boat attacks were made and failed, but I only wish to mention that afterwards the *Polyphemus*, a special vessel made chiefly to act as a ram, charged the eastern boom at her full speed, say seventeen knots. It was an interesting trial. I was watching carefully and considered that the boom bent a good deal and brought the ship's way up to about only a third of it, and then the steel wire hawsers, two parts of 5½-inch wire, parted, the boom broke in two, and the ship got by unhurt.

From Berehaven we went to Blacksod Bay on the west coast of Ireland, and in Co. Mayo ; a real out-of-the-way place, fit only for a manœuvring squadron. Here the Fleet was divided into two sides. One, the enemy, were to try and get into the Clyde, and the other, the defence being more powerful, to stop them if they caught them. We were the defence, and when our squadron went on were left outside Blacksod Bay, to report when the enemy, our attackers, left it.

There ensued a very dark night, and raining hard, during which the enemy, with no lights burning, chanced it, and got to sea without our seeing them. When daylight dawned we found it out, and our speed being much greater than any other ship present, enabled us to overtake and inform our Admiral.

Finally the attack failed, their ships being seen in the narrow north channel, between the Mull of Cantyre and Fair Head, the north-east point of Ireland.

Since then we have had—as is known—many manœuvres, summer and otherwise. No doubt they are useful, give much experience to those commanding them, and are a cause of thinking out defence and attack problems, that without them would not be well considered. Soon after the above cruise it was felt the *Oregon* had been sufficiently tested as a cruiser, and I paid her off at Liverpool, and handed her back to the Cunard Company.

As regards the question of employing such vessels as man-of-war cruisers in war time, my opinion is as follows:

ADVANTAGES:

1. Owing to their great speed they could escape from most men-of-war, and have the best chance of catching the enemy's mail steamers or merchant ships.

2. They would be at once available as somewhat armed troopships.

DISADVANTAGES:

1. You cannot make them decent fighting ships, for two great reasons, viz. that both their steering gear and engines are too unprotected.

2. They are not handy enough for men-of-war's needs. Turbine engines are much lower down and so minimise one of the above faults, but a mail steamer as a good fighting ship is an impossibility.

I was now on half-pay for nine months. For a time I was Chairman of an Admiralty Committee to revise naval officers' titles, and readjust the shares of prize money.

A discussion of the above would be tedious to the general reader; though on the former I could make many remarks. As regards the latter, the great days of prize money are probably gone for ever; when for instance Captain Digby made £60,000 one morning.[1] The proportions of prize money must, I suppose, always remain as of old, when before the battle the seaman knelt down, and prayed that the shot also might be allotted in proportion to the prize money.

I otherwise filled up my time partly by trips to France, sometimes staying in Touraine, a part of the country I am very fond of, and advise others to visit, as I have before said.

---

[1] This remarkable story of his being three times told when asleep in his cot to alter his course, and doing so with the result of meeting the Spanish treasure galleons at daylight, was told me by one of his family as a fact quite accepted by them as true.

CHAPTER XX

FLAG-CAPTAIN—NAVAL RESERVES

The old *Victory*—The Queen's Jubilee—Naval Manœuvres—
Submarine Boat—Earl St. Vincent—Portsmouth—Naval
Reserves — Coastguard — Heligoland — The *Hearty* and
her Cat — Coal Pit — The Forth Bridge — Stornoway —
Shetland.

In May 1886 I returned to England to become
Flag-captain to Admiral Sir George Willes at
Portsmouth. He was my captain when I was a
lieutenant in China in two ships, and was a strict
and very capable officer, and well up in all service
matters.

The Admiral's flag flew in the *Duke of Wellington* and the old *Victory* played only the humble
rôle of tender to us. She was of course under my
care, and a more rotten ship than she had become
probably never flew the pennant. I could literally
run my walking stick through her sides in many
places, and her upper works were mostly covered
by a waterproof coat of painted canvas.

One night they called me with the news that
the *Victory* was sinking. We, of course, hurried
on board her, and got all available pumps to work ;

249

with the result that we kept her afloat, till she could be put into a dry dock, where she was practically a good deal rebuilt, and will now I think go on as required for many years.

I must here remark à propos of the old *Victory*, that the recent idea of restoring her to look as much as possible as she was at the Battle of Trafalgar should be carried out. The late Commander-in-Chief at Portsmouth, Sir Arthur Fanshawe, took much interest in this, and did what he could towards it. The expense of doing what would make a great show would, I believe, be only a few thousand pounds.

Mr. Maxim, now Sir Hiram, brought his automatic machine gun to Whale Island to be tested; he let me work it at one time and said to me: ' You see, sir, you can set this gun going, then go into a house and have a gin sling, and come out and find a hundred men lying dead in the avenue.'

The duties of flag-captain at Portsmouth were very varied, but not onerous. Putting out fires even on shore came into them, and very useful our men were on one or two occasions. A real seaman is useful everywhere, and has well earned his name of the ' Handy man.'

I went to inspect the Naval Prison at Lewes, and found out that the young active seaman, with a good appetite, prefers hard labour, with more food, to its alternative. At that time the service was a good deal ' sheep ' and ' goats '; the former to become seamen, gunners, &c., went to the *Excellent*, while the ' goats ' came to me; and acted according to their title. Leave-breaking was the most common offence, and for this stoppage of pay was the most effective restraining measure.

In 1887 was the Queen's Jubilee. As an official I had a place in Westminster Abbey, and think I never felt a more affecting sensation than when her Majesty walked down the aisle, while 'God save the Queen' was sung. It was difficult for anyone to keep from tears.

Of course people differ immeasurably in their love—as in their knowledge—of music, but I believe it has an effect on the nerves of the brain in everyone. I have seen a dog sit up and howl when a musical instrument was played close to him; this, however, is perhaps departing from the sublime, and not a compliment to the player.

The Queen's Jubilee of 1887 I think stirred the nation more than that of 1897, because it was much more of a novelty to everyone; few remembering 1810! Our Queen, too, was able herself to play a more prominent part.

I commissioned my old ship the *Inflexible* for the Jubilee review and subsequent naval manœuvres; we first went to Portland to shake down into order, and then to Spithead for the review. At Portland I went over the convict prison there; it boasts having hardly ever had an escape from it, but a French prisoner once got clear away, it is thought by boat.

The Chief Warder amused us by lamenting the decline of the apparent popularity of the profession of convict. He said also that the long-sentence ones look down on the short-sentence prisoners as an inferior order of beings.

At Spithead on 19th July the Queen passed through the Fleet on her way to Osborne, being received with full honours; and I believe with the officers in full dress (on her Majesty passing in her yacht), for the first time since the death of the Prince Consort.

The Crown Prince and Princess—afterwards the Emperor Frederick and his Empress—with their three daughters, came on board my ship quite suddenly one day to see her. Nothing could exceed their natural charm and pleasant graciousness, especially that of the Crown Princess, who went round all the principal parts of the ship with me.

We now became flagship of Sir George Willes for the review, which took place on 23rd July. The Queen passed through the lines in her yacht, and then anchored for all the admirals and captains to come on board and be presented to her; and in the evening the whole Fleet was illuminated, and had fireworks. This is a matter much better done now, owing to our improved electric lighting system.

After this all the ships went to sea for a cruise; that was followed by manœuvres, the idea being that the defending fleet was to prevent the other from entering the Channel and passing up to the mouth of the Thames, which they did, and so won.

The *Inflexible* was soon after this paid off again, and I rejoined the *Duke of Wellington*.

In 1887 I went to Southampton to see Mr. Nordenfelt's submarine torpedo-boat, quite a novelty to me then. She was of steel, in shape a cylinder, quite round amidships and elongated at the ends. She was 125 feet long and her greatest diameter 12 feet; she was of 190 tons displacement. To sink her, forty tons of water were let in, added to which two down-driving horizontal screws when at work kept her under water. She was propelled by a single screw, and could go under water twenty miles at five knots, having a reserve of steam from a special boiler: this we were TOLD. She had two torpedo-tubes in the bow, one over the other. She must be kindly regarded as the forerunner or parent of the present submarine.

The Sailors' Home in Portsea was much enlarged while I was there. I was ex-officio Chairman of the Committee, and gave a cabin to it to be called the St. Vincent cabin, as I have great admiration for that iron-willed disciplinarian, who kept down the seamen's mutiny in his own fleet in 1797 off Cadiz. The story is shortly as follows:

H.M.S. *Marlborough* had just joined the fleet from home, a mutiny had broken out on board her, and a court martial had condemned a seaman to be hanged for it. Her Captain then told Lord St. Vincent that his ship's company would not permit the man to be hanged on board that ship, or at least that his own crew would not do it. The Admiral replied that the man should be hanged at eight o'clock the next morning, and only by his own shipmates.

General orders were then given for the *Marlborough* to be anchored in the middle of the fleet, her guns to be run in and her gun ports closed and secured. Armed boats from all the other ships were placed in position to rake her with their fire, and to sink her if required, which the other ships should assist in doing. At 7.30 A.M. next day all hands in the fleet were turned up to witness the execution.

The excitement was great, but at eight o'clock when a gun was fired from the *Ville de Paris*, Lord St. Vincent's flagship, the man was triced up to the yardarm of the *Marlborough* by his own shipmates and hanged, and ' The Earl ' (as Nelson usually called him) then said, ' Discipline is preserved.' It is in my opinion among the finest episodes in our Navy. And is not this real praise of Earl St. Vincent?—' that he was the tutor of Nelson, he taught and formed him—he made him greater than himself, and then did not envy him.' [1]

The great form of Nelson, whose meteor-like career closed with a bright additional blaze at Trafalgar, has eclipsed the fame of all other naval officers. But for solid service rendered to his country, both at sea and on shore, in days of difficulty, and periods of peril, the name of St. Vincent must to those who study naval history always stand forth prominently.

But I must not linger longer at Portsmouth, which place perhaps many look on only as the best known, or most visited by tourists, of our naval ports. Its history, however, is of much interest, without going back to the Roman times, about which details are doubtful. I believe the

[1] See Tucker's *Life of the Earl St. Vincent*, vol. ii. p. 252.

fortifications were begun in the reign of Edward III. The oldest dock is the one near the Admiral-Superintendent's office.

I was next appointed Captain, assistant to the Admiral-Superintendent of Naval Reserves. I was sorry to leave my Admiral at Portsmouth, and loath to leave all that was sea-life about it ; but I felt that short of going to sea, which is always the best thing, a new experience was desirable. I have often felt that you rarely know really what you have learnt in a given phase of your life, because you forget how much less you knew when you began it.

In December 1887 I took up my new appointment, the Naval Reserve offices being in Spring Gardens, but the house is now destroyed. They were very old fashioned and barely sanitary.

The inspections of the Coastguard stations from the head office in London are made mostly by the Admiral-Superintendent himself; it happened, however, while I was there as captain that, owing to an accident to the Admiral, I had to make a good many inspections, and among them to visit and inspect Heligoland, which then belonged to us.

Since our acquisition of it, from Denmark in 1807, we had not taken much trouble either to fortify it or make a harbour. It is very small, only three-quarters of a square mile in area, and is mostly a small high plateau off which the frequent strong winds threaten to blow the unwary pedestrian. Fishing was its chief industry, and about 30,000 lobsters have been got in the summer months ; and probably eaten also, by the 15,000 German visitors who came to bathe there.

No doubt it is very healthy—the wind I suppose blows the ubiquitous microbe away ; the average human life was said to be 63 years, but whether it was worth while to live in such a monotonous place in order to eke out one's life is a question. The Governor said it was a sort of Teuton Gretna Green ; ardent couples running over from the Continent to be married at the Lutheran Church here.

Germany is, of course, making it a war station, which we should never have done. H.M.S. *Hearty* conveyed me there and back. She was built for a river Hoogly tugboat. The officers' accommodation was right forward, in the bows, and the men were aft.

Coming back we had a gale of wind in our teeth, the ship pitched heavily, and every officer but the captain was down with sea sickness, I for one. In the *Hearty* they had a cat, about which the following story was told, and vouched for by both officers and men.

The ship was lying in the harbour and the tide was out ; it was a Sunday about 11 A.M., when a cat was seen to walk down to the shore abreast of the ship, unpursued by persons or dogs, wade through the mud, take to the water, and swim off to the *Hearty*, where it, of course, received a welcome worthy of the ship's name, and joined the crew.

Travelling along the north-east coast of England and east of Scotland in a snowy winter, I was kept at Sunderland by the snow and went down the Monkswearmouth coal pit. It is 1800 feet deep and runs out under the sea; at its extremity there is a large pool of water which is three times as salt as the sea, from evaporation of course. The thermometer was about 90° in the mine, and the contrast to it on the surface, covered with frozen snow, from which you descended in one and a half minutes, was great. I came to the conclusion that if I had to be a labouring man at Sunderland, I would be miner in winter and fisherman in summer.

The wonderful Forth Railway cantilever bridge was being built when I was there; they showed me over it, and let me walk over the highest parts of the piers, 370 feet above the water. They said six million rivets were driven in the bridge. The rails have to be ' tongued ' to allow of the expansion and contraction, for changes of temperature, and where the spans join fifteen inches as an extreme has to be allowed for. I asked how many fatal accidents had occurred to the workmen : but that was a secret.

The then recent terrible accident to a train on the Tay Bridge made one apprehensive about the effect of a very strong wind on so exposed a structure, but of this they had no fear. Experiments made had shown that the presence of wind is happily not uniform over a large area, but that the wind currents are restricted to small surface spaces, and differ a good deal, as pressing on a large perpendicular erection. Thus a wind gauge might show a pressure of wind at one spot much in excess of what another a very few feet off showed at the same moment. As an instance of this, a large gauge of 300 square feet area showed a maximum average pressure of only 27 lbs. on the square foot ; while a small gauge, near to, showed at the same moment a pressure of 41 lbs.

On the shore on the north side of the bridge, it was curious to see how the sloping field, on which an embankment had to be made, had given way and been turned from a smooth slope to a sort of ridge and furrow, as the weight of earth was put on to it.

My duty was, of course, to inspect the Coastguard, and the Royal Naval Reserve Batteries. I went on North, now and then in a sleigh, and crossed Scotland, then under snow from Inverness to Strome Ferry ; most people only know it in the autumn, but in its winter coat it looks most like ' Caledonia stern and wild,' &c. Then on by a small steamer to Stornoway, where the Matheson family have spent so much money on the ungrateful ' Crofters.' The Hebrides certainly produce for their size a numerous population of fine-looking people, but I have great doubts about the Naval Reserve men there being of much practical value to us.

A crofter's hut is a wretched hovel, with an ill-thatched roof ; inside one half is occupied by cattle and fowls, the floor is the natural earth, one door for both bipeds and quadrupeds, a turf fire in the middle, no chimney, a chain from the roof to hang the cooking-pot on, bed places in bunks at the sides. Then many of the older people only spoke Gaelic, but this was likely to change.

I visited the Orkneys and Shetland Islands to inspect. They are, of course, dreary in winter, as this was, but except that the length of the days, of course, varies more than in lower latitudes, there is really not so much change from summer to winter as regards the temperature as with us, because the sea and the gulf stream affect that so much.

Shetland shawls, &c., are, of course, well known and liked. The sheep they are made from have very fine fleeces, and their wool (or hair you may almost call it) is plucked from them and not shorn. They are smaller than Southdown sheep, and of various colours ; I have seen black, white and grey ones.

In July 1889 I was promoted to the rank of Rear-Admiral and therefore placed on half-pay. I was forty-nine years old and had been a captain for about sixteen and a half years. Now officers are less than ten years captain.

CHAPTER XXI

REAR-ADMIRAL

France — Russia — Caspian Sea — Caucasus — Taganrog—Sevas-topol—Odessa.

IT was quite uncertain when—if ever—I should be employed and hoist my flag, so I had to consider how best to occupy myself. First I went to France, and moving about in Brittany visited Brest and L'Orient.

Brest is certainly a first-class naval port, by nature. It is so thoroughly sheltered from the sea and from the enemy by its long 'Goulet.' I got into one of their signal stations, then very superior to ours.

While staying at Trez Hir, with some relations, we visited the Isle of Ushant. Of the two lighthouses one was electric, and one not; we were told that the latter—not electric--best penetrated a fog.

I went to see my old Port Said friend Admiral Conrad, who was Port Admiral at L'Orient, and he told me of the following sad and curious occurrence.

A picnic party of both sexes went to have

déjeuner on the sea-shore near there, at a place where the nearly flat sand had some large rocks scattered about on it. The tide was low, the day fine.

Preparing their food they found themselves short of something—say, water—and one of the party went off to the nearest house to get it. On his return he could not find his friends. At first he thought they had as a joke hidden behind the rocks ; but at last the terrible truth appeared, viz. that an abnormal wave—one of those most wrongly called ' tidal '—had broken on the beach, and had overwhelmed and drowned them all.

One often now hears such waves reported as being met with at sea—' seismic ' would be a good name for them ; they are, I suppose, caused either by submarine volcanoes or earthquakes.

I had long wished to visit Russia, and in August left with a cousin to do so. We crossed to Flushing and went on by rail to Petersburg. I think the three impressions one must form of Russia are: its space, its solitude, and its sadness.

Petersburg is too well known for me to describe it. I dined with our Ambassador, Sir Robert Morier, and for the first time saw the Russian custom of ' Zakousca,' i.e. that on entering the dining-room you take your partner first to the sideboard, where caviare, dried fish, strong drinks, vodka, &c., await you as a preparation for dinner.

We visited Cronstadt and I refreshed my memory about the Baltic War in 1854-5. I believe that in 1854 the allied fleets could have attacked Cronstadt on its in-shore side with good chance of success.

I was told that in 1854 the Emperor, watching one of our steamers reconnoitring on that side, said: 'She will soon run aground on the barrier I have had put to prevent attack on that side.' She did not because it had not been put, though paid for. Next winter it was put, and the conditions were altered.

We stayed at the Hôtel de France, and there got a Russian who spoke French as our courier, in place of an impostor from London. Beyond Petersburg a knowledge of Russian or an interpreter was necessary to travellers.

I was much interested at seeing, and having described to me on the spot, the murder of the Czar Alexander II in 1881. He was driving along the quay of a canal in Petersburg in a brougham with one A.D.C., when a man threw a bomb at the carriage; the bomb burst between the hind wheels and the shock unseated the Emperor and his A.D.C., but did not hurt them or disable the carriage.

The coachman pulled up and the occupants got out. The would-be assassin was seized. The coachman said, 'If your Majesty will get in I can drive you to the Palace,' but the Czar decided to walk. He had not gone many yards when a man leaning against the low parapet darted forward and flung a bomb at the Emperor's feet, which burst and mortally wounded him, the assassin being also killed by it. And this was the end of Alexander the liberator of the serfs.

I think the equestrian statue of Peter the Great, his horse treading on a snake, as spirited as any I know.

We went to Moscow, by the line made nearly straight in obedience to H.M. Nicholas's route as drawn out with a ruler on the map. Petersburg is half Russian, half French, but Moscow is Moscov. One should regard it from the Sparrow Hills, on its south-west side, and think of Napoleon doing so in 1812, and his army shouting for joy, not guessing what would follow.

The Kremlin is, of course, the chief attraction, and it is there you are impressed with the Asiatic characteristics of Russia. Here among other trophies are some of our field-pieces taken from the Turks in the Crimea in 1854. There are some 700 guns of various other nations.

The great foundling hospital in Moscow is interesting. It was instituted by Catherine II in 1763 to check infanticide. All babies are received; it had about 1100 children when I was there. In the wards some very delicate infants were in hot boxes, reminding one of incubators for hens' eggs. During Napoleon's occupation in 1812 it still went on, and some of his orders are shown you. Moscow is very noisy, both on account of its many bells and the stony streets.

The Russians are a very religious nation; for one thing it is striking to see the droskhy drivers taking off their hats or crossing themselves on passing certain sacred spots or pictures. The Russian riding school at Moscow impressed me;

it is said to have been, when built, the largest area building, unsupported inside. It is 560 feet long by 158 feet wide. In every shop is an icon, in respect to which you should take off your hat on entering.

We went on to Nijni Novgorod, where the great annual fair everyone has heard of was in progress. Here you see men and costumes from many parts of Asia, and the most extraordinary contrasts of goods for sale, Persian carpets in the same stall side by side with English toys, such as Ally Sloper, and men on bicycles. The contrast struck me as sad somehow, rather than ludicrous. At our hotel here none of the officials or servants spoke anything but Russian, and this we found the case at many other places.

We left Nijni in the *Grand Duke Vladimir*, a steamer of the Caucasus and Mercury Steamship Company, to descend the Volga to Astrakhan. She was a paddle-wheel vessel 280 feet long, speed nearly 12 knots; burnt oil, i.e. the refuse of naphtha after petroleum had been extracted from it. It was my first experience of such fuel, but now we are used to it. This came, of course, from Baku.

The stokehold surprised me—clean and quiet; and to take in fuel a trough was placed sloping down to the ship's tanks, and a liquid like chocolate ran down till the tanks were full—no labour, no noise, no dirt. Luxurious! There were few passengers, but much card-playing. The captain was a retired naval officer.

The Volga has many shoals; soundings were

got by a man with a long pole in the bows; the Russian fathom is the same as ours.

One of our fellow-passengers was an artillery officer who had served in Sevastopol during the siege ; he was then a gunner only, and was promoted from the ranks. He told me General Todleben often visited his ' Bastion,' and had a habit of asking the opinion of the men about matters concerning the battery, guns, embrasures, &c., to see if they could give him valuable hints.

The scenery on the Volga is not as a rule beautiful. You see much timber growing on both banks, too much for beauty.

We stopped at many places, the principal being Kazan (a town of 140,000 people), Saratov, and Tsaritzin. At these places you get an idea of what Russia is like. I have seen towns with the streets fifty yards wide and more, but left in their natural state ; one can imagine what traffic and rain make them like, and see why Russians as a rule wear long boots, coming up to their knees.

At Astrakhan we changed steamers to one called the *Constantine*. Astrakhan is a flourishing place, about fifty-three miles from the Caspian ; the town was lighted with electric light, then very rare in England. There were many camels, covered with long hair, and much handsomer than any I had ever before seen.

We went down the Caspian to Baku, of which place you can smell the oil two or three miles off. It was very hot when we got there ; the very streets might be said to be ' watered ' with oil, and the sea was covered with a good film of it—in a calm I believe you could light up the surface. I bathed in it, and when one came up after diving in, one had a cheap oil dressing on one's hair. The oil 'wells,' or rather oil fountains, look like trees of chocolate, and the froth like milk.

The ground is soaked with oil, which is said to be very good for chest complaints. Sometimes these fountains catch fire, and they must be left to burn out—a great loss of money. I was told that three years before one caught fire and burnt for three days, its flames rising to 900 feet: a splendid sight to all but its owners.

The Caspian is about 83 feet below the level of the Black Sea, and is, I believe, getting lower. Its water is brackish, but not nearly so salt as the ocean.

From Baku we went by train to Tiflis. All the locomotive engines about here burn oil. Tiflis, the capital of Georgia, is very picturesque, in an accentuated way—that is, with ravines and precipices. We arrived just in time for the opening of the Exhibition of Caucasus productions by the Grand Duke Michael, so the town was *en fête*; but at any time it would excite interest compared to most other places.

From Tiflis we drove across the Caucasus range to Vladikafkas. The scenery is very fine. One afternoon we encountered the heaviest hailstorm I ever saw; stones three-quarters of an inch across were very plentiful, and I picked up one, half an hour after it fell, that was by measurement over one and a half inches across.

At Vladikafkas we took the train to Rostov on the Don. In the middle of the night at a station the train was attacked by brigands who shot the engine-driver, and carried off a sum of money known to be in the train, but did not rob the passengers.

Rostov has a population of 70,000, but though we tried we could see very little of it, as a very bad dust storm was blowing, the worst, I think, I have experienced except in North China.

Next we visited Taganrog on the Sea of Azov, in the ' fragrant gardens ' of which Alexander I is reported to have died in 1825. The death chamber is said to be much as then ; we saw it, and an old grandfather clock, not going, which is supposed to have stopped when the Czar died.

Here in the Cathedral we saw the ensign of H.M. Gunboat *Jasper*, lost near here in the war in 1855.

Our Consul, Mr. W. G. Wagstaffe, who was a naval officer, had been many years here, and spoke Russian perfectly. He believes that the Sea of Azov has a double bottom, as suggested off Port Said.[1] I believe this sea is certainly getting shallower steadily.

The climate of Taganrog is trying, very hot in summer, and with bitter cold winds from the east in winter ; it is almost incredible how much milder the south of the Crimea is, and only 350 miles off.

We left by steamer for Kertch, and with us was a man in deep mourning with his two small sons, about whom I was told this story by our Consul.

[1] See page 227.

In the Taganrog Club, at baccara one night he lost £25,000, also his town house and his country house. He was nearly mad, and then staked his wife, a young and pretty woman, and lost again. He then by agreement had to give his latch-key to the winner, and not himself go home. The winner went there, but roused the servants, insisted on seeing the lady, told her the story and left the house. The wife became ill and shortly died.

From Kertch we went to Yalta, the Russian Riviera, a delightful place with first-class hotels. We visited the Czar's domain at Livadia, and went on to Sevastopol. It seemed to me very odd, with my former experience, to be quietly staying in this place in an hotel, which had actually been the house of Admiral Nachimoff, and in which he died after being struck with a piece of shell on the Malakoff.

We spent several days here, and visited the neighbourhood. Our Consul, Captain Harford, was most kind and useful. He had been over twenty years Consul here, and was so fond of the Russians that in 1878 he resigned his commission and joined them in their war against Turkey. After that war was over our Government reinstated him as Consul.

The Russian Government gave General Todleben a house in Sevastopol, which he presented to the town, and it is now a museum of the siege. In it you may see plans and models of the forts, bastions, and lines, of the place during the great siege, together with endless interesting relics.

I have known many Russian officers, and seldom one unwilling to talk of the defence of that place, of which they are very justly proud.

Count Tolstoy's work called 'Sevastopol' is most graphic in its descriptions of life in the town during the siege, and Russian officers then there, to whom I have talked, agree to its correctness. In these long-range gun-fire days that place shares the fault of Malta, and other sea garrisons.

As regards the climate of Sevastopol, the two winters of the Crimean War were very exceptionally cold. Captain Harford said he had never, if at all, seen one like those, he having also been there during the siege.

On 17th October, early, I swam about the harbour till tired, not cold ; and I could never do that in the sea in England in October.

When the Russian officers heard I had been in action on the first day of the actual siege, viz. our 17th October (then their 5th) they invited me to stay and take part in the regular celebrations, and I accepted.

On the morning of the day we went to a service in the crypt of the Church of St. Vladimir, which has been built as a memorial of the siege, and in the crypt is the tomb of the four Admirals— Lazaref, Cornilov, Nachimoff and Istomin ; the three last were all killed on the Malakoff during the siege.[1]

---

[1] The Malakoff is Bastion No. 2 of Tolstoy's book. The bastions were numbered in order from one on the Russian left next to the Grand Harbour.

The banquet was in the drawing-room of the Naval Club, the only dinner ever held in that room, and only officers who were in action on the first day could attend it. Our Consul had fought in the siege, but his regiment did not arrive till after the 17th, so he could not come.

It was a curious experience, I representing the enemy; we sat down fourteen in number. One said: 'At this date and hour, in 1854, I remember this room full of wounded and dying men.' I was the youngest; all were most friendly. One was about ninety, and he said: 'I was four times your then age on that day,' which was nearly true.

After dinner toasts began, and in turn our Queen and Empress of India was proposed, to which I replied; also to my health in turn. They said that after the Alma they made sure the allies would enter the north side and take the place, and sent many troops away to avoid capture. In consequence they were short-handed, and the sailors had to work very hard on, and in, the batteries; indeed that the battery work at first was nearly all done by them.

I, of course, heard many personal narratives. Admiral Manto declared he saw at Sinope a boy killed by the wind of a shot passing close to him, and that several bones were broken, though he was without external injury.

You could at that time quite trace out the lines, both of the defence and of the besiegers. The advanced French trench was only 25 yards from the Malakoff ditch; but ours was 120 yards from the Redan, which we had to storm—the nature of the ground making it very difficult to get nearer. But this is history.

I visited our cemetery on Cathcart Hill; it was then walled round and well kept, but I fear had not always been so. On the north side of the harbour is the Russian cemetery of the siege where about 100,000 men are said to be buried. That extraordinary vessel, the *Popoffka*, was laid up here; she was nearly round, with six screws to drive her, and was a failure.

We left Sevastopol with regret, for Odessa, which is a flourishing town with bad hotels. I went to the cliff below which we destroyed the *Tiger's* engines.[1]

In Russia our letters often had been opened by the censor, our newspapers always, some not let pass; others came with many parts obliterated with a stamp for that purpose. Books coming in were also examined.

At Odessa the English chaplain showed me a book of his that had been through the censor's hands; it was scored through and marked in many places, and had, he thought, been finally thrown by mistake into the delivery heap, instead of that for destruction.

One thing I remarked in Russia was that no driven horses have blinkers; are they required except to put your crest on?

We next went to Nikolaef, 32 miles up the River Bug, by steamer, passing Kinburn on our way. At Nikolaef is a dockyard where the ships of the Black Sea Fleet were all built and

[1] See page 16.

formerly floated down the shallow river on cradles; now the river is dredged deeper. Only one ship, the *Twelve Apostles*, was building. There was some absurd mistake made through her name, that several ships were being built there. There was in 1854 a three-decker of that name at Sevastopol.

From Nicolaef we went to Kief, a fine town, and held in great veneration by the Russians. Here we had to personally interview the police authorities, to obtain permission to leave Russia. Of course you cannot enter it without a passport, and the moment you arrive at an hotel it must be given up to be examined and marked at the police station, without which they would not entertain you. We returned to England *viâ* Vienna and Paris.

CHAPTER XXII

REAR-ADMIRAL (continued)

Channel Squadron—Pilgrims—United States—Mail Steamer—
Naval Manœuvres—France.

THAT winter I went for a cruise as the guest of my friend Admiral Sir Richard Tracey in H.M.S. *Anson*, he being Second in Command of the Channel Squadron. New signal books had just been issued to the Navy, and I was very anxious to see them tried.

Young officers now would be amused if they could see the ' Channel Fleet ' of that day. It consisted of four captains' ships, the *Anson* being the only one not obsolete, and one smaller vessel as despatch boat. Perhaps naturally manœuvres were not attempted, and little besides keeping the ships in order and moving from port to port was done.

Arosa Bay had just been ' discovered ' by us for the squadron as a port. From there we visited St. Iago de Compostella, and Tracey and I made a further pilgrimage to Coruña in the diligence. For over seven hours we were jammed up in the banquette, unable to move, with a fine view of the eleven wretched quadrupeds, some horses, some mules, who dragged us. On arrival I felt I would subscribe anything for a statue to the inventor of railways.

On our way we passed a real pilgrim, in ancient dress, with pointed hat, long staff with a cross, scollop shells on his coat—in fact 'he wore the sandal shoon and scollop shell,' as Byron says.

We next went to Gibraltar, where the usual winter entertainments and hunting with the Calpe Hounds amused us. At no place I know do the two services fraternise more than here.

I visited Ceuta, to form my opinion of its value. In 1879 I believe the Spaniards offered it to us in exchange for Gibraltar. Neither place has a decent natural harbour, so in that respect there is not much choice. But Ceuta is more commanded by the hills rising from it. Probably, had we made the exchange, we should at that date have acquired the land near it as a small colony, but the advantages of that are very doubtful.

I left my kind host in the *Anson* and went to a few places on the African coast and to the South of France for a time. Toulon always impresses me as a fine naval port, so long as the heights near it are safe from an invading army.

In the spring I went to the United States, my first visit there. I crossed both ways in the Cunard ship *Etruria*, then one of the fastest of the day. She was 12,000 tons, 505 feet long, and was built in 1885. Her best runs were 465 miles in the day; the passage from Queenstown to Sandy

Hook was made in six days and eighteen hours, and was considered a very good one then.

I visited various places in the States, receiving as one always does the greatest kindness and hospitality. An introduction or two to start with leads probably to more invitations than you are able to accept.

At Washington I much admired the splendid Capitol, their Houses of Parliament. The site it is on and the building itself taken together are nearly unrivalled.

A friend, a Mrs. C——, told me the following story about an occurrence at Baltimore; she knew the lady intimately to whom it occurred. This lady, who had a home both in that town and a few miles outside it, had occasion to spend a night in her town house, then half shut up. Her brother who lived in the town met her and they with a man friend dined at an hotel together. They then both saw her home to her house. She went into her bedroom to prepare for bed. She had come to visit a bank and get a considerable sum of money. This her brother and the friend both knew. Many rooms in the United States have over the door what is called a ' transom,' viz. a pane of glass on a swivel frame that can open. Sitting at her toilet-table with her back to the door she saw in the mirror a face at the transom.

She kept still and reflected that as she was alone in the house to ring the bell was no good, and decided that she would pretend not to notice the intruder for fear he should murder her; for though she recognised him as her brother's friend she felt he must be there for some desperate purpose. So she got into bed and pretended to sleep. Soon the man climbed in through the transom, took the money, and let himself out at the door and escaped out of the house, she seeming to sleep.

Next morning she went to her brother and told him about it. The brother, though incredulous as to the identity of the thief, took her to him, and told what she said. He at once gave in, and confessed that he was in great want of money and had acted as above.

There is a fresh, smart liveliness in American society, caused perhaps partly by the atmosphere of the country, which is certainly dryer and lighter than ours over here. But I think it is also because as a nation they are more mixed and cosmopolitan than we are.

Chicago to me was the most unlike an English place than any I visited, and no one can like its climate, or admire its beauty—there is none. One day at noon the thermometer fell about thirty degrees in fifteen minutes, owing to a shift of the wind to blowing from off Lake Michigan. I dined at a Debating Club that met periodically, and after dinner had a regular debate, only one speaking at a time—a very good idea, I think. We had politics, and the company seemed well up in ours.

Mr. Armour had me shown over his great ham and bacon place. One and a quarter million pigs are killed in a year. It is not an appetising sight, and I felt as if I could not eat ham for a long time after.

Pullman Town a few miles off is worth seeing, where the cars of that name are made. They had 4500 workmen, of whom 3000 were Germans and Swedes, and 40 cars were being finished daily. The wheels of the cars were filled in with paper squeezed very tight between the tyres and the axle to deaden the vibration. By the way, it sounds odd that the Japanese word 'Jin-rick-sha' means man-power car, or Pull-man-car.

Niagara must always fascinate, but its water is being robbed for electric power, and the sky-sign advertisements put up in the most prominent places are an outrage on nature.

I had introductions to a family who had lived here for some generations just above the falls. A very charming daughter took me about and said she had grown up overlooking the rapid just above where it fell over, and the falls to her were quite natural all her life, and she had seen a boat with people in it, that had lost an oar, helplessly swept over.

Below the falls it is calm for a mile or so before the lower rapids in which Captain Webb was drowned. One can pull in a small boat to within a hundred yards of the torrent, below it, quite safely. I did so, as the season for the excursion steamers had not begun.

The American works and tunnelling to use the water for electric power were just then beginning, and electricity is perhaps the problem of the hour now. I then heard the account of Mr. Edison trying to restore his first wife to life by it, and think I can understand its domination of the senses, in those who have immersed their minds in it.

I returned to England in the *Etruria*, as I have said. It was the height of the season, and she, being one of the flyers of the time, was crowded.

The floral offerings to the departing ladies nearly filled the saloon—ships made of flowers and other contrivances ; all meals had to be doubled ; on deck you could hardly walk at all for the long lounge chairs in which the passengers delighted. I should like to have put them all on board a man-of-war, and not allowed them to sit down on deck ! But the crowd was very amusing in its way.

Mostly the cabins were crammed, but I had one to myself by the kindness of my good friend the first Lord Inverclyde. On the way home we had a concert, as I believe all the mail steamers do, in aid of Sailors' Homes at Liverpool and at New York, this last having been latterly most properly added. I was made chairman of it; much money must be got in the year.

Our captain told me this story. One trip he was leaving New York, and on descending from the bridge when outside the harbour was accosted by a passenger, who said : ' Captain, I have looked at the compass, and see that the course you are steering will not take us to Queenstown, and I am a schoolmaster and know about these things.' The captain was not pleased and gave but a short reply. Having reached Queenstown as usual, they were leaving for Liverpool, and as he came down from the bridge he saw the learned pedagogue waiting for him, who at once said : ' Well, Captain, I see you did get here; but can you explain it ? ' To which the captain replied, ' Sir, you are a schoolmaster, and I am not, so I do not pretend to explain it.' My readers will understand the schoolmaster considered neither the variation nor the deviation of the compass.

I now spent the season mostly in town, but I do not write of my private life in England, as I cannot suppose it will interest others, and such personal monologues are usually overdone.

In the autumn of 1890 I again embarked in the *Anson* as a guest of my friend Admiral Tracey for the manœuvres. Our ' side,' the ' A ' or defending fleet, assembled in Plymouth Sound.

War was supposed to be declared at 5 P.M. on 8th August. Tracey was second in command. Our Commander-in-Chief, a most able man, had no expectation of hostilities that night, but at about 3 A.M. next morning the (supposed) enemy's torpedo flotilla came in, and harmlessly torpedoed three or four of our ships, which would have defeated our side, as leaving us too inferior to the other fleet.

What was to be done ? The Admiralty were consulted by telegraph; and the wise decision arrived at, that the manœuvres should proceed without prejudice !

Not much happened; we (' A ' Fleet) cruised mostly off the Scilly Islands for about ten days, and then returned to port. It is not easy to make naval manœuvres really instructive, but the general experience of getting ships and crews into order, and of organising and handling a quantity of ships, is all good experience ; and to have a supposed strategic object in view much exercises the imagination and scheming powers of those in command, at the same time exciting an interest in all concerned that sometimes becomes curiously great, and calls forth extra zeal. All this is good, but after all it does not matter one straw which side is supposed to have won.

I may add by my own experience that these mobilisations—certainly when I had to do with them between the years 1885 and 1897—showed us many weak points about ships supposed to be in the pink of condition, for commissioning and proceeding to sea on active service. No doubt these experiences were as salutary as unwelcome, and of proportionate advantage to the service. In which case, adding together all the above, we may say the game was, and is, well worth the candle, and that the expense of the manœuvres is not to be grudged.

I joined a friend in taking a shooting in Scotland for the autumn, and then went to France. As usual I went to Touraine, mostly, and lived among my old French friends. I am always struck with two or three things in French country life as different from ours. I think the life of the gentry is simpler and less ostentatious than in England ; cheaper too, both because a franc goes as far as a shilling in England, and also because French servants work much harder than ours, and one servant does the work of two here.

As regards the clergy, I have the greatest

respect for the country curés, and believe that, as a rule, they lead quite exemplary lives. The gentry seem to me to take little share in the management of provincial matters and politics— a state of affairs in my opinion almost disastrous to a nation. When talking to them about it, they seem often as if they had given the matter up as a bad job. I suppose Communism will some day produce this feeling in other countries than France —here perhaps.

I spent a few days at Bordeaux and heard much about wine, and dined with a French wine merchant. It was new to me to hear that Medoc, the name for wine so well known, and taken from the growth of the vines there, got its name from *in medio aqua*, meaning the tongue of land, about fifty-five miles long, situated between the River Gironde and the sea, on which so much of that red wine's grapes are grown.

I came to London from Bordeaux by sea in a small English steamer. Our weather was curious: we had in turn, first a snowstorm, then a thunder-storm, a waterspout, and St. Elmo's lights at the ends of the spars. Such a variety in two or three days I never saw. The Clerk of the Weather must have gone mad!

The captain knew the shoals about Ushant perfectly, and to show me how at home he was there, in a dark night, he passed through inside the Isle de Seine and Ushant with the utmost confidence; it struck me how useful such men would be to us if ever the times of a century ago returned. But they will not, I think.

CHAPTER XXIII

REAR-ADMIRAL (continued)

West India Islands—Training Squadron—Jamaica—Shark Story
— Panama Canal — North Pacific Mail Steamer — San
Francisco—California—Canada—Canary Islands—Emigrant
Story.

I SAILED in the R.M.S.P. *Orinoco* for Barbados
on Christmas Eve, and spent a nice quiet Christmas
Day in the Bay of Biscay ; a very good place too
for it.

At Barbados I went to the post-office and got
one letter asking me to stay at Fonthill in England,
the other at Fonthill in Jamaica. Rather odd ;
once, as is known, both belonged to the same owner.

Barbados is one-seventh larger than the Isle of
Wight. I always think comparisons like that are
much better than to say so many acres or square
miles. The fact of the coffins in a well-closed up
and dry vault, in a churchyard in Barbados, being
found on more than one occasion moved about to
new positions when the vault was re-opened for
another burial, is well known and I believe quite
unexplained.

I then took to the local British Royal Mail
steamer and went to Santa Lucia, but will not

weary my readers with an account of these well-known islands. I believe there is only one of our West India islands in which the ' Fer de lance ' snake is found, viz. Santa Lucia. Kingsley in his ' At Last,' I think, gives Dominica the palm as being the most beautiful of the Antilles, and I know no island anywhere that to my mind surpasses it ; but such is a question of feeling, not fact.

I visited several more of these islands, and could advise anyone fond of yachting to spend a winter among them.

On 12th January 1891, as I was driving through the Island of Antigua to English Harbour, and passing the churchyard of St. Paul's parish, I stopped and went in to look at the graves, and found one with its stone slab covering fallen off, but on it was engraved :

' Here lie the remains of Honble James Charles Pitt—Son of the Earl of Chatham—Commander of H.M.S. *Hornet*, who died in English Harbour 13th November 1780, aged 20 years. His early virtues and dawning promise bespoke a meridian splendour worthy the name of Pitt.'

One brother was buried in Westminster Abbey, and the other at St. Paul's—Antigua. I was able to communicate with relatives, who restored the grave.

I spent some very pleasant days in Grenada with my friends the Hon. Sir Walter and Lady Hely Hutchinson, he being the Governor there, and the possessor of a beautiful collection of orchids.

At St. Thomas, which is Danish, the Governor was most kind. I heard all about the great hurricane of 1867 and the seismic wave that visited the island a few weeks afterwards, but had no connection with the former. Residents told me that concerning the wave, they saw the sea much higher than usual at the mouth of the harbour, and were alarmed and ran up the hillside on which the town stands. That after the wave had come in and flooded the lower town, and wrecked some ships, the sea receded many feet below the normal position, and for a very short interval left dry parts that are usually many feet under water. Then by degrees with ebbs and flows of waves the ordinary condition was restored.

At St. Kitts Island I became the guest of Commodore A. T. Powlett, my old messmate in the *Terrible*—he being in command of our training squadron ; and with him I went to Jamaica in the *Active*.

The Exhibition there of 1891 was in full swing and was a great success. I thought not the least interesting thing in it was the ship's papers that were found inside a shark, concerning which the following is a true account.

The *Nancy*, a brig of Baltimore, left that place in 1799, and on her way to Port au Prince was captured by H.M.S. *Sparrow* and taken to Port Royal, her cargo being contraband of war. The case was being tried in the Vice-Admiralty Court at Kingston, and would have been dismissed, had not Lieutenant Fitton of H.M.S. *Abergavenny* produced certain papers which he found inside a shark caught off Jacmel by the *Ferret*, tender to the above ship. These papers, together with others of an incriminating nature found in the *Nancy*, led to the condemnation of the brig and her cargo on 25th November 1799.[1]

I stayed with my cousin, Captain Seymour Spencer Smith, at his estates, Fonthill and Hampstead, which adjoin. In his great-uncle's time the owner could lay by £10,000 a year ; that being the palmy period of slaves and sugar. Now there is not a cane on the property ; but pimento, logwood and cattle are the staples of it, and the income is, I fear, very little.

Both the grand old planter's houses of the two estates had vanished. I visited other estates, and stayed at one called the ' Retreat,' owned by Mr. W. Farquharson. This was a sugar-cane one, and the harvest was in full swing when I was there. The cane-crushing mill was close to our small house. It was a scene of great animation ; work went on for about eighteen hours, certainly for far more than the hours of daylight. Negroes and negresses big and small joined in. When a certain amount of cane was crushed the big bell was tolled loudly, and each operative knew that he, or she, had earned so much harvest money, and was stimulated thereby to fresh exertions.

The negroes are, of course, utterly unfit to govern themselves, but if governed with a strong

[1] The shark's jaws are now in the United Service Museum, Whitehall.

and kind hand, are happy, healthy, and, to my mind, very amusing to deal with.

I have talked in the Southern States of the Union with people who remembered the slave times. Of course it was an abuse that should not exist, and all history, I think, shows, not only in the so-called 'New World' but also in the 'Old,' that slave-owning had always a very bad effect on the masters; worse morally than on the slaves.

From Jamaica I went to Colon to see the Panama Canal, and to do so stayed in Panama, and from there visited the works. In the *Nineteenth Century Review* for February 1892 I published the result of my visit, with my opinions, that were shortly as follows:

That the work had gone on about nine years, in which about sixty million pounds sterling had been spent, and only one-third of it really well; and that a lock canal, with an artificial lake to aliment the locks, seemed the only practical plan. I was much impressed with the deadly climate of the Isthmus. The heat is very trying because the climate is so damp and steamy; the thermometer while I was there ranged from 77° to 87°. As regards the Panama railway, the expression is that a man was buried under every sleeper. The growth of the vegetation is such that they say if the railway was quite neglected for a few weeks the creepers, &c., could make the line impassable till cleared away.

In the town of Panama were many hairless dogs (called 'Fever dogs') when I was there, of whom the superstition is that they are an antidote to the fever.

We were at Panama on Easter Day. In the morning we attended High Mass at the Cathedral, where a company of soldiers were present in full dress, and presented arms at the 'Elevation of the Host.' In the afternoon we were present at a cock fight, the only one I ever saw, and I cannot understand how English gentlemen can have taken pleasure in so degrading a sport.

We all admire Count Ferdinand de Lesseps, but so great a work as the Panama Canal was surely never elsewhere so lightly undertaken.

I left Panama in the U.S. Mail steamer *Acapulco* for San Francisco. We called at many ports on our way; in Guatemala we went by rail to the capital—of no great interest. At a station on our way up we were visited by some tiny native women selling fine and excellent pineapples for what equalled in our money 2*d.* each.

Our steamer had lately had a tragic event on board. She was coming south, and anchored off St. José, the port for the country. She had on board a Guatemalan General proscribed by law. He hoped to get by unnoticed, but the authorities heard he was in the ship, and the police boarded her, and demanded his being given up. He retreated to his cabin with arms, and locked the door.

Free firing began and he was killed; there were many bullet marks to be seen. A United States gunboat was at the anchorage, and her commander was blamed for not having taken the victim on board, kept outside, and so saved the above scene in a vessel under the United States flag. But as things were the local authorities acted within their rights.

All the servants, and many of the stokers and others in these steamers are Chinamen, and with all a bargain is made that if they die on board their bodies are embalmed and sent back to China for interment at the cost of the steamer company. The Pacific coast of Central America is very badly off for harbours; usually there was no shelter where we anchored.

In about a month we arrived at San Francisco and found two celebrities there, viz. the President of the United States, and Sarah Bernhardt, who was in the same hotel with me, and her rooms being on the same floor, the landing was usually covered with presents from her admirers—floral gifts, of course, but also wild animals of sorts, luckily in cages ; anything she asked for, if it could be got.

The climate of California in spring is delightful, and indeed all the year round is, I believe, one of the best in the world. As a harbour San Francisco has the fault of being too large inside, like Rio de Janeiro.

Among other places I visited the Yosemite Valley and the famous Wellingtonias, or Sequoias, at the Mariposa Grove. We drove through the hole cut in the tree, which everyone knows on the wine brand advertisement. Near by there is a store where all sorts of things are sold and all said to be made of the wood cut out to make the above hole.

A Yankee friend with me bought a stick, and when another man doubted its genuineness, replied, ' The man said it was so, and I carried it off, and the lie is on his conscience.'

I drove many miles on a ' buckboard ' with an American and his daughter, and our driver, whose father had driven the mail cart for years, told us several stories of the highwaymen. One only I will repeat, as follows : His father had by his side a lady who had on a watch and chain round her neck, which she much valued, and hoped if stuck up by the robbers she would not lose it. The driver said : ' Give it to me, for if we do what they tell us it is a point of honour not to rob the driver.' They were stopped by the brigands. The fashion was for one or two brigands to stand in the road and call out ' Stop,' while others from the roadside kept their rifles pointed at the car. The driver was expected to pull up, and get out and stand at his horses' heads till the affair was over ; the passengers all to alight and toe a line along the road, and hold their hands up while searched.

This procedure went on, and was all but over, when one of the highwaymen said to the driver : ' Hullo, Bill, that 's a fine chain you 've got on, what's the time ? ' Bill coolly looked at the watch, and was about to reply, when the owner called out : ' Oh my dear watch, don't take it.' ' Oh, Bill,' said his querist, ' that 's the game, is it ? Hand over the watch and chain and never try that trick again.'

Everyone knows there are no end of rattle-snakes in California. One day with some companions we saw a snake on the road that had been hurt and could not get away. I jumped down and got my foot on its head. They said, 'Pull his rattles off.' I hate touching a snake, but did so, and gave them to the lady mentioned above, as women out there sometimes wear them as brooches. This snake had nine rattles; eleven are said to be about the greatest number found, and the snakes, I am told, get one more each year they live.

From San Francisco I went to Vancouver's Island, and thence across Canada to Montreal, but a description by me is not wanted. Travellers in the United States know what the newspaper reporters are. I have been 'interviewed' many times. But at Seattle they put in an invented conversation with my opinions, I not having been even asked for an interview. As a rule I used to see the reporters to save worry, and they are often amusing. Besides the interview I have been requested to come round the corner and be photographed 'right away' for to-morrow's issue ; and I have once or twice seen the portrait of another naval officer put in as mine. These things do no harm, and it is best to be amused by them. Contradiction of invented opinions rather pleases the journalist, as drawing attention to his organ.

I returned to England in an Allan Line steamer, with no event to relate except seeing some icebergs.

In the autumn of 1891 I had a cruise in the *Sans Pareil* with my friend, now Admiral Sir

Cyprian Bridge, to see the naval manœuvres of the year. The ship was sister to the ill-fated *Victoria*, and the only other one of that class.

In December I went to the Canary Islands. We arrived at Santa Cruz on Christmas Day, and to show what odd mistakes the telegraph codes may make, I will mention that two of my fellow passengers—husband and wife, he being in business in England—on landing at Teneriffe got a unicode telegram saying, ' Your house is burnt down, but business can still be conducted.' Only one letter, or figure—I forget which—was put wrong and made the above instead of ' A merry Christmas and a happy New Year.'

I visited all seven of the Canary Islands, and it is curious how much they differ. The three western ones—Palma, Gomera, and Hierro—are the smallest, greenest and dampest. The two eastern ones—Lanzarote and Fuertevertura—are the driest, both for climate, soil and vegetation. In some places in the former island the end of a stick put two feet into the ground is charred by the heat. The two central and largest—Teneriffe and Gran Caranaria—are midway in climate, as in position, regarding the others; and they are both the most populous for their size, as well as the best known.

I took it into my head to try and ascend the Peak of Teneriffe in January. Perhaps partly because Lord M—— had tried it two months before and failed.[1] It is no feat at all. Alpine

---

[1] See a letter to the *Times* in November 1891. I sent my account to the *Times*, but being only a common naval officer it was not published.

climbers would laugh at it. But so far as I could learn it had never been done in winter, and the guides did not wish to try it. Everything is comparative !

The peak is 12,198 feet high above the sea, and rises in all about 15,000 feet from the bed of the ocean.

About 7000 feet above the sea you come to what are called the Cañadas—'cañada' meaning in Spanish a glen or dale between mountains. It is supposed that this plateau, which is about eight miles in diameter, was the ancient crater of eruption while still submerged ; and that before its upheaval from the sea, the second part of the mountain had been thrown up, and replaced it as the active part of the volcano. This second part rises to a height of 10,702 feet above the sea, at a place called Alta Vista, and from there springs the present cone.

At the time of my visit the upper half of the mountain, including the Cañadas, was covered with snow. I first went up to them, made my plan and returned. I then started early one morning with three native guides, also Harold Douglas, a young friend, Mr. Egger, the landlord of my hotel at Orotava, and two mules.

We rested at a hut on the Cañadas, where the guides strongly advised our returning. But in spite of them we went on up the ' Lomo Tieso,' perhaps best translated as the ' Stubborn Ridge,' a steep ascent of frozen snow ; of course no mules could face it. I had chosen full moon, and, with axes to help cut steps, we at last reached, at Alta

Vista, the hut called the 'Casa Inglesa,' into which we got and spent a chilly night. My companions were mountain sick, I much the same, and all very cold. Next morning we climbed up the cone, and so accomplished our object.

In summer only patches of snow are left on the mountain. I could say much about the Canary Islands, but will cut short any further account of them, as I did my own visit, on hearing that my turn for employment seemed to have come, and I was most anxious above all things to hoist my flag, and I wished therefore to be on the spot.

I therefore got a passage home in a New Zealand frozen-meat ship, called the *Maori*, as the quickest means of going. She was not a passenger ship. We fed on frozen sheep got up every morning from the refrigerating room, thawed gradually and then cooked. The cooling of the refrigerating chambers was done entirely by very great compression of air, which is then passed through pipes cooled by the sea water; after which it is allowed to expand suddenly and then becomes very cold, going to far below zero even in the tropics at times, I am told.

The captain told me the following story. He was first mate of a sailing ship taking emigrants to New Zealand. One afternoon an emigrant apparently died. He reported this to the captain, who said: 'We will bury him at sunset.' But as the man had a wife on board it was put off to the next morning. That evening the supposed deceased was being sewn up in canvas, which at sea takes the place of a coffin. The face is usually covered last, and when it came to that stage, my informant agreed with the sailmaker to leave the face exposed till the next morning, so that the wife might take a last look at it. The body was in a place by itself. In the morning the bereaved one went in alone to say farewell. A loud yell was heard, others entered, and found the supposed widow fainting across the 'corpse,' whose eyes were rolling in its head. Finally husband and wife both landed in New Zealand. Moral, when you emigrate take a wife with you.

We arrived in the Thames, and I proceeded to urge my claim for employment into the always most sympathetic ears of the Lords Commissioners of the Admiralty!

CHAPTER XXIV

SECOND IN COMMAND CHANNEL SQUADRON

H.M.S. *Swiftsure*—Manœuvres—H.M.S. *Anson*—Ferrol—Salving
H.M.S. *Howe*—Spaniards—*Serpent's* Cemetery—Ferrol Ball
—H.M.S. *Empress of India*—Winter Cruise.

ON 21st July 1892 I hoisted my flag for the first
time in H.M.S. *Swiftsure* at Devonport for a
month's cruise as Second in Command for the
summer manœuvres.

I had then been three years on half-pay as
Rear-Admiral, and, having no particular interest,
began to think that the Admiralty did not
intend to employ me at all; the more so that
some of my juniors were already afloat in good
appointments.

At the time I was much annoyed, but reflection showed me two things: one that selection
must always be ruled by some favouritism, which
when in *our* favour we call good judgment; and
the other that your character and your sympathy
with others benefit much by some personal disappointment. But I was very glad to get afloat
anyhow.

My superior officer in these manœuvres was

the late Admiral Fitzroy, an old friend, and a very capable officer. We rendezvoused in Torbay to organise; this with a lot of scratch commissioned ships means hard work for all concerned, but it is capital training for what will probably occur in case of war.

A description of the manœuvres would not be interesting, so I will only say we were called the Red Fleet, and the others the Blue; that the seat of the supposed war was off the northeast coast of Ireland mostly; and we were considered to have won. Outsiders can hardly realise how interested and even excited the actors in these sham campaigns get; and it is well they should do so. In this one in Belfast Lough, the officer of a steamboat put his helm over and rammed an enemy's boat, excusing himself by saying he thought the order called out to run was to ram. But I am sure he much preferred what he did do. Happily they were not ships.

The next month—September—I was appointed as Second in Command of the Channel Fleet, my flag being in the *Anson*, a ship I knew already. She was one of the six 'Admiral' class, and, like most other armoured vessels, was soon severely criticised, and almost condemned. Their worst point, perhaps, was that their barbettes did not have sufficient armoured protection below them. For accommodation the men were very well off in the central and highest part of the ship.

The ends of the ship were very low, and I have seen her battened down forward, and also aft over all the officers' cabins and mess places, for two or more days. But they were better fighting ships than those before them.

The flag-officer commanding the Channel Fleet then was Vice-Admiral Fairfax, a delightful companion, and a great friend.

In October the squadron rendezvoused off the Start, and comprised the *Royal Sovereign* (flag of Vice-Admiral Fairfax), *Anson*, *Howe* and *Rodney* (ironclads so-called then), two cruisers, and a despatch boat.

We went to the north coast of Spain, and then to Coruña, the scene of that battle ending with our splendid retreat in 1809 and the glorious death of our General. A retreat may be as creditable as a victory, and Sir John Moore's was so; but, perhaps, a battle can hardly be called a victory unless you either hold the field or advance beyond it.

On 2nd November we went to Ferrol to pay an official visit to the Spanish Captain-General, meaning to stay there only three hours; I remained seven months. What happened was this: Our squadron, as enumerated above, was passing through the long entrance to Ferrol harbour, with a flood tide in its favour. The ships were in single column line ahead, as was right, the *Royal Sovereign* leading. As soon as she had cleared the passage and entered the very spacious harbour, the Admiral said to his Flag-captain, 'Reduce speed,' naming the revolutions. This he did not mean for a signal to the ships astern of him, but by an error it was hoisted.

At that time the *Howe* was passing a small bay on her port hand, and seeing the signal she reduced her speed. She was already rather too much in the bay, and this, the slower speed, and the flood tide taking her on her starboard quarter caused her to be swept on to an uncharted rock, where she remained with her port bilge ripped open. Her captain was a very good officer, also young for his position, already distinguished, and with the best of service prospects. The result was his professional ruin. I only mention this, not so much to blame him—it might have happened to others—but to show how precarious is the career of a naval officer, and how one minute's error (even in peace time) may mean professional ruin, or the loss of the ship.

As regards the tribunal part of the matter and myself, I will only shortly say that I was told to hold a court of inquiry at once to say if the rock was known or not, and a few other details, but not to apportion the blame.

The Vice-Admiral and some ships were ordered home, and a court martial was held at Portsmouth to try the Captain of the *Howe*, but with very little result ; so a second court martial was, several weeks after, held at Devonport to try the Vice-Admiral. For this I was ordered to England, and put in the, I think, rather unusual position of being distinctly asked to state what were the causes of the *Howe* running aground.

As my flagship was astern of her, with only one ship between us, I, of course, knew all about it. and said what I knew, and gave the four causes.

But it is now long past, and I will proceed .. some account of the *Howe's* being salved.[1]

By daylight on 3rd November the ship assumed the following position, heeling 20° to starboard, and her bow tipped down 10°, and in this position without the least movement she remained for 101 days.   At high tide her forepart and all her starboard side were well under water, and she had 12,000 tons of sea water inside her.   Had she been exposed to wave action she could, of course, not have been saved, but would have broken up.

The Admiralty left me at Ferrol in charge of a small squadron to guard the wreck and help to salve her : the contract for the salvage being given to the Neptune Salvage Company of Stockholm, on the excellent principle of ' no cure no pay,' i.e. that the Company agreed to convey the *Howe* within six months to the gates of the dry dock in the ' Darcena ' or floating basin at Ferrol for £35,000.

The superintendent of the Salvage Company's people sent was Captain Edlind, who was both a very able man and one perfect to work with. Three steamers were sent, and were lashed along-side the *Howe*, all having very powerful steam pumps on board.   The *Howe* was on a rocky shoal of hard granite for quite half her length, the bow and stern off the ground, with deep water on her starboard beam, and this we were always

---

[1] If anyone wishes to study this subject let them read the admirable account of it by the late Rear-Admiral G. T. H. Boyes, then my Flag-captain, called *Salvage Operations : the Floating of H.M. Battleship Howe.*

afraid of her tumbling off into, or indeed of her capsizing.

The damages were mostly on the port side, and it may give some idea of them to say, that after the ship was got into dock at Ferrol, I could stand on a temporary flooring where the bottom of the ship used to be, and holding one hand over my head could not touch where the ship's bottom plates had been driven up to. It was mainly a question of divers' work.

The Salvage Company had, of course, first-rate divers, but our own were specially useful for the intricate inside of the ship. This was a very dangerous part, and one day we nearly lost some men at it, by their air-pipes getting jammed. The steps to be taken were, generally speaking, these :

1. Remove by blasting the rocks that had penetrated the ship.
2. Build a wooden coffer dam, or flooring, to do temporary duty as ship's bottom on port side.
3. Stop up also by this or other means any holes on the starboard side not at first possible to discover.
4. When sufficiently watertight pump her out and float her.

For the first the blasting charges had to be small so as not to injure the ship's frame, &c.

For the second careful measurements had to be made by the divers, and wooden frames made in accordance.

For the third, if and when possible, as for the second.

For the fourth, the pumping power of the three salvage steamers and of all other pumps the squadron could provide.

By degrees we made watertight and pumped out the uninjured after compartments of the ship, and, of course, we moved all weights not fixtures in her, except her four 67-ton guns. There would have been immense difficulty in getting them out, owing to the great heel of the ship and the very strong shears required, so they were left in place.

It was most important not to let the ship move on her bed till ready to lift, because if she did so she would destroy the work referred to in the second and third categories above. Partly to prevent this and also to prevent her slipping off to starboard into deep water, we got every steel wire hawser we could, at least ten of them, and made them fast from the ship to anchors and rocks on the shore. These hawsers at low tide were as taut as harp strings, and the chain cables of the salvage steamers lay over them like a watch chain would over your finger.

Indeed I wrote to the Admiralty and said: ' If one of these wire hawsers parts, the name of the hero of the 1st June 1794 will have to be scratched off the Navy List ! '

One great difficulty was that the so-called watertight compartments were not so, but leaked very much, besides which water passed through the ventilation arrangements; the mud, slime and dirt covering everything as the water was cleared from below, and the bad smell was almost beyond belief. The plan of salvage, the skilled diving work, building a false bottom to the ship, and pumping her out, were all entirely due to the Salvage Company; but we in the squadron were constantly at work at the *Howe*, and without us a far larger staff and number of men from the Company must have been necessary, and probably more steamers.

On the 3rd February, just three months after she grounded, the first attempt was made to pump her out and float her off the rocks, but it failed. Steps were now taken to keep the water out by coffer dams inside the ship. As a result of this on the 11th February, after no movement for 101 days, she righted one degree, which was hailed with as much delight as a first-born infant's first articulate word is by its mother. After this the ship gradually righted more, and our hopes rose in proportion.

The *Howe's* complement had been reduced to her Commander, Charles Windham—now a Rear-Admiral—and a few officers. Windham lived in the wreck, and showed a good example to all, which was followed. The carpenter, Mr. J. Rice, was a host in himself, and was afterwards rewarded by being made carpenter of the Royal Yacht.

We now set to work to make collision mats to place under the ship, and in all seven such were placed. Divers with iron bodkins, some twelve

H.M.S. HOWE

Salved after 148 days on the rocks at Ferrol
1892–1893

feet long, worked them through under the keel, a rope being fast to the bodkin's eye, and to this rope a chain made fast to the mat.

Of course we had complete stations prepared and known for the duties required if the ship was floated; in view also of the possibility of her sinking again in deep water, arrangements to try and save the men in her. The *Seahorse*, a man-of-war steamer, all steamboats, and the pulling boats of the squadron had their stations, and knew if the signal BX was made at any hour what to do; and two possible beaching places were examined and selected. The above ' stations ' employed on board the *Howe* 412 officers and men, besides those belonging to her.

On 27th March the first attempt was made to float and haul the ship off the shoal, but failed, as did two subsequent attempts.

At last the great day arrived; on 30th March at about 2 P.M. the *Howe* was floated off the shoal that she had lain on for 148 days. Everyone was at their station by the signal BX. The steamers and steamboats were ready and only high water awaited. The pumps were set to work, the decrease of water anxiously watched inside the ship, as well as at her water-line outside. Soon a slight movement in the vessel was apparent, the securing hawsers were slacked, and the towing vessels started.

The *Howe's* head pays off slightly to starboard; she is alive again; her winter fetters are cast off; she moves ahead; she is free. Will her tender patches give way, and will she sink in deep water ?

This question may just occur to the mind, but success is the predominant feeling.

I cannot express our delight, it was almost like winning a victory. The men cheered, and the ships' bands as we approached them played ' Rule, Britannia.'

We anchored the ship in Malata Bay, an inlet of this splendid harbour, and there placed under her a specially prepared pad made of thin deal planks, so fitted as to be flexible and fit tight round the ship, and frapped firmly round her, outside all the other mats and patches. We now were able to pump out nearly all of the 2500 tons of water still in her when floated.

On 13th April we got the *Howe* into the floating basin, and on the 17th into the dry dock and in safety. On arrival off it, we were still uncertain if she would get in owing to her size and abnormal draft, but the Salvage Company had earned their money.

I should now say a few words about our social life at Ferrol.

It is a purely naval port and was once the scene of much activity. By nature it is, perhaps, the finest naval port I know, being thoroughly sheltered from the sea, with a narrow entrance, having high sides that, fortified, could keep any enemy out, and also keep him far away from the town and inside shipping ; yet approachable by ships at all times and tides, if properly surveyed, buoyed, and lighted.

Inside is a fine expanse of water deep enough, but not too deep ; and beyond this hills round its land side on which forts could be put for inland defences.

The Governor was the Captain-General Vice-Admiral Jose de Carranza, a dignified Spanish Don, speaking English well, and always assisting us in every way he could.[1]

He and his Señora had a reception every Thursday evening, to which some of us always went. There were many ladies there, and our acquaintance among them was large; but among them not one spoke English, and only five spoke French.

Our nation are bad linguists. My Flag-captain, Boyes, already knew Spanish, but hardly one other officer in the squadron knew a word of it. I, my Flag-lieutenant (now Captain Douglas Nicholson), and another officer set to work to learn it.

There was only one English family in the neighbourhood. Our Vice-Consul, Señor Emilio Anton, did all that was possible to help us, as did the officials generally; but an extraordinary thing was that the peasantry were, as a rule, very rude, and became if anything worse during our stay. Why I cannot say, unless it is religious animosity, and in order to show their disapproval of heretics.

While I was at Ferrol the Admiralty told me to look after the cemetery of the crew of the *Serpent*. H.M.S. *Serpent*, a steam sloop, was lost on 10th November 1890 close to Cape

---

[1] The Queen was pleased to appoint the Captain-General to be a Knight Commander of St. Michael and St. George; and various pieces of plate were presented by the Admiralty to Spanish officials at Ferrol. Captain Edlind, of the Neptune Salvage Co., was also made a Companion of the Order of St. Michael and St. George.

Trecé, about thirty miles north-east of Cape Villano in Spain. Both these names are of ill-omen. 'Villano' means villain, and 'trecé' is thirteen in Spanish, and held by them as an unlucky number.

The *Serpent* was outward bound to the west coast of Africa, and of a crew of 175 only three were saved—no officers. Most of the bodies were washed on shore and buried by the Spaniards near the spot. The graves were surrounded by a wall, whose interior was divided into two-thirds and one-third by a high wall. In the smaller space they buried all they considered to be Roman Catholics, and in the larger space the others. I tried to find out how they arrived at the above, but could not. I suppose every man who had a woman tattooed on him was taken as a Roman Catholic. Many sailors have women tattooed on them. Probably the *Serpent* had, at most, a dozen Roman Catholics.

It was a question of putting the place to rights. I suggested that as on board ship they had got on all right together, a wall was not required to keep order, but this I fear shocked the natives.

The cura of the parish was a delightful man, and a very sporting character. The Admiralty had, in reward for his attention after the wreck, offered him a present, and he had asked for a first-rate sporting gun; and I was now able to supply him with a lot of cartridges of the same gauge.

Several other vessels in the last few years had

been lost near the same spot, and there is no doubt often an inset on that coast.

The *Howe* having been got off, we resolved to celebrate the event, and so hired the theatre in Ferrol and gave a great ball in it. Dancing took place in the auditorium, which was arranged so that such a thing could be done. We had the supper on the stage, but before it began I made them a speech in my best Spanish—not very good at that ; but I am bound to say I worked it well up beforehand.

We were at Ferrol in Lent, and at Easter. On Good Friday there was a great religious procession, the officers walking in it in full dress. The ships had their yards topped at angles, and rigging slacked off. Several images were carried in the procession, and on Easter Eve a religious salute of fifteen guns was fired.

When the *Howe* had been got into dock we felt she was safe ; but shoreing her up there, with her bottom nearly gone, was a difficult job. Finally a sort of temporary bottom of wood was fitted to her.

When the engine-room was emptied of water, instead of the machinery being found all rusty it was in good condition, as the great quantity of oil afloat on the water deposited itself on the metal as the water fell, and so kept the air off and prevented rust.

The *Howe* was fifty-eight days in the dry dock ; her stores, &c., were then replaced, her engines tried running round the harbour, and on the 18th June, after 229 days, we left Ferrol with her for England. Everything was prepared to tow her, but she steamed home at eight knots, and I deposited her safely at Sheerness.[1]

I returned in the *Anson* to Devonport, and on arrival heard the dreadful news of the loss of H.M.S. *Victoria* in the Mediterranean.

Our next job was the naval manœuvres off the coast of Ireland and in the St. George's Channel. I will not describe them, but only say that one day an odd thing occurred. Our Fleet was just sighting the 'enemy' at sea, the two approaching each other, when a thick fog came on and lasted some hours. What a difficult position had it been real war!

After the manœuvres I was ordered to Chatham to change flagships, the *Anson* turning over to the *Empress of India*. On our way a man was lost in a curious way. The sea was calm, the weather fine and warm, the ship steaming full speed. A seaman fell overboard and the life-buoy was let go close to him, but it being in the centre of the stern it was towed along in the wake of the ship, and the man could not reach it, and was drowned.

The *Empress of India* was a new ship, sister to the *Royal Sovereign*, and a great improvement on the *Anson* in nearly all ways. As regards her personnel, I never was in a ship where all the officers, from the captain downwards, got on so well and so happily together.

[1] She was at once docked at Chatham, and repaired with all despatch. In a few months she was re-commissioned and went to the Mediterranean.

In October the Channel Fleet assembled and we went to Gibraltar and to the Balearic Islands.

At Palma in Majorca we made acquaintance with the Austrian Archduke Lewis Salvador and visited him at his country place Miramar He lived alone there, abjured all ceremony and state, and almost the comforts of life ; spoke several languages, English for one. The Archduke was most kind to me, and gave me the copy of a large book he had written about these islands.

At Majorca, the Canary Islands, and the Philippine Islands, the Spanish Captain-General, or Governor, was forbidden to return any visit afloat ; the reason given being that one such official was once carried off in a ship.

We were much at Gibraltar, and enjoyed both the Calpe Hounds and some paperchases, perhaps the last most.

CHAPTER XXV

SECOND IN COMMAND CHANNEL SQUADRON (continued)

A Duel at Gibraltar—Madeira—Canary Islands—Vigo Treasure
Ships—Ceuta.

I AM fond of looking at old cemeteries ; you may
find interesting inscriptions.   In one of the above
at Gibraltar, now disused, I found this :

> To the memory of Midshipman Seth Amiel
> Wheaton, of the United States Frigate
> *Washington*, who fell a victim to a misplaced
> sense of honour 8 February 1817.

The story was told me by Captain McCleverty
when in the *Terrible*, and is as follows.

The above frigate came to Gibraltar, and was
lying in the anchorage. A party of her officers, who
had stayed on shore late one night, came down to
the ' Ragged Staff ' to go off to their ship. The
rules about entering or leaving the garrison at
night are now strict, and were even more so then.
The sentry stopped the officer, and sent for the
sergeant of the guard, who in his turn called out
the officer of the guard, a subaltern, who conferred

with the U.S. officers, and regretting his inability to let them embark, offered what accommodation he could for the night.

They, however, got angry, and made out they were insulted. The next day the subaltern received a challenge to fight a duel, and as such things were done then, and he was young, and the other was a foreign officer, he felt he must fight, did so and was killed.

The surgeon of his regiment, who was a great friend of his, was very angry, and happened to be a very good shot with a pistol. He waited till the officer who had killed his friend landed, and then insulted him, so that he had to challenge the surgeon whose reputation as above was well known, and who gave out that he would kill his man.

They met on the neutral ground outside the Rock lines; the American had his hand in a bucket of water to cool it, seeing which the Englishman said: 'It is not much good for I'm certainly going to shoot you,' which he did and killed him. He then turned to the dead man's second and said : 'This will do for to-day, but whenever any of you land I will insult them, and kill them all in turns.'

The United States Commodore, i.e. Captain, complained to the Governor, who said he would not interfere, so they sailed.

Leaving Gibraltar we spent Christmas at Arosa Bay, again visiting St. Iago de Compostella, which in 1889 had for me completed the four great Christian pilgrimages of the world, viz. Jerusalem, Rome, Loretto, and this last. The town is essentially sombre of aspect, and the Cathedral of dark stone is especially so.

I twice visited Oporto, a pleasant town on the high banks of the Douro. They say no one has the gout there because they drink enough port wine, and that medicine is certainly good. You see it kept in immense wooden vats where it is refined. I was told that one vat held 237 pipes of 115 gallons each, and that in six or seven years it was fit to drink. I was also told that the Russians like white port, and that England buys most of the best wine. Many of the houses in Oporto are covered outside with bright glazed tiles with patterns on them, which much enliven the aspect of the streets.

From Arosa we went to Vigo, and thence to Madeira. Here the *Empress of India* distinguished herself by giving a performance of ' Romeo and Juliet,' travestied, in the theatre on shore to a crowded audience. I wrote a song for it, which was sung. The performers were officers; the present Commodore Rosslyn Wemyss, then a lieutenant in the *Empress*, was one of the actors, and I think was also stage manager.

We left Madeira with great regret, and went to the Canary Islands, calling at Las Palmas in Grand Canary; our ship rolled here though angle of 20° at anchor. This class of vessels all rolled heavily till bilge keels were fitted to them, with a good result that surprised all the scientific authorities; but naval officers had pressed for them. Here we came in for the carnival, and saw much of the Spanish society.

Opinions differ about the Canary Islands and Madeira as winter health resorts for invalids. Of course the Canaries being nearer the equator, and with no other thing to interfere, their climate is warmer than that of Madeira. But in favour of Madeira it is to be remembered that it is about one thousand years ahead of the Canaries by nature, and one hundred years by civilisation.

We returned in a few weeks to Gibraltar. On reaching Cape Spartel in the night we got suddenly into a strong levanter, and the ships pitched so that the Vice-Admiral's cabin was suddenly flooded about four feet deep, to the astonishment of his guest who was in bed, and to the destruction of his furniture.

I again visited Ceuta and confirmed my opinion that, though a mole harbour could be made more cheaply than at Gibraltar, it is not as suitable for a defensive fortress.

At Gibraltar our theatrical party from the *Empress of India* gave 'Romeo and Juliet' in the Assembly Rooms to a full house, and had great applause.

From the Rock we went to Vigo. There had lately been efforts made to recover treasure from some Spanish galleons that ran in here at the beginning of the eighteenth century. I first heard the story when here in 1873, but the company was only starting then. Our Consul—a Spanish gentleman—told it to us, and said that before investing any money he made inquiries in the archives of the province, and decided that the treasure had been landed before the English squadron followed the Spanish ships in and sank them. However, in spite of this a company was promoted in Paris to get the treasure. Their ship entered Vigo harbour with great *éclat* ; a diver went down and came up with an ingot, which was sent off to Paris, and raised the shares for those who were in the swim to benefit by.

Much later I was approached in London to join another company on the same ground, and I related to them the above at greater length—with what result I am not aware. I know of several other treasure hunts in different parts of the world, and I quite understand their fascination, but I have never known one that succeeded.

From Vigo we went to Arosa Bay. Near here are streams in which trout fishing should be good if the natives did not poach the fish anyhow they can.

We arrived in Plymouth Sound, and on 24th April 1894 I hauled my flag down and went to London to a new appointment.

The Second in Command of the Channel Squadron then was a very unsatisfying position, because he had not enough work to do. Now squadrons are larger, this fault has been somewhat rectified. When with a rear-admiral under me I have tried to improve this matter by giving him work, for all good reasons.

No good officer likes to find himself without work and responsibility, and if he has none a fault exists somewhere. I was truly sorry to leave my flagship and all the officers and men in her, also to part from my friend and superior, Vice-Admiral Fairfax, but I was not sorry to end the appointment.

CHAPTER XXVI

ADMIRAL-SUPERINTENDENT OF NAVAL RESERVES

The Naval Reserves and Coastguard—Naval Manœuvres—
Coastguard's Duties—Eagle Island.

ON 25th April 1894 I relieved Vice-Admiral Sir Robert Fitzroy as Admiral-Superintendent of Naval Reserves. This was a very interesting appointment. The position of Admiral-Superintendent of Naval Reserves then combined all the Coastguard both afloat and on shore ; also inspections of all Royal Naval Reserve drill batteries and stations, the Royal Naval Artillery Volunteers, and the inspection of the *Worcester* and *Conway* training ships for young officers for the mercantile marine ; and of all those boys' training ships round our coasts, that were *not* in any way reformatories, and from which we might take boys into the Navy.

Added to the above was more strictly naval work, viz. inspecting the Coastguard ships, and organising and commanding in the summer the squadron composed of them, and of other mobilised ships, for that year's naval manœuvres. Much of the above is quite changed now, and the appointment is quite different.

In the summer I went to sea with my flag in the *Alexandra*, and commanded one of the manœuvring fleets. I had to visit (or should visit) and inspect every Coastguard station in the United Kingdom, and see that all the houses for the 4500 men were kept in order. I have been into every room of, I may say, the 4500 houses! In short, there was plenty to do.

The office was in London near the Admiralty, and I had a very fine official steam yacht called the *Hawk* to go about in as I felt right.

The naval manœuvres this summer, of course, specially interested me because I was in command of the two squadrons on one side. We were the Blue Fleet, and our enemy the Red one. Red consisted of two squadrons, called A and B ; Blue of two also, called C and D.

They united were superior to us when we also were united, but they had to start their two squadrons from different places and meet if they could. My object was to catch them singly. Each of the four squadrons started from different places—out at sea. These places were not known to the other side.

We knew Red's object was to unite in the St. George's Channel, and had reason to believe that one of them to do this would pass in round the North of Ireland.

I joined company with my D Squadron off the Isle of Man, then united and went to patrol the narrow channel between that island and the Mull of Cantyre. The details of our cruise are, of course, many, but would weary the reader ; so

I will only say that eventually my object was attained. I got into close quarters with B first, and afterwards with A, both singly ; and was adjudged to have won.

I must however remark, as I have before, that which side is supposed to have won matters not a bit, and winning is very much chance. Also that each fleet after fighting a supposed action, even if victorious, should be lowered as to her ' points ' of power ; for in real warfare, though victorious, she would certainly be weakened till repaired, &c., even if no ships were actually sunk, which I think some would be.

I had this appointment just over three years ; one did not want much leave, because the duties and localities were so varied, that the series of changes did instead.

In the beginning of 1895 we had the hardest frost I have ever seen in England : it began 26th January and lasted till 19th February. The Serpentine bore immense crowds of skaters, and the Thames was frozen over at London, and was covered with seagulls, who now learned to come up for *their* season, and have continued to do so since.

I place a high value on the Coastguard, as a thoroughly dependable body of well-trained men for a Naval Reserve ; and for what the term ' Coastguard ' means, also as applied to the protection and saving of life and property in cases of shipwreck. One of my predecessors in the office made out a list of various duties that the Coastguard performed. I added to them, making about sixteen in all, and I had some hundreds of copies printed, one of which was put up in every station's watch-room, so that any inquirer could see how important the Coastguard is.

I was often agreeably struck with the great respect with which both the officers and men were invariably treated by their civilian neighbours. This is a subject I could enlarge on, and I regret that a recent influence at the Admiralty, guided by a spirit that thought any change in the Navy must be an improvement, has begun to largely reduce the Coastguard.

In 1895 we again had large squadrons at sea, but we were all combined for tactical exercises, probably quite as useful as manœuvres, but not so popular with the journalists.

I landed once on Eagle Island off Blacksod Bay on the west coast of Ireland, and saw an astonishing proof of what the sea can do. Its west side faces the open Atlantic, the cliff being almost precipitous, but having in one part a very steep incline, slightly curved in—a cleft, in fact, running down it. On the top of this, and 180 feet above the sea, were two lighthouses, and between them houses for the lightkeepers and families, with a joining wall. In December 1894, during a violent westerly gale, the sea dashed up the 180 feet—in green seas, I was told—pouring over the summit of the cliff, and with such force as to destroy some of the houses.

In 1896 we again had manœuvres; our side, the Reserve Fleet, was called C and D Squadrons, and was opposed to the Channel Fleet, called A and B

Squadrons, who united were superior to us ; our object was to defeat our enemy separately if we could, or in any case without their defeating us to get into Lough Swilly.

My Second in Command was the present Admiral of the Fleet, Sir Arthur Wilson, who devised a very wily plan, and we succeeded in accomplishing our object.

In May 1897 I finished my appointment as Admiral-Superintendent of Naval Reserves, with the knowledge that there is a great deal of naval patriotic feeling in the country, only requiring to be encouraged and trained to usefulness. But any sea training must be thorough to be of value.

CHAPTER XXVII

CHINA COMMAND

Chusan Island—Occupation of Wei-hai-wei—Nagasaki—Hankow
—Nankin—Hong-Kong—Manilla—Formosa—Corea.

THAT autumn (1897) I was given the appointment
of Commander-in-Chief of our squadron in China.
This was without doubt the best, most important,
and most interesting appointment I ever held.   I
do not mean only as events turned out, but I
consider as follows.   If we were engaged in a
European war, the command of our principal
Fleet in home waters must always be the most
important naval post ; and it certainly is so now
for reasons known to everyone.   But the China
station with its large area, its very varied shores
and interests—commercial and diplomatic—and
with the momentous questions relating to the new
power of Japan, the awakening of China, and the
Eastern aspirations of Russia, certainly yielded
to none in interest ten or twelve years ago.

I left England in the end of 1897, and arriving
at Hong-Kong by mail steamer, I hoisted my flag
there in the *Alacrity*, which is the Admiral's
official yacht, and proceeded to Chusan Island,

where I relieved Admiral Sir Arthur Buller and took command of the China Station.

Chusan Island, off the mouth of the Yang-tse River, was occupied by us in the Opium War, 1839-42. Its strategic position is undoubted, and after discussing with Admiral Togo in Japan the question of where China, when she got a navy, should make her principal naval station, he gave it to me as his opinion that it should be at Chusan. Captain Mahan has said that the first requirement of a naval port is being in the right geographical position, and few, I think, dispute that.

Chusan has a poor harbour, and the tides are strong ; and I think an island, *qua* island, inferior to a port on the mainland of a nation.

In April our squadron all met at Chifu, in consequence of strained relations with Russia, and we prepared for any eventuality. I went to Pekin to confer with our Minister, Sir Claude Macdonald, and found much changed since I left the Peiho and Tiensin twenty-eight years before.

The Russians having now got a lease of Port Arthur from the Chinese, our Government got one for Wei-hai-wei—the period named being ' as long as Russia holds Port Arthur ' ; and we took possession of our new territory on 24th May, Queen Victoria's birthday, surely an auspicious date.

To please the Chinese we arranged that the Japanese who were in possession should haul their flag down on 23rd May, and the Chinese flag be hoisted then and fly till the 24th ; so that we should receive the place from them.

Perhaps I should briefly state that our possession called Wei-hai-wei comprises the Island of
Leu-kung-tao — which practically shelters the
anchorage in the bay, so named from the walled
town called Wei-hai-wei, which is on the mainland
at the west side of the bay. This town is a 'Fu'
or fortified city, and as such is highly valued by
the Chinese ; and it was arranged that it should
preserve its autonomy, though it actually stood
within the radius of ten miles measured inland
from the shore all round the bay of the same name,
which from its eastern to its western extreme was,
with the exception of this town, to be British
territory.

Outside the ten-mile radius was to be another
ten-mile one, neutral to us and the Chinese—
like the neutral ground at Gibraltar ; and the
land beyond that was to remain Chinese territory
as of old. This arrangement held good for about
eighteen months, when we got the Chinese to agree
that the neutral territory should be simply defined
by an imaginary line running north and south at
longitude 121° 40' E. across the Shantung pro-
montory—a sensible plan.

As a comparison of sizes, I may state that the
island of Leu-kung-tao (or Prince Leu's island)
is about two-thirds of the area of the rock of
Gibraltar.

The Navy had the management of Wei-hai-wei
entirely for over a year, and it interested me
immensely. Captain G. F. King Hall of the
Narcissus actually took over the Island of Leu-
kung-tao, and I appointed his First-lieutenant

(now Captain Ernest Gaunt) to be the actual Governor. Both these officers showed what is well known, viz. that a real sailor can fit himself into almost any office, as if bred to it.

The Chinese had fortified both the island and the mainland well, but the batteries were all ruined by the Japanese siege and capture of the place. Indeed the word 'ruin' best describes the state in which we found the island, town, dock-yard, &c.

Prince Henry of Prussia, as Admiral in command of the German squadron in China, visited me at Wei-hai-wei a few days after our occupation, and walking through the town with me said: 'It looks as if there had been an earthquake, and all the people had run away.' And that was what it did look like.

We set to work to make the place as useful as possible to us as a naval station; for this, much had to be done. I will not inflict details on my kind readers, but in praise of Wei-hai-wei geneıally I have no hesitation in saying, that no place I know of exists, that is better than it for the health and discipline of a squadron.

I set my officers to examine and survey the whole of our territory, both afloat and on shore. Later on, to perfect these surveys, a surveying ship and a corps of Royal Engineers were sent, and forts were commenced to be adequate, as the expression is, to refuse the anchorage to raiding cruisers. These forts were well in hand when I left the station, but the home authorities then altered their minds and left them unfinished.

One of my captains taking a passage in a local steamer found sitting next him a Chinese gentleman, who talked good English and said : 'So I see we have got Wei-hai-wei.' He replied : 'Yes, but I do not quite understand,' to which the Chinaman answered : 'Oh, I'm English, I was born at Hong-Kong.'

> A celestial who came from Hong-Kong
> Said 'In spite of my pigtail so long
> I'm a Britisher born,'
> And he spoke with much scorn
> Of the heathen Chinee and his gong.

It is sometimes amusing to hear how the British Bluejackets mispronounce some ships' names. For instance the *Hermione* is called as three words, 'her my own.' When that ship joined my flag I thought the following doggerel might cure the above error:

> Cried the yeoman in rapturous tone,
> 'She is coming, it is Her my own ';
> Said the Midshipman, 'Fie on ye,
> Call her "Hermione,"
> One would think you were Darby and Joan.'

The summer of 1898 I spent mostly at Wei-hai-wei, but I visited Japan, for the too short time I could spare ; we always looked upon it as our holiday resort, and every ship was pleased when I sent her there.

Nagasaki was the best known place, partly because it was the first port opened to Western nations, but also because, besides being a very good harbour, it was the nearest to get to. The Russian men-of-war most of all frequented it, as a delightful retreat in winter from ice-bound Vladivostok.

In the autumn I went up the Yang-tse to Hankow, where I called on the Viceroy Chang-Chih-Tung, who is a very up-to-date Chinese official.

Lord Charles Beresford was at Hankow at the same time on his commercial mission to China,[1] and soon after my interview with the Viceroy, he also had one. When I again came up there, the Consul, who always was present as interpreter at official visits, told me that the next time he saw the Viceroy after Lord Charles's visit the Viceroy said: 'Is Lord Charles Beresford a rebel?' and on being answered in the negative, explained that he thought so because at one time he had said to the Viceroy, 'Well, if our Government won't do [something] my party will make them.'

The Yang-tse differs immensely in the height of its waters; in the late spring when the snows far inland melt, the river at Hankow rises fifty feet. But as regards Hankow it is not fifty feet deeper because the stream brings down much mud which raises the bottom temporarily by many feet.

I called at Nankin, and had an interview with the Viceroy, who is styled Viceroy of the 'Two Kiangs'; his name was Liu-Kun-yi. We made great friends then, and while I was in China; and he was the ideal of what a great gentleman in such a post should be. During the disturbances

[1] See his book *The break-up of China.*

325

of 1900 it was he who kept the Yang-tse region quiet.

The question of Pekin being the capital of China, instead of its former one, Nankin, seems to me much as if, in the days when we and the Scotch were foolish enough to be cutting each other's throats, instead of combining together, they had got the better of us, and then moved the capital from London to Carlisle.

I visited the Kiang-yin forts, by permission of the Viceroy. They are on the heights a few miles below Nankin, a commanding site which, if properly armed and held, with the river passage well mined, would quite bar the river to an enemy.

That winter was spent mostly at Hong-Kong, which is our China headquarters. It is said that more tonnage of shipping—including, of course, all Chinese junks and other craft—passes through Hong-Kong harbour in a year than through any other port in the world. The hospitality and agreeable society of Sir Henry Blake, our able Governor here, and of Lady Blake, added to that of other friends at Hong-Kong, made it a sort of home for our squadron.

The importance of Hong-Kong to our squadron and our trade can hardly be overrated. It is fortified of course, but neither in its defences nor its garrison could it pretend to stand a siege. This might be said of many of our possessions ; the reply I suppose being, that we hope to command the sea—a hope not so easy of fulfilment now as it was before those modern navies, not requiring my mention, arose.

I went to Manila to visit Admiral Dewey of the United States Navy in his new conquest, and to see what was going on. I had known him several years before, also since, and class him as a real friend. As regards his Manila work, he risked uncertainty, and did all that could be done quite well. That he had not a hard fight is no part of the question.

I found them expecting civil war in the island, and on inquiry learnt that I could by going several miles into the country have an interview with Aquinaldo. Perhaps I was anxious to see him, but I intended to show him the absurdity of his hoping to get the better of a contest with the United States.

I found him in no way impressive, in build medium height, slight, and rather like a Japanese. He spoke little, perhaps because his Spanish was only passable, and the island patois his usual tongue ; our interview was most friendly, but did no good.

I cannot praise what I heard of the Spanish rule and conduct generally in these islands, but details are best omitted. The United States have in the Philippine Islands a task which requires the British special ability to carry out.

In March 1899 I visited Formosa ; it is not well off for harbours. The east coast is precipitous, and the west the more approachable. The Japanese were getting the better of the mountain tribes, whose only weakness was a wish to acquire as many human heads as possible. They had souls too lofty only to care for money.

In the autumn I went to Corea, riding up from Chemulpo to Seoul, the capital, twenty-five miles of dreary road. Our Resident sent down for me a horse considered worthy of my exalted position; it took two men to hold him while I mounted, and so impressed was he with the event, that as soon as I was on his back he immediately reared up and threw himself backwards prostrate on the road—a demonstration I could easily have dispensed with. However no harm was done, and eventually he carried me up to the capital of the 'Hermit Kingdom.'

It is curious to reflect that thirty years ago Corea was as little known as Thibet was then. I never saw a race so devoid of energy, either mental or physical, as the Coreans are. My journal shows me that I then noted Japan's influence as predominant; her intentions were no doubt fixed before that date.

I had an interview with the Emperor of Corea, during which Captain A. Smith Dorrien made an excellent sketch of his Majesty which appeared in *Vanity Fair* of 19th October 1899. The Emperor I believe has never got over the shock he experienced in 1895, when some Japanese broke into the Palace and murdered his Queen. He then took refuge for a year in the Russian Legation.

Corea has great possibilities, and no wonder the Japanese wanted it. Besides its inland value, its good harbours so near Japan, especially Masampo, must attract a rising naval power.

CHAPTER XXVIII

CHINA COMMAND (continued)

H.M.S. *Bonaventure* grounding—Vladivostok—Russian Tartary —Convict Prison—Japan—The Yang-tse Rapids.

THAT autumn (1899) I took the squadron to Russian Tartary. On entering Kornilof Bay we nearly had a disaster. Our previous squadrons had several times been there, and the charts were thought good.

We were in single column line ahead, when I ordered the *Bonaventure* to quit the line and take up a berth arranged previously for some intended manœuvres. To do this she came up on my starboard beam, about two cables off. I was looking at her, when I saw her bow rise into the air a few feet, and the ship stop. Of course I knew she was on a rock. We at once anchored, and set to work to lighten the *Bonaventure* and get her off. In about three days, with very hard work and two vessels towing her astern at full speed, we got her off, and she was saved.

These accidents, however, have their bright side, as they do not only exactly call forth, but they show, the immense zeal in our service, among both the officers and the men. No excitement of action with an enemy, no hope of promotion or distinction for war service, no prospect of prize money, or other reward exists ; but the strongest emulation is there to save a ship of their squadron, and to assist her unfortunate crew. It is this sort of thing that, even in time of peace, shows that the right spirit still exists in our Navy.

We were very fortunate in two things : first, that the sea kept fairly smooth ; secondly, that she was not a very large ship, and was sheathed with wood, which both helped to protect her and facilitated patching her up. It might have been one of my battleships that grounded, and if so, from my experience of the *Howe*, I consider she would have been lost.

I finished the matter by a court martial, which showed that the only thing to blame was the rock for being there ; unless indeed it were the fault of those who surveyed the harbour, and had not discovered the above offender.

I went to Vladivostok, where the Russians received us with that friendly, half informal and warm-hearted hospitality they always show, in my experience. Admiral Dubasoff, afterwards Governor of Moscow in the troublous times, was the Commander-in-Chief.

Vladivostok, which means 'Dominion of the East,' is a splendid harbour, its almost only drawback being that it is frozen over in winter.

They showed me the ice breaker with which they keep the passage pretty clear in winter ; it was built at Copenhagen, and is about 200 feet long ; it has a very great shear, in shape like a crescent moon of seven days old on its back ; it is driven ahead by a screw in the stern ; the bow rides up on any ice it meets, and a small screw forward is then turned astern to suck the water from under the ice, and the weight of the forepart of the vessel, then helped if required by filling a water chamber in the bows, is said to be able to break through thirty-three inches of ice for a distance of a mile in an hour.

It interested me very much to consider how Vladivostok should be attacked from the sea, and I could not help thinking I saw a means. Plans, however, are easy, and practice is another thing. No doubt the Muscovite would show his tenacity of possession, as well here as at Sevastopol and Port Arthur.

The Russian regulation limiting the number of men-of-war that may be in one of their ports at the same time makes visiting a series of them rather difficult with a large squadron. I believe it originated from the entry in a thick fog of our China Squadron to Vladivostok under the command of Admiral Sir V—— H——, a fine piece of pilotage, and worthy of our Navy.

Talking of animals, I was told in conversation that wolves and dogs breed together at times, and the offspring are not ' mules,' but continue to do so ; the first cross is said to be fully as savage as a wolf, but further on they tone down. The Russians also said that wild horses, to protect themselves from the wolves, form a circle of the mares with their heads inwards towards the foals, and their heels outwards, while the stallions patrol round outside them.

I gradually worked North as far as Castries Bay, but we were not allowed to enter the Amur River.

Our chief sporting amusement was to fish— sometimes the ships' companies with the seine net —often trolling from boats, sometimes with a fly for salmon. Fish are abundant in some places.

To fish I went a few miles through a forest, and found what I had heard, viz. that the flies and midges are almost maddening ; you can hardly rest for them, and cases have occurred of their bites causing the face to swell so as nearly to obscure the sight.

I went to Saghalien Island, as I was anxious to visit the great convict prison there, at Alexand-rovski ; they showed me, I think, everything there. The island is a little larger than Scotland. There was a strong garrison of troops ; the soldiers are kept here five years, and I was greatly struck with their fine physique. Several men raised a weight of eighty pounds with one hand over the head, and some tossed it over and caught it with the other hand.

The prison contained about 1300 convicts, a great number being murderers. They fell a large number in, and let me walk along the ranks and inspect them. They looked well fed and healthy; I also saw and tasted their food. A very few spoke English, and were allowed to speak to me. They have not solitary cells, but a good many are lodged in one room. For severe insubordination in the prison, or attacks on warders, the knout is administered. It is a fearful scourge, and only a few blows with it can be made to kill. But for lesser offences being chained to a wheelbarrow is the punishment. I saw some men so situated; one they said had been so for three years, but he looked pretty jolly on it; the chains allow them to lie down. I would much rather be chained to a wheelbarrow than to a good many men I know of. Some of my readers will remember the remark of the Scotch lady when she heard her son was fastened in a chain gang : ' I pity the man who is chained to our Sandy ! '

But as regards Saghalien and its prison life : according to the convict's sentence and behaviour, it depends on when he shall be let out of prison, and be given land to live on and cultivate, and he may have a wife, and the comforts—or otherwise—of domestic life. But he may not return to Russia. However, in view of the interesting works by Mr. de Windtz, I should apologise for even the above digression.

Russian Tartary along the sea coast consists mostly of land densely covered with forest ; the climate is no doubt very severe in winter, but it is healthy. I visited ' Pallas Bay,' so called because in 1855 the Russians there burnt their frigate of that name to prevent her falling into our hands.

We next went to Yezo Island and spent some time in Hakodate harbour ; I happened to be there on the day when England's agreement, that in future the Japanese might try the offenders of our nation if living in Japan, became valid.

It seemed a parody on this (as a rather uncivilised custom) that the same day boatloads of natives, many evidently ladies, came off to see our ships, the boats being rowed by men perfectly naked ; and no one thought more of it than if they all were negroes in tropical Africa, not so much perhaps. After all custom seems everything.

The Japanese war with Russia was no sudden and unexpected accident ; looking back to my journal of 1899, I there see I was often told of the hostile feeling existing, and that 1903 was the date of preparation looked forward to, when great events might be expected.

That autumn, by kind invitation of Prince Henry of Prussia, Admiral commanding the German Squadron out here, I visited him at Kia-chow Bay, the real name of the German settlement being Tsingtau. We rode about the country near, and I was struck with the very practical way everything was planned out and pushed forward. The commercial prosperity of the port must, I think, depend on the railway communication with the interior.

In October I found time to go up the Yang-tse as far as Kweichow. At Hankow one took the local steamer to Ichang, and then embarked in H.M.S. *Woodcock* (Lieutenant and Commander Hugh Watson). She was one of a class sent out from England in boxes, and put together at Shanghai. She had a flat bottom, and only drew about eighteen inches. She could steam about twelve knots, and in passing up the rapids at that speed she sometimes was stationary, which shows what the current was. It was quite exciting work, and even more so coming down. Rocks abound, and to strike one, of course, means to be sunk.

The Chinese trade is done by light junks which are tracked up the river to Chung-king. For this work some 300,000 men are employed. At Ichang there is a large establishment called the Tracker's Guild-house, where these men lodge while awaiting a job. Having got to Chung-king, they work their way back to Ichang, partly in the returning junks, and partly carrying loads by land. Junks aıe often lost at the rapids, and many men drowned. We saw a good many wrecks scattered about.

The scenery of the Yang-tse in the gorges is magnificent ; I remember one gorge, the Ninkau, with a perpendicular cliff 700 feet high, the width of the river there being about 280 yards. In such a place the river rises 70 feet from low to high water.

CHAPTER XXIX

CHINA COMMAND (continued)

H.R.H. Prince Henry of Prussia—Siam—Borneo.

NOVEMBER 1899 saw me again at Hong-Kong, where I found H.R.H. Prince Henry of Prussia with most of his squadron. We exchanged more than civilities—very friendly hospitalities; and as he was soon to be 1elieved in his command, I took leave of him, but with real regret, and the feeling that he had a great regard for England, and a true sailorlike warmth of heart.

The China Station is so large that no Admiral can in three years visit it all, or even its important parts; but I was anxious to see what I could of the southern parts, and left in December for Siam.

We anchored outside the Menam River, on which is the capital Bangkok, where I proceeded in a gunboat. The (now late) King, Chulalonkorn, lodged me in the house of Admiral de Richelieu, a Dane, who was the head of the Siamese Navy—a not very onerous task; but its chief was a most agreeable host.

The King struck me as unusually energetic

and intelligent. In fact, I described him as a little German Emperor. He also spoke English quite well. He gave a large banquet in the Palace, at which the servants who waited were said to be gentlemen.

Siam is a very hot place; but to cool the dining-room, instead of punkahs, men stood behind the guests waving immense ornamental fans.

I never was at a place so infested with insects of all kinds as Bangkok is. We had a banquet on board the King's yacht, at which small flying things innumerable kept descending, so that all the wine-glasses were covered over, and the covers only lifted while you drank. In your bedroom you had the cheerful company of lizards of kinds, besides things aerial; but I believe they were nearly all quite harmless.

Siam is, of course, the land of elephants. In the King's stables at least one white one—so called, really grey, or dirty white; they are albinos, I believe—is kept as a kind of fetish. I rode on an elephant and found its paces, when going fast, rough beyond expectation. They are said often to live a hundred years in captivity, and it is thought much longer when wild.

The Siamese may be shortly described as rather darker than the Japanese, better looking as regards the men; but the women on the whole rather less attractive, though by no means without charm. Both sexes wear their hair short; the women would look nicer if they did not chew betel nut!

From Siam I went to Singapore. The importance

of it to us is undoubted, and efforts have been made to fortify it; but it is a very difficult place to defend.

I visited the prison, which I had done before in 1877; it was much the same, only increased in size. The Chinese form the greater part of the gaol birds. I was told that men were put in prison here for running off with other men's wives. How would that answer in England?

We got at Singapore a small black bear, which became the devoted friend of my dog 'Jim,' a pointer. They used to play together till tired, and then lie down and sleep in company. Alas! both came to untimely ends by falls in the ship in 1900.

I was anxious to see Borneo, and went first to Sarawak, where I was very kindly entertained by the Rajah, Sir Charles Brooke, at his house, situated near Kuching, the capital. I believe his kingdom is kept in very good order, to do which he had both a regiment and a prison.

This is, of course, the land of orang-outangs. I saw none alive but several stuffed; they are difficult to export, being very sensitive to change of climate. While here I saw a crocodile's egg opened, and a young one eleven inches long came out and ran about merrily.

I visited the Sultan of Brunnei, an old man, very courteous, and almost dignified. He had several curious old brass cannon, about 6- and 9-pounders, but highly ornamented with figures of men and animals.

Brunnei lies between Sarawak and British

North Borneo, which last place we acquired in 1880 from the above Sultan. It has an area of 30,000 square miles, almost the same size as Scotland, and should become very valuable. Its harbour, at the Island of Labuan, is an important position, and especially valuable on account of the coal found there ; and, being about midway up the China Sea and opposite Cochin China, it might in a war be of great strategic value.

I stayed in the Government House at Labuan, with our Resident, Mr. Keyser. It is said to be haunted by the ghost of a pirate who became a Roman Catholic priest, but again reverted to his former indiscretions. I tried at midnight to see him by visiting his haunts, but with my usual bad luck in such things, I failed.

I went to Sandakhan, which is the capital of British North Borneo, and was informed here that orang-outangs—or mias—are very human if kindly treated, and become not at all savage; that they live sometimes for forty years ; but I was told the story of one who proved his actual civilisation by drinking himself to death.

I was given what is extremely rare, viz. a ' Buntat Klapa,' which is a white stone as hard as marble ; they are found inside cocoanuts, but you would probably not find more than one in 10,000 nuts. Pearls, emeralds, &c., are quite common in comparison, as regards facility of acquisition—only a little money is wanted for them ; but you might search all London and not get a Buntat Klapa, no matter what sum you offered.

I returned to Hong-Kong *viâ* Manila, where I

z 2

found our friends the Americans busy trying to pacify the wily Philippino.

While at Hong-Kong I made a trip up the west river—or Si Kiang—in our river gunboat the *Sandpiper* (Lieutenant and Commander the Hon. Arthur Forbes Semphill). This river runs into the Canton River; it was infested with pirates, and our gunboats have been very useful in suppressing them.

In the spring as usual I went North, visiting many places, and in May found myself at Wei-hai-wei, and went to visit our Minister at Pekin. I stayed there till 18th May, and then returned to Wei-hai-wei; no one having the slightest suspielou of what was very soon to happen in North China.

China indeed is a land of surprises, and partly because there is no semblance of a universal patriotism. The north and the south have no more community of national feeling than has Germany with Spain. Railways, telegraphs, and Western education may gradually bring about the existence of a united and homogeneous China, and if so then she may become a powerful and armed nation. But I think the danger of the ' Yellow peril ' is still very far off.

CHAPTER XXX

CHINA COMMAND (continued)

The Boxer Rising—Our Preparations—Our Expedition starts—
Tiensin—Lang-fang—Desert Trains—Taku Forts—Peitsang
—Hsiku Arsenal.

THIS memoir of mine is in no way a history, and therefore as regards the Boxer Rising of 1900 I shall only attempt to say what came under my personal notice, with such other short remarks as seem necessary for coherency. The actual account of the affair has been better dealt with as history elsewhere, in various books.

I will only here remark that the Taiping rebellion was anti-dynastic, and the Boxer rising was anti-foreign, i.e. intended to turn the Western nations out of China. The Boxers were called I-ho-chiian, meaning, 'the patriotic harmony fists.' The word 'Taiping' can, I believe, be translated as 'great tranquillity.' If so, and they named themselves, perhaps they had read in Tacitus' 'Agricola,' 'Solitudinem faciunt pacem appellant'—applicable possibly to their awful destruction of human life.

My first notice of anything unusual was on the

28th May at Wei-hai-wei, when I got a telegram from Sir Claude Macdonald at Pekin, to say the Boxers were troublesome and a guard was wanted. Some Marines were at once sent in compliance.

On 31st May more serious news arrived, so I at once proceeded with some ships to the anchorage off the Taku Bar, where we were joined by other vessels of various nationalities.

Let me here remark as follows. The general history of our dealings with China has been that we have forced ourselves undesired upon them and into their country. I believe we are too apt to forget this, and not to make those allowances in consequence, that we certainly should make for our own behaviour in case any foreign nation tried to intrude themselves by force on us. But Crabbe's well-known lines beginning—

> How is it men, when they in judgment sit
> On the same faults now censure now acquit

apply to nations as much as to men. I might easily enlarge on this subject by dilating on the religious question, on the opium trade, on the war of 1840, and on events both before and after that ; but that is not my theme.

Arrived off the Taku Bar, affairs soon got more serious, but it was quite easy for me to see what to do. Fortunately for me I was the senior of all the admirals on the station, so it was my place to initiate proceedings.

Men-of-war of the following nations were present—Russian, French, German, and United States with admirals in command ; and Austrian,

Italian and Japanese with captains. I at once invited these officers to consultations on board my flagship, in order that we might all act in harmony if possible. We agreed that, if required, an allied Naval Brigade should be landed, and advance on Pekin.

This brigade, I felt, I was the proper person to command, and I telegraphed to the Admiralty certain proposals regarding it, for the Foreign Office to consider, and, if approved, to act on. I might add that I was, of course, anxious that my own officers and men should not be under foreign command, which my going would avoid.

However, time was not given us for any reply, when on 9th June Captain Jellicoe,[1] my Flag-captain whom I had sent to Tiensin for information, returned about 11 P.M. with a message from Sir Claude Macdonald to say that unless help was immediate it would be too late. This was, of course, enough ground for me to act on.

Our arrangements for landing if required had been made, so we were ready, and at 1 A.M. on the 10th we were off. I went in the *Fame*, a destroyer commanded by Lieutenant Roger Keyes,[2] who managed very well, though in a dark night and with a falling tide, to get us to the landing place at Tonghu, where we got a train and left for Tiensin.

Of course I had to act without any home authority, but in such cases, whether success or

---

[1] Now Vice-Admiral Sir John Jellicoe, K.C.V.O., C.B.
[2] Now Captain.

failure attends you, England nearly always approves an officer who has evidently done his best. I never could understand why anyone minds taking responsibility. You have only to do what seems proper, and if it turns out badly it is the fault of Nature for not having made you cleverer.

I, of course, informed my foreign colleagues of my start, and their various contingents followed as soon as possible. I may here with pleasure truly remark that throughout the operations in China in 1900 I always met with the most kind co-operation and help from all the naval foreign officers I had to deal with, with perhaps one exception, which did no harm, and is best not described. Also that the foreign officers under my command invariably acted in perfect harmony with me.

This may be accounted for as follows : First, I was the senior naval officer on the station, and a head was necessary ; secondly, we had all one common object ; thirdly, that we were all sailors, among whom a certain sort of freemasonry, or brotherhood, always exists.

At Tiensin we had some trouble in getting trains to go on towards Pekin, but no excuses were listened to, and we were prepared to use force if necessary to get them. In a couple of hours we were off on the Pekin line.

At Yang-tsun, about fifteen miles above Tiensin, is the railway bridge over the Peiho River ; here we found General Nich's troops, some 4000 strong, but we exchanged friendly greetings, crossed the river, and went on till that afternoon, when we had to stop and repair the line which the Boxers had torn up.

Next day we were joined by other trains, making our force up to about 1866 all told of eight nationalities, which I give in the order of their numbers : British, 915 (double any other), German next, then Russian, French, United States, Japanese, Italian, and Austrian. My own staff was: Flag-captain, Captain J. R. Jellicoe ; Secretary, F. C. Alton; Flag-lieutenant, F. A. Powlett; and Lieutenant G. M. K. Fair, R.N., as Intelligence Officer, and Midshipman E. O. B. S. Osborne as A.D.C.

At Tiensin my staff was joined by Captain Clive Bigham (late Grenadier Guards), and by Mr. C. W. Campbell, of the Chinese Service ; the latter was most useful as a Chinese interpreter, and the former from a knowledge of more than one foreign tongue.

From now onwards till further progress became impossible owing to the destruction of the railway, we were constantly repairing torn-up rails and broken bridges ; but a difficulty not less than these was to get water for the engines, the Boxers having destroyed the station water supplies.

Our first encounter with the Boxers was on 11th June, just below Lang-fang station, where they attacked us, and came on with decided courage, losing some thirty-five men killed. It was said—I believe with truth—that these fanatics had been persuaded that they were invulnerable, and, after some had been killed, it was added that they would in a few days revive.

Lang-fang station was the farthest we could get the trains to, the line above it being very badly destroyed. It is about forty miles above Tiensin and half-way to Pekin.

A party of Marines under Major J. R. Johnstone, R.M.L.I.,[1] reconnoitred on nearly to the next station, Anping, but the line was too badly damaged for us to repair it. We were now isolated, with no transport or means to advance, and cut off from our base behind.

For this position I make no apology, for in view of the Pekin message mentioned on p. 343 an immediate dash to save the Legations was the only course to pursue. For five days we held on to Lang-fang station, unwilling to move backwards, and in hopes of better pros-peets ; and desultory fighting with the Boxers went on.

On the 16th it became evident we could not approach nearer to Pekin, and that therefore our stay here was both useless and impracticable, and that our only course was to return to Tiensin and then act according to circumstances—a possible advance by the river, in view of the railway's destruction, being in my mind.

By great exertions we were able to repair the line so as to move the trains back nearly to the bridge across the river at Yang-tsun, but we then found the bridge there so damaged that it was impossible to cross it. But it was important

---

[1] Now Major-General and C.B.

to have got so near to the river, because we were then able to seize some Chinese junks and in them get transport for our wounded men, and our provisions, our field-guns, and ammunition.

The forced desertion of the trains was sad, and we had to leave much private property behind us ; in fact, to go on with only our arms and what we could carry, besides the junks for the above purposes.

The Taku forts were taken on the 17th, about which various opinions have been held. First, as to the propriety of taking the forts ; and, secondly, as to the effect so doing had on the Chinese authorities and their subsequent conduct.

One view (*pro*) is that as things appeared to be, with fighting already going on up country, it was a grave error to leave such forts in the hands of the enemy in our rear, and to cut off our inland communications with the Fleet and the sea. The other view (*con*) was that we were only at war with the Boxers, a sort of rebels, but that we were friends with the Chinese Government and authorities who held the forts, and so that we had no business to attack them.

The question was of necessity settled by the conclave of Admirals off the Peiho in my absence, so I had nothing to do with it. The Chinese said afterwards that had we left the forts in their hands they would not have countenanced the Boxers as they did. Of course our attacking the forts, held as they were by the Government's troops, was nothing more or less than an act of war against China. All the national representatives

347

in fact did not consent to it, but there was a sufficient majority.

My own unbiased opinion is that under the peculiar circumstances we were right to act as we did and to take the Taku forts. It is a curious fact that my flag was flying on that occasion on board the *Algerine* (Commander R. H. Stewart)—a unique instance perhaps of an Admiral's flag flying in action, he not being present.

This was the second occasion of the Admiral's flag of one of my family flying at the capture of the Taku forts (see Chapter VIII). I may also remark that I have gone three times to China, and that each time we went to war, and took the above forts.

General Nieh's troops had now become hostile to us. On the 18th we abandoned the trains, and escorting the junks, started towards Tiensin, on the left bank of the river. The weather was very hot, but it was curious how few succumbed to it; I suppose because it was a dry heat. It caused much thirst, to quench which the very uninviting river had often to be resorted to. No doubt to campaign in a moderate temperature is the pleasantest ; but if it must be extreme either way, by all means give me heat rather than cold, especially for rest at night.

We could already hear the firing of heavy guns in the direction of Tiensin, which hastened our efforts. The distance by river was about thirty miles, but owing to the shallow water the junks often grounded and delayed us. We also came to numerous villages held by Boxers, who caused much delay while our guns were brought into action, and the places attacked and taken.

All this time on our flank were Chinese troops with light guns, from which they frequently fired on us. Our provisions were reduced to something like half rations, but it is astonishing how little food you can do with for a short time.

On the 20th I see noted in my journal : ' Fighting nearly all day, and only made about eight miles' progress.' I sometimes noticed that on attacking a place, the fire seemed to get heavier when we got close to, but the bullets much fewer ; and the explanation was that at the last, if retreat was decided on, the Chinese set light to a large quantity of crackers that made a great noise and emitted much smoke.

On the 21st we had, perhaps, our hardest fight, at Peitsang, a large town, which after some hours we took. Here my Flag-captain (Jellicoe) was very seriously wounded, after which I requested Captain von Usedom, of the German Imperial Navy, to act as my Chief of the Staff ; and authorised him if I were killed to command the expedition. His services to me were most valuable, and as loyal as if he had been in our Navy, showing the unanimity with which our mixed nationalities' force acted.

A curious episode occurred that day. We had got one or two more junks to hold the wounded, and I sent some men on board to examine and prepare them ; no sooner had they reached the decks than, as if in a pantomime, the closed hatches flew open, and out popped some women and children and leaped over the side into the river, preferring drowning to falling into the hands of the 'foreign devils.' Some of my people jumped after them to save them, my Flag-lieutenant for one. Though it was warm weather it was not pleasant for those who did so to get their only suit of clothes wet ; no one having two suits.

On another occasion we had just taken a village, when a Chinese woman threw herself into a well to escape. It was covered with a large stone slab, and the hole was so small it barely admitted a human being. The Germans saw this happen, and managed cleverly to move the stone and fish the woman out alive ; then coming to ask me what to do with her. She was young and good looking, but, of course, dripping wet and nearly dead with fright ; but she had preferred death to captivity.

That night was rather a trying one. We were all tired and hungry. The sound of firing towards Tiensin and occasional shells falling near us were adverse to sleep, but mattered less as we had not time for it.

I decided that as soon as we could get the freshly wounded ready in the above junks we had fortunately found, we must push on in the night. Of course our position was an anxious one ; it appeared quite possible we might be surrounded and a disaster occur ; the Chinese never give quarter, and any of our officers or men who fell into their hands were at once killed. It often occurred to me what a very curious scene such an international holocaust would be. But I never regretted our coming on the expedition, and should not have regretted it whatever occurred, as I considered it was the proper and only thing to do. The wounded men were our chief anxiety.

On the 22nd we started at 1.15 A.M., and before daylight carried the first village that resisted us, by a charge of our Marines. About this time a junk with some of our guns in was sunk, but happily no wounded men were in her.

About daylight to our surprise we found ourselves abreast of a fortified position on the right (or opposite) bank of the river. Out of this came a few soldiers in uniform. They hailed us to ask who we were, &c., and we answered ' A friendly force on our way to Tiensin.' I thought at first they would let us pass, but instead of that almost at once a heavy volley of small arms was opened on us from their ramparts, showing that they had been on the look out and known of our approach.

I should here say that the reason we were surprised was that the existence of Hsiku arsenal, which this proved to be, was before unknown to us ; and further I may add that though, of course, not so intended by the Chinese, their firing on us probably saved our combined force, because it led to our taking the arsenal, and sheltering in it, which without this hostile act on their part I could not have done ; and had we continued on towards Tiensin with our junks of wounded, through the narrow and intricate watercourse just above Tiensin, and with forts on both sides of it, we should almost certainly have met with a complete disaster.

It was at once evident we must take the arsenal. To do this I sent our Marines under Major Johnstone, R.M.L.I., to cross the river higher up and attack Hsiku at its north-east side, while the Germans did so at the south-west part, and so it was taken. We found it a complete enclosed work, rectangular in shape, and about 700 yards long on the river side, and its area some 30 to 40 acres. Inside were several edifices, a temple, barracks and other buildings, but most important of all a large stone arsenal containing a great quantity of field-guns, rifles, ammunition for the above, and other warlike stores.

Some of us found arms and ammunition like our own here. In fact it was an arsenal of great importance. There was also a very large store of rice. I decided at once to rest here at least for a day, everyone being nearly worn out for want of sleep and food.

We were almost immediately attacked by General Nieh's troops in great force, who tried to recapture the place, but were repulsed. In this affair the Commander of the German cruiser *Hertha*, a very fine officer, was killed.

Early next morning we were again attacked by a large force, some of whom had actually got over the walls in the darkness. Again we repulsed them, but with loss to ourselves—among others Captain Beyts, R.M.A., of the *Centurion*, being killed.

It was now plain that the forces between us and Tiensin made it impossible to make our way there; especially with our large number of wounded. Our force was distributed as seemed best, the French under Capitaine de Vaisseau Marolles occupying the arsenal itself at the south-east part of the enclosure. The constant firing in that direction was, however, a sort of comfort, as showing that the European settlements still held out, and our immediate objects were to fortify our position and communicate with our friends in the settlement.

This last was accomplished on the 24th by Captain Bigham's Chinese servant, who took a cypher message from me, which, however, being searched, he had to eat; but he got to the Consulate and told where we were.

On 24th we had a very bad dust storm; you could only bear to look to leeward, and then could see but a few yards, and had we been attacked from windward, the enemy would have had a very great advantage.

As soon as our position was known in the Tiensin settlement, a force to relieve us and help us to reach that place was arranged. It consisted mostly of Russian troops, lately arrived from Port Arthur, and commanded by Colonel Sherinsky, with some of our own and other nationalities. Early on the 25th they appeared in sight, and soon closed us on the other side of the river.

The Colonel said he was told to return as soon as possible, and I agreed to start early next morning; but would not move that day as it took long to prepare the wounded and get them across the river ; and also because I must have the contents of this important arsenal destroyed, to prevent their falling into the enemy's hands.

Our relief was especially welcome because, though we could defend ourselves and had plenty of ammunition, food was very scarce, and hunger was becoming a very serious question.

During the night we crossed the river and at 3 A.M. started on a circuitous route to the settlement, which we reached in about six hours.

The arsenal had been prepared for destruction by the French, and I entrusted to Lieutenant E. G. Lowther Crofton, R.N., of the *Centurion*, the duty of actually firing it.   The explosions and conflagration lasted more than one day, and the loss to the Chinese was very great.

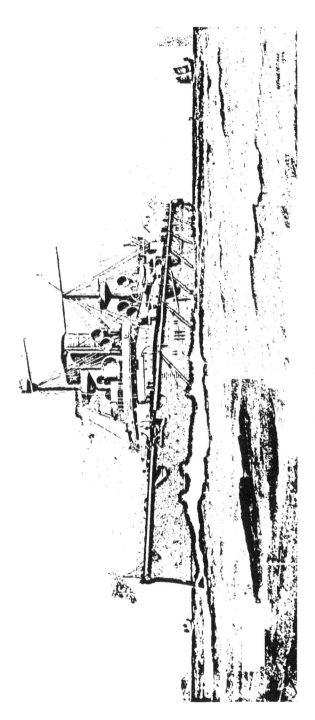

H.M.S.   CENTURION
My Flagship in China
1898–1901

CHAPTER XXXI

CHINA COMMAND (continued)

Defence of the Tiensin Settlements—Capture of the Chinese Arsenals—General Fukusima.

I FOUND the European settlements in a complete state of siege ; they are all on the right bank of the Peiho, and situated just below the Chinese walled city of Tiensin ; from which a rather desultory fire both from guns and small-arms was constantly kept up. No place was safe ; many houses were pierced both by shell and rifle bullets, and it was never known from what quarter an attack might come.

Since we left, sixteen days before, much fighting had taken place ; many troops had arrived, the most numerous being the Russians under General Stössel (afterwards the defender of Port Arthur), and of ours the 2nd Battalion of the 23rd Welsh Fusiliers, from Hong-Kong, under Colonel the Hon. Reginald Bertie,[1] and the 1st Chinese Regiment from Wei-hai-wei—both under the command of Brigadier-General Dorward[2] ; also some Japanese troops under General Fukusima, with whom I have become most friendly. The Russians were

[1] Now C.B.
[2] Now Maj.-Gen. Sir Arthur Dorward, K.C.B.

2 A 2

encamped in the country across the river, and Vice-Admiral Alexeieff, the Russian Viceroy of the East, had arrived at their camp.

It was a nice question whether he or I should pay the first visit, he being junior to me as an Admiral, but, of course, of higher rank as Viceroy. However, he called first and our relations were always very pleasant. He was a dignified man, with pleasant manners.

I have already mentioned my German and French colleagues in our expedition, but I must also refer to Captain McCalla of the United States Navy, whose energy, and devoted efforts to help me, nothing could excel. He was wounded more than once, but managed to lead his men till we got back, and he remained my valued friend till his lamented death.

The Russians were commanded by Captain Shaguin, who has deservedly risen in his profession, and is now a Rear-Admiral, and lately commanded his Emperor's yacht.

I hired a house in the English quarter for myself and my staff, and in concert with the three Generals mentioned above conducted the operations.

On our return to Tiensin we all much wanted clothes. I got a suit made by a Chinese tailor, who then said, ' Maskee me catche dollar pigeon more better my makee whilo chop chop,' to which I replied that he must stop and make clothes for others as fast as possible. I fancy there are in London at times people who would not object if their tailor preferred bolting to having their bill paid !

Captain E. H. Bayly, of the *Aurora*, was senior naval officer at Tiensin till I arrived, and had been most active and efficient.

The position was now rather a peculiar one; such a mixed force of nationalities, both naval and military, and such a variety of commanders, with no one authorised head, perhaps never were associated before on active service, but it worked very well. Though it was hard to say who had the chief command, I was the senior in rank and was often referred to, but a sailor is not supposed to command soldiers on shore.

Nearly in the middle of the settlement was the Town Hall, from the tower of which one got a fine view all round. It also made a good mark for the enemy's guns, but though shell often flew by when we were up there, it suffered but little. Several horses were at times grazing in a paddock, into which the shell after passing this tower sometimes fell, and I used to look to see what happened, and was surprised to observe how little the horses noticed the shell, unless of course they were hit. The lower part of the Town Hall was used as the general hospital. Outside Tiensin were two arsenals, one to the north-east and one to the west, close to the city walls. The north-east one was taken on 27th June by a mixed force of Russians and British.

By this time we had further Naval Brigade men up from the Fleet ; many from the *Barfleur* and other ships, Captain J. H. T. Burke, of the *Orlando*, being in command of the Brigade. The *Terrible*, lately arrived from South Africa, also supplied some gun mountings as designed by Captain Percy Scott, and on such carriages as Captain Hedworth Lambton had taken to the defence of Ladysmith.

Among our garrison was the 'First Chinese Regiment,' whose behaviour did full justice to its officers. It was raised at Wei-hai-wei for the defence of that place, and was commanded by Colonel Hamilton Bower, and officers from various regiments of our Army. I had watched its growth with great interest, and now it proved its success on active service. Major Bruce of this regiment was dangerously wounded in the settlements, but happily recovered.

The regiment became 1200 strong, consisting of Chinamen of very good physique and behaviour; but the ways of the British Government are 'inscrutable,' and after finding that the regiment was really efficient they disbanded it.

On the 28th, while writing in my house, a bullet came in and hit me fairly hard. Luckily for me it was spent or from the direction I should have been killed. Perhaps scientifically speaking I was wrong, but after that I felt quite safe in the same place, and believe many others would do so too, on the doctrine of chances; no second bullet being likely to take the same course.[1]

One of our anxieties was that Yuan-shi-kai, the Governor of Shantung, had a well-drilled and armed force, supposed to be 4000 strong. If these also came against us our position would at least

[1] Some of my readers may here be reminded of the midshipman in *Peter Simple*, and the calculation by Professor Inman.

be desperate, and any day it might occur. There is no doubt we have to thank the Viceroys of Shantung and Nankin that our task in China in 1900 was not a much heavier one.

I was anxious to get all the women and children away, both for their immediate safety, and also not knowing what might happen, and I took every opportunity to send them down the river and lodge them on board our ships. Our excellent Consul was Mr. W. R. Carles, who had a wife and some children; these last I got away one morning, and that very afternoon a shell came in and burst in their nursery.

Lieutenant P. N. Wright of the *Orlando* was dangerously wounded by a shell bursting close to him. I telegraphed to the Admiralty to ask them to promote him at once, which they did, and I had the pleasure of telling him he was a commander. Unhappily he did not recover ; but his promotion was some satisfaction to his widow.

The railway station was, I think, quite the worst position. The rolling stock in it was all destroyed and the walls that still stood were like sieves, for the holes in them. Those ordered to hold it mildly remonstrated, and I remember telling the Russians and Japanese to relieve each other—a rather curious thing looking back from a few years later ! Sometimes I had an assortment of field-guns out, and a small artillery duel with the guns on the city walls, where a pagoda, till we destroyed it, was an interesting mark.

On 8th July we were much pleased at getting a complimentary telegram from 130 members of the Royal Navy Club at their annual dinner in London to the First Lord of the Admiralty. Sailors appreciate the good opinion of their brother sailors ! It is sincere.

On the 9th we took the west arsenal called Hi-kuan-su, mentioned on p. 357. To do this a mixed force including Russians, all really commanded by the Japanese General Fukusima, started before daylight, and first made a détour to the south end. I went with them. Our seamen were under Commander Beatty [1] of the *Barfleur*, who, though wounded only a few days before, insisted on keeping to his duty.

When approaching the arsenal we had to descend a steep bank of some ten feet. I was with General Fukusima and said to him : 'Go first and I will ease you down '—with a staff I had ; he did so and I followed, and while so doing heard a noise just behind me and looking round was told by Major Aoki, the General's A.D.C. : 'It is lucky you went quickly as a shrapnel shell [coming across us from our left] just passed between you and me' ; which it did, and then burst, wounding for one Lieutenant G. Fair of my staff.

If we could have held this position, it would have helped to keep down the fire from the city on the settlements. I had hoped to be able to do so, but when I saw its condition, and how it was commanded from the walls, I felt I could not order men to remain in it.

On the 12th I felt I must return to my squadron.

[1] Now Rear-Admiral David Beatty, M.V.O., D.S.O., the youngest Flag-officer for 130 years.

There were now three general officers at Tiensin, and the matter had become mostly a military one, while my duty was of course afloat. During my absence of over a month my place had been most ably filled by my colleague, Rear-Admiral Bruce.[1]

I did not like to leave the province of Chili, in which Pekin and the Peiho River are, but I was very anxious about what might happen at Shanghai, and in the Yang-tse region ; and a telegram from the Admiralty, taking the same view as I did of the possibility of an outbreak down there, decided me on going at once to Shanghai.

There should no doubt have been a clasp given for Tiensin, including the defence of the settlements and capture of the city. When the long duration of the fighting, the large number of casualties, and the importance of the episode in North China are considered, no one, I think, will dispute this, especially when it is compared with what some clasps were given for in another continent at about the same time. I did my utmost to get the clasp for my officers and men ; why it was not given I know, but the poor reasons I do not feel at liberty to mention.

The saying ' Surgit amari aliquid ' is very true, and so is its converse, and I could relate several little international incidents during the above period which were very amusing, and might even be of interest ; but although not at all to the detriment of our gallant and friendly allies, they

---

[1] Now Admiral Sir James Bruce, K.C.M.G.

are perhaps best omitted lest their mention be misunderstood.   Who was it said—

> He surely must be good for nought
> Who is not humorous prone ;
> Who has not got a merry thought
> Can't have a funny bone—?

But I may express my thanks to my foreign brother officers who so kindly advised and supported me, especially to Vice-Admiral Bendemann of the Imperial German Navy, and to Rear-Admiral Courejolles of the French, and Rear-Admiral Kempff of the United States, Navies ; I can only hope that their memories of me are as agreeable as are mine of them.

CHAPTER XXXII

Shanghai — The Yang-tse—Pekin relieved — Shan-hai-quan — Chen-wang-tao—The Pier.

ON my way south, I looked into Wei-hai-wei, and found it full of people, hospitals, and work, the immediate base in fact of our operations.

At Shanghai I found things quiet, but people very apprehensive of what might happen, and meetings took place to arrange for its defence in case of attack.

I went up to Nankin to see the Viceroy Lu-kung-yi. There we had to drive about seven miles through roads and streets mostly lined with Chinese soldiers. This is a curious illustration of what China is like : we had just been fighting with Imperial troops—as well as with Boxers— and the fighting was still going on at Pekin ; yet here we were entirely in the power of troops of the same nation. But I felt it right whatever occurred to visit the Viceroy.

Between Woosung and Nankin lay a squadron of Chinese ships of war, with whom we exchanged friendly salutes as if their Empress and her Government were not at war with us and attacking

363

the Legations, but China is at present an exception to all ordinary rules—and unanimity of action in its different provinces does not yet exist.

Our Consul at Nankin, Mr. Sundins, was in an isolated and anxious position, and any moment disturbances might have broken out and his life been in danger. I offered to send one or two naval officers to keep him company, but he declined.

It is a proof of the great power these Chinese 'Satraps' wield, that peace was preserved in this region though affairs were much strained. We had to be prepared for any eventuality. I had pilots subsidised and all things ready to force our passage up the Yang-tse if required,[1] and to attack the Kiang-yin forts. In that case I had a most able colleague in General O'Moore Creagh,[2] V.C., commanding the troops at Shanghai ; and I think he will forgive me if I say he would not have blamed the Viceroy if he had quite failed to prevent an outbreak of hostilities.

The Viceroy, who I have already mentioned in Chapter XXVII, received me as before, and our interview was both pleasant, friendly and satisfactory.

In August we heard of the death of the King of Italy, and a full-dress funeral service was performed at the Roman Catholic Cathedral with great state.

With the military expedition to Pekin that relieved the Legations I had nothing to do except

---

[1] If killed in action the pilot's widow was to be pensioned like the widows of naval lieutenants.

[2] Now G.C.B. and Commander-in-Chief in India.

to arrange our Naval Brigade under the command of Captain G. A. Callaghan[1] of H.M.S. *Endymion*. The expedition, as is known, succeeded in its object on 14th August.

The ' Forbidden city ' was then for the first time entered by foreigners. The details are matters of history. Pekin was mercilessly looted, which with eight different nationalities was perhaps inevitable. ' Inter armas silent leges,' and looting is the legalised robbery of war; very few souls are noble enough to resist the temptation. I should think the booty taken at Pekin in 1900 was as valuable as any so got in the lifetimes of the present generation.

I remained at or near Shanghai till the middle of September, when I felt it time again to go north. I found Wei-hai-wei amply showing its great value to us as a base of operations, as a naval station, a military depôt, a general hospital, and a sanatorium. We shall be foolish if we give it up voluntarily.

Off Taku Bar I found ten Admirals, with ships-of-war in proportion.

Soon after the German Field-Marshal, Count Waldersee, arrived, having been sent by the German Emperor with the accord of some of the other nations concerned, to take the place at Pekin of the senior international military officer. I, of course, called on the Field-Marshal, and I found him a courteous gentleman full of vigour, both of mind and body, and seeming young for his age, which I believe was sixty-seven. His

---

[1] Now Vice-Admiral Sir George Callaghan, K.C.B., K.C.V.O.

position in China was a difficult one, as all present were not prepared to accept him as their chief. I could say a good deal on this question, but had better only again remark that I am not writing history.

It now, however, became my duty again to have conferences of the allied Admirals, and arrange for an expedition to Chen-wang-tao and Shan-hai-quan. The latter place is where the great wall of China runs down to the sea, and though it is not exactly the line between China and Manchuria, which begins a few miles farther north, it is so virtually ; and at Shan-hai-quan are many forts, and the question of how to deal with them had to be considered. It was thought we should have to bombard and take them, and the part each nation should take in this had to be arranged.

But at the last moment before we were going to start with the above object, our gunboat, the *Pigmy*, arrived early one morning to say the forts had surrendered to her. It was truly a case of *du sublime au ridicule,* and the gunboat's name was very appropriate.

I pass over details, but the end was that we all proceeded up there, and I then had to visit all the forts with my brother Admirals, and arrange how they should be shared out and garrisoned.

The Commander of the *Pigmy*, Lieutenant J. Green, carried out a difficult position extremely well. A comic paper at Shanghai—a sort of *Punch*—hit the situation off so ably with a cartoon, that I sent it to the Admiralty, and think it helped to the officer's promotion !

Our Russian friends, with that liberal desire for the occupation and civilisation of the Far East of Asia for which they are justly renowned, had contemplated saving their allies the trouble of occupying the Shan-hai-quan forts by doing so themselves. Unfortunately for the Russians this did not at all suit me or my other colleagues, and their troops arrived too late.

The circumstances of the occupation of Shan-hai-quan were a little complicated, though relieved by several touches of humour ; but I will confine myself to saying that we agreed that the principal coast fort should be common property, and that all our national flags should fly on it. Their order of precedence was difficult to decide. I might have made it according to the Admirals' seniorities, but thought it best to go in alphabetical order of the nations' names, using French as the language of diplomacy. The other forts were divided among the various nationalities for occupation during the coming winter.

As senior national officer present, much devolved on me, and to me were addressed the complaints of the Chinese as to what had occurred in the city of Shan-hai-quan. I shall mention no names, but only remark we are yet very far from the ideal of what civilisation even in war time should be.

It being our intention to occupy these forts, as mentioned above, and as the ice in winter made communication with the shore in the Gulfs of Pechili and Liau-tong very difficult, we had to seriously consider how best to solve this problem. My brother Admirals did so by agreeing to leave it all to me ; in this, of course, they showed their sense, as they avoided both the trouble and responsibility.

Having then found out all I could about the matter, I decided that the best way was to build a pier at a place called Chen-wang-tao, a few miles south of Shan-hai-quan, and comparatively very free from ice in winter. There were many difficulties, but a contractor was got and the work began. Paying for the pier had to be arranged among the nations ; we tried to divide it according to the numbers of the garrisons ; but in this my first experience of financial assessments, I found it not easy to give general satisfaction ! I fancy it often is not.

That winter the ice formed to thirteen miles off the land at Shan-hai-quan. The Peiho River, which is frozen on an average for seventy days every winter, is only one degree south of the Tagus.

I then visited Tiensin, and found peace and some order again prevailing, with a strong garrison of troops. The German Field-Marshal, with his headquarters, was there for the present. There was much to settle with our foreign allies, but after a few busy days I returned to my naval duties.

CHAPTER XXXIII

CHINA COMMAND (continued)

The Yang-tse—Death of H.M. Queen Victoria—Hong-Kong—
Tiensin—Pekin—The Forbidden City—Newchwang—Nankin—Wei-hai-wei—Relieved in Command—Arrive Home.

I WENT to Shanghai and the Yang-tse, and again
visited my friend the Viceroy of Nankin, and
then went on to Hankow to call on Chang-Chi-
Tung, the Viceroy of the Hukuang. I have
mentioned him before in Chapter XXVII. This
was my third visit to him. He was then about
sixty-five years old, but looked much more. The
Chinese often ask you how old you are, and when
told, it is considered polite for them to say,
' Dear me, I should have thought you were much
older,' meaning because you look so worthy of
the greatest respect.

The Chinese Viceroys occupy positions unknown as subjects in Europe, and any foreign
officer in a prominent position should visit and
treat them accordingly.

I had to leave the *Alacrity* at Kiukiang, fifty
miles below Hankow, and go up in a destroyer,
for want of water. On our return we had to go
full speed, and I fear our wave did much harm

369   2 B

to many Chinese small craft, but no time could be spared.

The birthday of the Dowager Empress of China was on 1st December ; I happened then to be in company with a Chinese squadron in the Yang-tse, and we saluted and did honour to the old lady as if she had been still reigning at Pekin instead of a refugee in hiding.

I felt it right to stay at Shanghai till February in view of possible occurrences. So I was there when the melancholy news reached us of the death of our great Queen Victoria. We heard it on 24th January, our time being eight hours in advance of England. Her reign was the longest of any English Sovereign.

On the 27th was the birthday of the German Emperor, and all men-of-war present dressed with flags to honour it ; except my flagship, which remained with the Royal Standard at half-mast.

On 2nd February we had a memorial service at the English Cathedral here to do honour to the interment of our late Queen. Besides our own, about seventy foreign officers, naval and military, attended, all, of course, in full dress. With the bands, and with the Indian pipers from Indian regiments here, the ceremony was very impressive. In the afternoon we fired eighty-one minute guns, for the age of our late Sovereign, and so timed as to end at sunset.

While at Shanghai I got a telegram from the Admiralty, asking me to remain out six months longer than my proper time ; this I felt to be a great compliment, but I had anyhow no hesitation in accepting it, as besides my love of sea service. I took the greatest interest in the China Station.

. H.M.S. *Glory* about now arrived from England, a new class of battleship quite superior to the *Centurion* in size and power. The Admiralty offered me to change to her as my flagship, and perhaps, had I expected soon to be in a ship action, I would have done so ; but one is loath to leave one's old ship and shipmates.

In February I went down to Hong-Kong, a place one was always glad to be at in the winter. It is just cold enough to enjoy a fire and feel it is not summer. The walks about the island are beautiful, and as a winter climate there is no place in Europe I like so much.

In April I was again at Shanghai; this place is like no other I know of, being a thoroughly cosmopolitan trading settlement. The chief nations have their own quarters, presided over by their Consuls, or elected committees, and society therefore has the charm of being very varied, and by no means narrow-minded. It is hardly a port at all, as only moderate-sized vessels can get up to it, and the anchorage off the mouth of its river is a poor one; however, its position is central for China, and it does, and will, flourish.

I paid a last visit to Tiensin and Pekin; the wreck of our railway trains just above Yang-tsu was a most melancholy sight. The railway stations were still all garrisoned for protection.

On this occasion I saw the wreck of a train, caused by a sand storm. The sand was so hard that the engine left the rails, unfortunately just as it approached a bridge, over which it fell, and remained with its wheels in the air. Strange to say the driver and stoker were saved by the cab, and not badly hurt, though others in the train were killed. This accident occurred near Lofa station, and by one of the bridges that we had repaired. The North China sand - storms are really bad simoons, as I have mentioned before.

At Pekin I was received in the most kind and complimentary way at the station by our Minister, our General, and others; and I was now able to visit and see what before 1900 was jealously secluded; but other pens than mine have well described it all, so I must refrain.

It was most interesting to have the siege of the Legations exactly explained on the site by actors in that drama. Their defence was most creditable, and it will always be a curious question why they were not destroyed. Probably it was owing to vacillating counsels, and disunions.

Riding out to the new Summer Palace, about nine miles to the north-west of Pekin, I passed the ruins of the old one destroyed by us and the French in 1860, and since then quite neglected and left as it was.

The 'Forbidden City,' i.e. the Emperor's palace and demesne inside Pekin, is a striking instance of how the Chinese, when a building has been completed, even with great care and expense, neglect its upkeep: spacious halls with ill-kept walls and ceilings, and flights of marble steps with weeds on them, are not uncommon sights.

Perhaps the most interesting spot in the vicinity of the 'Forbidden City' is the Peitang (or North Church) where the Roman Catholic Christians were besieged at the same time as the Legations. The marks of shot on it were innumerable, and five hundred people are said to have been killed or died in its defence; one mine exploded near it is said to have killed a hundred. When the relief of the Legations took place I believe the Japanese first reached the Peitang.

But I must not let myself enlarge on these too interesting subjects. I left Pekin with regret, paid a farewell visit to Tiensin, and went to see our pier at Ching-wan-tao—mentioned above.

I afterwards visited General Reid, in command of our troops, occupying with our allies the Shan-hai-quan forts. He had spent the winter here, and seen much of the special characteristics of our international co-operators, which he detailed with Caledonian humour—and some severe strictures.

Such a combination of several nations' garrisons in close quarters during a severe winter perhaps has never occurred.

I could not resist again going to Newchwang, the great port for the export of beans and bean cake from Manchuria; 136,363 tons of the above are said to have gone from here in a year, of a value of three million pounds sterling. The freedom of this place from other than Chinese control had often exercised my mind.

I had another visit to pay to Shanghai and the

Yang-tse River, and calling at Wei-hai-wei heard I had become an 'Admiral'—or as called in contradistinction to the lower flag ranks, a Full Admiral. I went first to Hankow to see again Chang-Chi-Tung, the Viceroy of Hukuang. Here also I found the Austrian Admiral Count Monticucolli in his flagship; my relations with him had always been most agreeable, and he possessed a sense of humour at times quite refreshing.

My last Chinese visit was to my friend Lu-Kung-yi, the Viceroy of the Liang Kiang at Nankin. I was sorry to take leave of him, and regret that death has since deprived his country of his services.

The Taotai of Nankin brought his children to see me; one, a little girl about ten, was most intelligent, and being brought up as a young blue stocking was learning several of the awful Chinese ideographic characters a day, and now knew two thousand of them. But what a waste of time learning such an alphabet seems to be.

I then paid my last visit to Shanghai, where I was entertained as the guest at a large dinner by the Shanghai branch of the China Association. No naval officer who has served much in China can fail to take great interest in our commerce there, or to realise how greatly our mercantile community there appreciate any efforts of the Navy to protect and assist them.

Once more I went to Wei-hai-wei, and while there the 1st Chinese Regiment, of which I have before spoken, was paraded before me, about 1200 strong; a fine and well-drilled body of men, showing what can be done with the Chinese by British officers, who I believe are superior to all other nations in dealing with natives other than European.

My Captains gave me a farewell dinner on 21st June which I very much appreciated. Sailors are honest and straightforward.

On 25th June H.M.S. *Glory* arrived with my friend Vice-Admiral Sir Cyprian Bridge, who next day relieved me in command of the China Station.

On the 26th I left in the *Centurion* really sorry to vacate my command. We called at Hong-Kong, where the Governor, Sir Henry Blake, and the China Association, respectively, gave me farewell banquets, and on 3rd July I sailed for England.

In 1858, at just the same season of the year, when in the *Pique* [1] (as before related) we were fifty days on our passage from Hong-Kong to Singapore ; in the *Centurion* we were now only five days, or one-tenth of the time.

After Singapore we coaled at Pulo Weh, a small Dutch island off the north end of Sumatra, with a good harbour ; it may become a very important strategic position to some nation—which ?

We called at Colombo and again filled up coal, having to contend with the full force of the south-west monsoon, which as you approach Africa is very strong with a heavy head sea.

At Mount Lavinia, near Colombo, I visited our Boer prisoners of war, and talked to many who

---

[1] See page 70.

spoke English ; mostly they said they still expected to win in South Africa.

We coaled at Perim, which nature has surely put there for the purpose, and for England ; the story of our taking possession of it is too well known to repeat.

Going on to Suez we found the absurdity of the bogey quarantine awaiting us, in the news that because the plague existed in China—though we had not had a case—we must hoist TWO yellow flags, and not take in a pilot. This last we did not mind ; but being, as we were, in strict quarantine the rest of the way to England, viz. at Port Said, Malta, and Gibraltar, was equally ridiculous and tiresome.

On 19th August we arrived at Portsmouth, and went into harbour. We got a most hearty reception, cheers from the ships and the shore, and visits from many friends ; all really inspiriting and touching.

Next day, Lord Selborne, then First Lord of the Admiralty, paid us the special compliment of coming on board to receive us, and to give us His Majesty's message of approval, and of welcome home—an honour we all immensely appreciated.

On the 21st I left the ship, and my flag was hauled down : such leave takings are things not easily forgotten. These endings of the chief phases of our lives are the milestones of our existence !

CHAPTER XXXIV

ADMIRAL

The King's Telegram—Decorations—Portsmouth Banquet—
Royal Visit to Devonport—With H.R.H. Duke of Connaught
to Madrid—Order of Merit—The Coronation.

ON our arrival in England the King was abroad, but honoured me with a most kind telegram on my return. On 11th September the Mayor of Portsmouth, with the Corporation and Borough, entertained myself, the officers and ship's company of the *Centurion* at a banquet in the Town Hall of Portsmouth. Lord Selborne, the First Lord of the Admiralty, also was present. There were, of course, speeches ; we (the guests) regarded it as a great compliment, and I think such welcomes do good and are valued by the men.

About now the King arranged with the German Emperor that decorations should be exchanged between England and Prussia for the war service in North China in 1900. I had to nominate the German officers, while the German Admiral had to nominate ours, and it had to be considered what decorations on either side were

377

equivalent to those on the other. This is a little difficult; but all was arranged satisfactorily, I think.

That winter I visited Italy, Malta and France; it is very good for sailors after long foreign service to get a real variety of scene and society.

In March 1902 the King and Queen visited Devonport in the Royal Yacht, and on 8th March Her Majesty the Queen launched the ship called after her; and then the King laid the first keel-plate of the ship to be honoured with his name—a very apposite double function.

Previously the King honoured me by presenting us with our China medals at Keyham. I was given a second Chinese medal, having one already for the former wars there. It is probably rare for anyone to have two medals for wars in the same country.

This spring the King sent the Duke of Connaught to Madrid, as the head of a mission to invest the King of Spain with the Order of the Garter, on his assuming the reins of government; and I was selected to go in the Duke's suite as the naval representative.

We went out in the Royal Yacht, the *Victoria and Albert*, to Bilboa, where we landed, and went on to Madrid. There was, of course, a grand reception.

Her Majesty Queen Christina (the Queen Regent), as the Sovereign of Spain received the Duke, and the missions from other nations that arrived at the same time.

The first evening a great banquet was given

in the Palace, and the Queen conferred various Orders on the members of the different missions.

The Palace at Madrid is among the finest in Europe, and its site is good, being on an elevation. While we were there the magnificent Goya tapestries were displayed in the Palace ; they were so large and numerous that they were hung round the immense staircases.

The next day the investiture of the King with the Garter took place in one of the large salons of the Palace ; for such functions everything should be carefully planned and rehearsed beforehand. We had done so.

The various members of the Duke's suite carried on cushions the different emblems of the Order of the Garter, which in proper order were taken by the Duke of Wellington, who as a Grandee of Spain had very fitly been selected for this office, and were by him handed to H.R.H. the Duke of Connaught, who carried out the investiture.

The ceremony of the King's taking the oaths was not performed till the next day, in the Church of San Francisco.

The King of Spain is not crowned, but the Crown is placed on a cushion by his side as he publicly takes the oaths. The whole ceremony and service, with a ' Te Deum,' were very impressive.

Madrid was *en fête*, the houses decorated with flags and festoons of all sorts, and I am glad to say no contretemps of any sort occurred to mar the harmony and gaiety of the whole proceedings.

No great festival in Spain seems perfect

without bull fights (if in season, which is summer) ;
many bull fights took place during the week we
were in Madrid, but the State bull fights on the
last day were attended by the King, the Queen
Mother, and all the Royalties and their suites
who had come to the celebration.

Most people know pretty well what a bull
fight is like, but I may briefly remark that its
chief cruelty, at least to my mind, consists in the
brutality to the horses ; the bull it is true is always
killed, but till killed, his sufferings are not much,
and his excitement and anger no doubt minimise
them, such as they are ; but the occasional treatment of the horses is such as I will not describe.

However, on the occasion of the State bull
fights, one of them is what is called 'Caballeros en
plaza.' The riders in this are gentlemen mounted
on valuable horses which are their own property,
and every precaution is taken to prevent their
being hurt. I believe this performance is very
rare.

The bull seems to me a very stupid animal on
the whole, but is very active ; I have seen one leap
over the boundary fence of the ring, which was
about eight feet high. Much commotion ensued
among the spectators. The men are seldom hurt,
and if they are, one feels their being there is quite
voluntary on their part. The 'Matador'—or
slayer (from *matar*—to kill)—is the hero of the
Spanish feminine world, and often makes a great
deal of money. The theory is that he always
kills the bull with one thrust of his sword : but
in practice this is, I believe, rare.

I will not inflict on my readers any description of Madrid, but only say that the ceremonies lasted about a week, after which the Duke of Connaught with his suite returned in the Royal Yacht to England.

This spring I was a member of a committee on the question of manning the Navy, and of a Naval Reserve. Our very able chairman was Sir Edward Grey. The committee lasted several weeks, and its recommendations were in great part adopted by the Admiralty.

The 26th June 1902 was to have been the Coronation Day of His Majesty King Edward VII. The sorrow and anxiety created by his serious illness that caused its postponement will be long remembered by survivors.

On that day the King instituted the Order of Merit, the naval members of which were Admiral of the Fleet the Hon. Sir Henry Keppel and myself.

I consider the Order of Merit to be the highest compliment paid by the Sovereign to a subject, not only because the number is very limited, but because it is awarded for prolonged work, or service, of the kind specially germane to the individual ; and not only for a short or sudden action.

The King having happily recovered his health, preparations for the Coronation were resumed ; in them I played a small part, being selected to ride in the Coronation procession and join in the Abbey ceremonials. Participants in the procession through the streets see nothing of the procession, but they see the streets of London in an extraordinary guise, and it is a sight well worth seeing.

On 16th August the King reviewed his Fleet at Spithead, and I was honoured with a command to attend on board the Royal Yacht, from which the scene was most impressive.

In October 1902 the King made me his First and Principal Naval A.D.C., which I continued to be till I became Commander-in-Chief at Devonport ; when I was relieved from the above position, which I think is right, as the holder of it should be free, and at the immediate call of the Sovereign.

The same month I and all the other King's A.D.C.'s rode in His Majesty's procession to the Guildhall banquet.

In March 1903 I became Commander-in-Chief at Plymouth.

CHAPTER XXXV

PLYMOUTH COMMAND

House Book—Cambridge Degree of LL.D.—Visit of T.R.H. the Prince and Princess of Wales to Devonport—German Squadron's Visit—Three Admirals—Promoted to Admiral of the Fleet.

THE First Lord of the Admiralty kindly offered me my choice of either Plymouth or Portsmouth, but I chose Plymouth, partly because it was vacant six months sooner than the other, and I could only hold either till two years after that date.

Admiral in command of a home port is as a rule the end of one's service ; its duties are greatly social ones, but when all is considered such appointments do not leave one much spare time.

I know both Portsmouth and Plymouth well, and have always considered as a residence the latter preferable to the former, because you are living more in the county society, and the kindness of your Devon and Cornish neighbours is endless.

I succeeded my friend Admiral Lord Charles Scott, in whose time, and with whose assistance, plans had been made by the Admiralty to alter both the Admiralty House and the grounds about it; and these were now carried out.

This partly induced me, with the help of my Flag-lieutenant (Lieutenant C. N. T. Carill-Worsley), to start a 'House book,' by which I mean a volume containing a history of the house, so far as known, with plans and views, &c.; to be continued and kept up to date, with any details of the inmates, or of events, that seem worthy of record. I never heard of such a book anywhere else, but only fancy the immense interest of one such that had long been kept in some of our historic mansions. I mention the above in hopes some one may read this and copy my example.

During my command at Plymouth but few events occurred worth relating.

A great dinner of welcome home was given in the Guildhall, Plymouth, to the 2nd Battalion of the Duke of Cornwall's Light Infantry. I was present and had to speak, and I think surprised them by saying I had probably known the regiment longer than anyone else there, as I made their acquaintance on board the *Prince* on their arrival in the Crimea in 1854, when they were the 46th Regiment, and had they arrived a few days later they would probably all have been lost in that ship, as she was wrecked in the gale of 14th November.

In June 1903 I had the great honour of having the degree of LL.D. 'Honoris causa' conferred on me by the University of Cambridge. The meaning, of course, is Doctor of both Civil and Church Law —once I believe it was called ' J.U.D.' or 'juris utrusque doctor.' The ceremony was to me very interesting, and the compliment I highly appreciated.

In July 1903 their Royal Highnesses the Prince and Princess of Wales, now our King and Queen, visited the port, for H.R.H. the Princess of Wales to launch H.M.S. *King Edward VII*, whose keel-plate was laid by the King in March 1902.[1]

In July 1904 a large German squadron visited us at Plymouth, commanded by Admiral von Koester, with two Rear-Admirals. I think I may say that the visit went off in the pleasantest and most friendly way in all respects.

When I dined with the German Admiral on board his flagship in Plymouth Sound, he did me the honour to ask to meet me such officers of his squadron as had been under my command on shore in our Chinese expedition in 1900, and he also had fallen in on deck as a guard of honour the seamen who had served on the same occasion. It was a compliment that touched me greatly, and was well worthy of German heads and hearts.

On 20th February 1905 I was promoted to the rank of Admiral of the Fleet, which meant my vacating my post as Commander-in-Chief at Plymouth.

I may here just mention that a very extraordinary position in the Navy List had occurred about a year before, viz. that the three senior Admirals next each other at the top of the active list had all been boys together at the same school

[1] See p. 378.

2 C

fifty-two years previously—viz. Lord Walter Kerr, Lord Charles Scott, and myself—at Radley.

When the number of boys, schools, and naval officers of the United Kingdom is considered, I think it would require a Senior Wrangler to calculate the arithmetical chances against such an event.

My flag as Admiral of the Fleet flew for a month in the *Impregnable*, that ship by chance having the same name as the last one that ever flew an Admiral of the Fleet's flag for more than a day.

On 20th March 1905 I was relieved by Vice-Admiral Sir Lewis Beaumont, and went on half-pay, as I supposed, for the last time.

CHAPTER XXXVI

ADMIRAL OF THE FLEET

Remarks on Title and Flag of Admiral of the Fleet—With H.R.H.
Prince Arthur of Connaught to Berlin—Trafalgar Fête at
Boston—Southern States—Go with Prince Arthur of
Connaught to Japan.

I MUST make a few remarks both on the title and
on the flag of an Admiral of the Fleet—objecting
as I do to both.

As regards the title, it is not significant enough,
being too like the title ' Admiral *in* the Fleet,'
which means, the next lower grade of Admiral.
The result is, as I know well, that most people
neither use, nor understand it.

What would be thought of changing the title
' Field Marshal' to 'General of the Army'? What
would the Field-Marshals say? When the title
' Admiral of the Fleet ' was instituted about the
end of the seventeenth century, there was to be
only one such officer at the same time, and I
believe he at first only held the rank and title
while employed on full pay.

In the latter part of the eighteenth century
there was still only one such officer at one time.
The increase in numbers seems to have taken place

2 C 2

in the nineteenth century. While only ONE such officer existed the title no doubt had a meaning it has not now. I may just remark that at this moment Admiral Dewey, of the United States Navy, holds the special title of ' Admiral of the Navy,' he alone having it.

In May 1905 the King attached me to the suite of H.R.H. Prince Arthur of Connaught for his mission to Berlin to be present at the wedding of the Crown Prince of Prussia. We were there over four days, and the ceremonies were as well carried out as German thoroughness would make probable. Whatever I may think of the ulterior aspirations of United Germany, I have the greatest admiration for their intelligence and practical organisation, in whatever they undertake.

On the day of the wedding it was very hot, and we were in levee dress for about seven hours. The Schloss is far larger than Buckingham Palace, and on this day about 1500 guests dined in the Schloss, of course in different rooms, at dinners as well served, and attended on, as if the guests had been only a tenth in number.

In the autumn of 1905 a community in Boston decided to celebrate the centenary of the Battle of Trafalgar—Captain Mahan, the great naval historian, kindly consenting to make the speech of the evening, of course, on Lord Nelson and his career.

It was wished that some British naval officer should represent our Navy ; and being asked to do so, I consented for the sake of our service.

The day chosen was, of course, 21st October,

when about 2500 people assembled in the Tremont Temple in Boston. Those who have read the illuminating works of Mahan can imagine how he did justice to his subject. I had the pleasure of staying in the same house with him, and found him equally interesting as a companion as he is as a writer.

From Boston I moved south, visiting many places, among them New Orleans, which has an old-time charm. It is the most straggling city for its population that I know. It lies very low, and a bund, or sea wall, is necessary to protect it from the Mississippi River. It has several cemeteries; the two oldest are dedicated to St. Louis, and the inscriptions on the tombs are nearly all in Spanish or French. One was in memory of Dominique You, a celebrated pirate who seems to have died in his bed instead of his boots.

The old French Creole quarter is interesting, but too old-fashioned as to hygienic arrangements, and as regards its street pavement.

A yellow fever epidemic was going on, and I was much interested to hear about it. The doctors said the mosquito is what takes it from a patient to another person, and that only in that way is it infectious. Then if a draught of air, or low temperature, prevents the above conduction, no fear of infection exists. This I believe. They said that in a week (at most) you could be sure if a patient would recover or die, that no ill after-effects are usually left by it, and that a young person nearly always recovers, but that a patient over fifty usually dies.

From New Orleans I went to Atlanta, the capital of Georgia, where old inhabitants told me that after General Sherman burnt it on his march to the sea, only a hundred houses or so remained. Now it is a very fine city.

I then went to Charleston, famous, perhaps, as the scene of the beginning of two wars; now alas, since the slave days much decayed like other southern places are. As servants I heard the negroes mostly praised.

Intoxicating drinks are not legally sold here, but if you name them in your hotel, where no wine card is allowed, they appear. If thirsty in the streets one goes into shops known as 'Blind Tigers,' and gets a dose of medicine in the back parlour.

I must not prolong my account of the United States, but whenever I have been there, the great kindness I have met with, and the interesting people and places, made me both unwilling to quit the country then, and tempt me to say more about it now.

I returned to England before the end of the year, having been selected by the King to join the suite of H.R.H. Prince Arthur of Connaught for his mission to Japan, to invest the Mikado, or Emperor, with the Order of the Garter.

The Prince's suite numbered six; we left London on 11th January 1906, and at Marseilles embarked in the P. & O. steamship *Mongolia*, arriving at Hong-Kong in twenty-eight days.

From there we proceeded in H.M.S. *Diadem* to Yokohama, where we arrived on 19th February and went by train to Tokyo. The Emperor himself came to the station there to receive our Prince—a very extraordinary honour for His Majesty to pay to anyone.

The reception was in all respects very striking, and the streets were crowded with people, though it was very cold, and snowing at times. The Prince and his suite were all lodged in the Kasumigaski Palace, a very fine stone building.

Next day the ceremony of investing the Emperor with the Order of the Garter took place in the Emperor's residential palace. It was interesting to me to compare the whole scene with the same ordeal at Madrid; the surroundings and the costumes were different, but the Japanese lack nothing in courtly forms and state ceremonies, and certainly never in courteous manners.

We were nearly a month in Japan; to do justice to an account of our visit there would not only be too long for me to attempt, but is far better described than I could do by Lord Redesdale.[1] I will only relate that so far as time allowed we travelled to the most interesting places in Japan, and so far as possible with great comfort, in the Emperor's special train.

The enthusiasm of our Prince's reception everywhere we went—though often in very cold or very wet weather—was quite astonishing, and almost beyond belief.

People were often drawn up at, or near, the railway stations the train did not stop at; where

---

[1] In his book *The Garter Mission to Japan* (Macmillan & Co.).

391

it did stop addresses of welcome were given. When we arrived at a town and left the station, the streets were thickly lined with spectators, all most orderly, the children always ranged along in the front rank, and each child holding in one hand a small Japanese flag, and in the other a Union Jack; of these flags we must have seen many thousands. The populace bowed frequently and shouted 'Banzai.' 'Banzai,' I believe, means 'ten thousand,' i.e. 'may you live very long.' The more official naval cheer is 'Hoga,' meaning 'respectfully saluting.'

In short, I can only say that had the British fought on the side of Japan and saved that nation from defeat, our Prince could not have been received with greater enthusiasm.

To me, perhaps, our most interesting visit was to see the Russian prizes at Yokosuka; the *Nicholas* 1st, and the *Admiral Apraxin* were repaired and in commission with new names. But some of the others were as brought in after the action, and the havoc done to them by shot, shell and fire was almost beyond belief. Wood splinters in action do much damage to the personnel, but I suspect that the steel or iron ones are much the same. When you have not plating intended to be protective, I think that the slighter your scantlings—except for constructive strength —the better.

Admiral Togo accompanied the Prince about everywhere. A more modest and retiring man than the Admiral has never worn a naval uniform; and these characteristics he particularly showed during the Prince's visit to the captured ships—so much so that it was impressive.

I was very much in Admiral Togo's company; though he was a boy for a time in our mercantile cadet ship the *Worcester* in the Thames, he conversed with difficulty in English. I am told he is naturally of a silent disposition, but all allow that it was he who designed and carried out the naval campaign. His face in repose has a rather sad expression.

One evening while at Tokyo a slight earthquake shock occurred, but so little as to be merely interesting. Earthquakes are, of course, very common in Japan; this shock was repeated the next morning, more severely.

On the afternoon of that day a charity concert had been got up by Lady Macdonald, the wife of our Ambassador (Sir Claude), and a rather absurd joke was played, by whom I know not. When the concert was about half over, a telegraphic message arrived to say that an earthquake might be expected at any moment. No disturbance was caused in the audience, but as the message was believed by the management who received it, our Prince was quietly requested to leave, followed by his suite, and by degrees the whole house was then quickly emptied, but no earthquake followed, and, as I understand, such things are as difficult to foretell as a really fine day in England.

I visited the military hospital and saw many wounded men. The Japanese, I believe, almost rival the Turks in their endurance of pain. I saw

393

one soldier who had lost in action both arms and
both legs, high up. Yet strange to say his face
and body looked healthy, and what I believe the
doctors call ' well nourished.'

I would gladly say more about Japan, but
it is wiser and kinder to leave my readers to Lord
Redesdale's book mentioned already.

CHAPTER XXXVII

ADMIRAL OF THE FLEET (continued)

Leave Japan—Cross the Pacific—Vancouver's Island—Canada
—Indians—Niagara—Quebec.

ON 16th March we left in the Pacific R.M.S.P. *Empress of Japan* for Vancouver's Island, quite sorry to part with our Japanese friends, who had left nothing undone to render our stay delightful.

On leaving I see that with other remarks in my journal I said : ' The courtesy, self-command, quietude of manner, and general refinement, of the Japanese, surpass those of any other nation I know of.' These expressions are pretty strong ; but it must be remembered that being with the Prince we mixed in the best society. Ordinary ' globe trotters ' do not do this.

I also said: ' It is not easy to know the Japanese, they are retiring in manner, and not expansive to foreigners.' In short, as Rudyard Kipling said, ' But East is East and West is West, the twain will never meet.'

When I was going to China in 1897 I said to the First Lord of the Admiralty : ' It seems to me not to matter what nation we go to war with singly, except Japan; because she is about 12,000 miles off.' Subsequent history has not at all altered my views.

The Japanese are like our neighbours across the North Sea, in that they know what they mean and want, and steadily prepare for that. ' Nec temere nec timide' might well be their motto. Japan's army in 1902 was, I believe, the bravest civilised one that ever took the field.

Our passage across the Pacific Ocean to Vancouver's Island occupied twelve days—eleven only by the calendar, but an extra one occurred, called 'Antipodes' day, when we crossed the longitude of 180° as we were moving eastward. This, of course, seemed like an extra day gained; and if going westward passing the 180° would have appeared like one lost.

I believe we were fortunate in our weather; this passage has at all seasons a bad weather reputation, but the ships of the company are fine steamers and well managed.

I see I noted her as the most comfortable mail steamer I was ever in, and I have been in several. The servants are all Chinese, and none are better servants.

Across the Pacific Ocean from west to east there is a set called the Japan current, and somewhat comparable to the Gulf Stream; bottles with papers in them to test the ocean drifts are often used, especially perhaps on this passage just now, to find the best routes. On one occasion such a bottle was found on the coast of the State of Washington, south of Vancouver's Island, ten years after it had been thrown overboard off the south-east part of Japan, having drifted across the Pacific Ocean for a distance of 4300 miles.

At the end of March we arrived at Victoria, the capital of British Columbia, but situated at the south end of Vancouver's Island, which country is about half the size of Ireland.

The Prince was received by the Governor, Sir Henry Joly de Lobiniere, a French Canadian, and a perfect specimen of a kind and high-bred French gentleman. With him we stayed a few days. We had a fishing excursion in the island, which was more remarkable for the constant rainfall than for the fish caught—I dare say not the only such instance !

From Victoria we went to Vancouver Town, and thence by the Canadian Pacific Railway across the Rocky Mountains. As everyone knows, the scenery there is sublime ; we viewed it partly from a seat in front of the engine, over the ' cow catcher '—a plan I can recommend.

As a place to recover the health of a thoroughly ' run-down ' invalid, commend me to Banff, and it is both well known and much patronised.

Our train for the Prince was a special one. We lived in it for a fortnight, and I could not wish for more comfort on the rails. My compartment had a private bathroom.

The Prince and his suite were the guests of the Canadian Government during his visit to that country, and we were shown all that could be seen in three or four weeks.

Canada is so well known now that I will only venture on one or two remarks about it. Calgary and Edmonton stand out most to my mind as new and very crude, but rising and promising, places.

Near Gleichen a large band of Indians were assembled to greet the Prince, and to show off their native sports. Some of their names sound to us ridiculous, but are not so to them. Such are, when translated, ' Dying young man,' ' Bad dried meat,' ' Red wolf,' ' Running rabbit,' &c.

The Indians struck me as being mostly of a yellowish and red tint ; prominent features, nose and lips large, hair black—the men wear it with two plaited tails in front. Both sexes paint the face, often yellow or red. Some of the young women are nice looking. The old chief took off his clothes and wished to exchange garments with the Prince. This is, I believe, the *ne plus ultra* of civility and friendship !

Chinese immigration is dreaded in British Columbia, and the tax for a Chinaman coming in was then £100.

One has often heard that large families were common among the French-Canadians. I was assured by friends that they knew a case of a man who has seventeen sons by one mother, working with him. An instance of—

> Where children are blessings and he who has most
> Has aid to his fortunes and riches to boast.

as the old colonial song said.

At Ottawa we stayed at the Government

House, as guests of Lord and Lady Grey, who made our short stay with them very agreeable. Here with much regret we parted from our gracious chief, H.R.H. Prince Arthur, who was to remain rather longer in Canada.

Though it was now the middle of April, snow and ice were still about in plenty. The salubrity of Canada is indisputable, and its prosperity assured; yet as a country to colonise in, the long and severe winter appears to me a great drawback. Its population is now about seven and a half millions; but when we were there it was much less, and was calculated at fewer than two persons to a square mile, including its most northern parts.

We then visited Montreal, Toronto, Niagara and Quebec, all known to me before.

At Niagara we were shown the new electric development company's works, then in construction; they divert a small part of the water just above the falls, on the Canadian side, into a basin having eleven shafts down which the water falls for 160 feet and in doing so turns several turbines placed in the shafts, and the collective power of each of the eleven is expected to give 15,000 horse-power.

A visit to Quebec is always of vivid interest; when there on this occasion, General Sir Thomas Kelly-Kenny and I were conducted over the route of Wolfe's landing and ascending the cliff, and the scene of the battle on the plains of Abraham, by Major W. Wood of the Canadian Militia, whose excellent work 'The Fight for Canada' I can strongly recommend. The cliff Wolfe ascended was about a hundred feet high.

The name ' Plains of Abraham ' is not taken from the Bible patriarch, but from Abraham Martin, a Frenchman who fed his sheep there.

I should like to dwell and enlarge on the half pathetic, half romantic, wholly heroic, close of Wolfe's career ; but I must remind myself again that this is not history, into which, being of course much more interesting than I am, I can hardly resist digressing.

I like to think the legend of Wolfe's repeating Gray's ' Elegy ' in the boat that was landing him is true ; the poem would then have been out about eight years.

From Quebec we went to Halifax, and there embarked in the Allan Line steamship *Victorian* for England, arriving at Liverpool early in May.

My next three years were entirely those of private life, varied by occasional travels abroad, that probably would not interest any kind readers I may have.

CHAPTER XXXVIII

H.M.S. *INFLEXIBLE* AND NEW YORK

Hoist Flag in *Inflexible*—Hudson-Fulton Celebrations at New York—Processions — Banquets — West Point Academy—Return—Retirement.

IN August 1909, I got a telegram from the Admiralty saying that both they, and the Secretary for Foreign Affairs, hoped I would go out to New York, with my flag flying in command of a squadron, to join with other foreign ones in the coming ' Hudson-Fulton ' celebrations there. This function was not actually an official one of the United States Government, but was instituted by the State of New York to celebrate the tercentenary of Henry Hudson's discovery of the river there, which is named after him ; and the almost centenary (really 102 years) of Robert Fulton's launching the first steamer on the Hudson River.

Immense preparations were being made in New York for this commemorative festival. Foreign nations were invited to send representatives and ships of war ; and our Government was anxious both to have there a squadron worthy of our Navy, and an officer in command of it higher in rank than any other one present.

I accepted the appointment, which, besides its special and historical interests, combined my hoisting my flag at sea as Admiral of the Fleet, with the Union Jack at the main, which had not occurred since H.R.H. the Duke of Clarence (afterwards King William IV) did so in 1814, to receive the allied squadrons at Spithead, on the occasion of Napoleon's going to Elba.

It will be understood therefore that as a naval officer only the appointment had an intrinsic value in itself. The immediate questions were my staff and my flagship. For the former I got the officers I wanted, viz. Captain Douglas Nicholson, who was my Flag-lieutenant in the Channel Fleet, Mr. Alton my Secretary, and Commanders Powlett and Lowther Crofton, who all three had been with me in China in 1900.

After some consideration the First Lord gave me as my flagship the *Inflexible*, a new first-class cruiser, one of our three newest and largest, and really the most powerful class of cruiser afloat anywhere—in fact the sort of ship worthy to fly the flag of an Admiral of the Fleet. Captain H. H. Torlesse, an able officer who commanded her, continued to do so.

Arrangements somewhat unusual had to be made for the social and domestic requirements of such a service, but these were easily got over. On 16th September I hoisted my flag in the *Inflexible* at Portsmouth, and left for New York.

Circumstances had made it most convenient

H.M.S. INFLEXIBLE

The first Steam Man-of-War to carry the Flag of an Admiral of the Fleet

1909

that part of our squadron, viz. the *Drake* (with the flag of Rear-Admiral F. T. Hamilton), the *Duke of Edinburgh* and the *Argyll* should precede us at a slower speed to the anchorage off Sandy Hook, where we arrived early on the 24th.

That forenoon we weighed, and followed by our squadron entered the Hudson River and moored off General Grant's tomb. The United States Fleet, a powerful collection of modern ships, under the command of Rear-Admiral S. Schroeder, were moored the highest up the river.

Next to them came our squadron, and below us the remaining foreign ships in order according to the seniority of their commanders. The German squadron was commanded by Grand Admiral von Koester, a former friend ⸢of mine at Plymouth in 1904; the French squadron by Admiral Le Pord.

New York was *en fête* in the energetic way worthy of the sea capital of the United States. The population of that city including its suburbs was said to be just over four millions, and I was told that on some days during our stay two million extra visitors were in the town. We lay in the Hudson River for a fortnight, the days being well filled up.

I will not attempt an account of all the feasts and receptions ashore and afloat, but only mention some of them. On, I may say, all occasions uniform of different degrees was worn by all officers.

On the 25th there was a full-dress reception by Mr. Sherman, the Vice-President of the United States, he representing Mr. Taft, the President, who was unable to come : this was really the only national, and therefore ' levee dress ' function.

That afternoon the river procession of vessels took place to escort the two 'lions,' viz. the duplicate of the *Half Moon*, and that of the *Clermont*. The former had been built in Holland, and Captain Colenbrander of the Dutch Navy assured me she was an exact copy of the ship Hudson made his voyage in. She was 68 feet long, and drew nine feet of water, she had three masts, her bow was very low, and her poop very high, but narrow. There was only three feet of height between her decks. The *Clermont* was a copy of Fulton's ship, a paddle-wheel vessel of course, but steaming very slowly.

On the evening of the 27th there was a great reception in the Metropolitan Opera House, we, the delegates, being ranged along the front of the stage like actors. The house holds some four thousand people, and was about full.

We each read our official addresses in turn. It was my first experience of addressing so large an audience, but I was told that they could hear me at the back part.

To give some idea of how any spare time was spent in visits, I may mention that this day we travelled fifty-five miles by river and land at New York to pay visits.

On the 28th we had a great lunch at a round table quite twenty feet across—things are mostly big in the United States !

In the afternoon we witnessed the great historical pageant, viz. a procession in the Fifth

Avenue of people and of cars carrying figures and models designed to show the phases and fashions of life and the chief events in North America from bygone times. It took about three hours to pass by.

On the 29th we visited the West Point Military Academy, which holds over 500 cadets. They were reviewed for us, dressed in the picturesque uniform of a hundred years ago. They were a fine set of young men, and no expense is spared to make the academy perfect.

That evening we dined at an official banquet in the Hôtel Astor. The dinner lasted six hours; from 7.30 to 1.30 we were at table. Two thousand two hundred guests sat down, all men, at round tables each holding about eight to ten persons. The galleries round were filled with ladies. When one had to speak one was led up to a special pulpit or rostrum, which was required in so large a place.

On the 30th there was another great procession in the Fifth Avenue, when about 25,000 men of various nations passed, both civil, naval, and military.

The foreign ships present were invited to land contingents of their crews with their arms, and of course did so. There were of course more Americans by far than any other nation, and the procession lasted about three hours.

On 5th September the St. George's, and other British societies—English, Scotch and Welsh (not Irish)—gave us a great dinner of about 500 people at the Waldorf Astoria. Much friendliness was expressed.

On the 6th we lunched with Mr. Pierpont Morgan, who showed us his wonderful library and collection of manuscripts.

On the 7th we were entertained at a great dinner at the Waldorf Astoria Hotel by the German community of New York, at which Grand Admiral von Koester was, of course, the principal guest. Much good feeling and cordiality prevailed.

On the 8th I had a trip out on an express train electric engine ; and back on a steam one, doing the mile in forty-three seconds ! The journey to Chicago of 960 miles is done in 18 hours, at 53 miles an hour. The American mode of fixing the rails on the sleepers never to me looks as good as our ' chairs,' but it seems to answer : the rails are heavy 100-lb. ones. Their engines are larger than ours ; the biggest with its tender loaded weighs close on 200 tons.

On 9th October we left for England, having had what is called a ' strenuous,' but very interesting, time at New York.

Such national representative congregations must, if the participants are sensible men, conduce to friendliness between their countries : and no people are better hosts than our American cousins.

Among my many kind entertainers whom I should like to name, I must mention one, viz. Mr. R. A. C. Smith of 100 Broadway, New York, who had special charge of myself and my staff, and whose kindness and attention left us nothing to wish for.

On our passages both out and home we encountered just enough bad weather to form some judgment of the ship's performance in a sea way. As a splendid modern ' sea-girt citadel ' no cruisers surpass her, but owing to her great steadiness, which is, of course, valuable as a gun platform, the sea soon sweeps over her upper deck.

On 19th October we arrived at Portsmouth, and I obeyed my last order from the Admiralty, which according to the old formula is to ' strike your flag, and come on shore '—and while doing so I felt a pride, I think pardonable in a naval officer, of having served at sea as an Admiral of the Fleet.

On 30th April 1910 I became seventy years of age, and so, in compliance with the very excellent rule of the Navy, I was placed on the retired list.

Human nature is often weak, and so we may even regret what we have both expected to occur, and believe to be proper. Retirement from a career is professional euthanasia ; yet—especially if Dame Fortune has kindly wafted us successfully over the billows of our active existence to the haven of retreat—I think the pilgrim of life should then comfort himself by taking the same view of his present condition, as did the great Francis Bacon of the canticle ' *Nunc Dimittis.*'

CHAPTER XXXIX

ENVOI

China and Japan—Importance of our Navy—Steamships—
Armourclads—Turret Ships—Navy in 1844—Naval Changes—
Knowledge required—Engineers—Modern Personnel—Marines
—Navy's Duties—Coastguard—Size of Ships—Conclusion.

I WISH to add to my personal memoirs a few
remarks on China, a part of the world of much
interest to me, and also to the profession in
which my life has been mostly passed. As
regards the first the Far Eastern question is quite
unlike any other in the world, especially since the
late wonderful rise of Japan to be a first-class power.

Japan seems to be in the happy condition
that nothing but a combination of nations can
harm her, and at least for the present I see no
prospect of any such alliance against her, if only
because very great mistrust of each other is now
prevalent in the happy family of Europe.

The position of Japan merely geographically
speaking as regards Asia is like ours towards
Europe, and possibly a parallel may be drawn
between our once actual possession of (and for
long our advanced claim to) certain provinces in
Europe, and Japan's occupation of Corea, but

all through such similes runs the one pregnant fact that whereas we were always in presence of other warlike nations, Japan's only real neighbour is the unmilitary empire of China. Thus the position of Japan is really a very enviable one.

As regards China, no greater evidence of her ultra-conservative immutability seems required than the fact that in spite of all her lessons of humiliation by encroaching enemies, and still more by the military triumphs of her once despised neighbour Japan, she yet hesitates to provide herself with the only real protection for a nation, in spite of Hague Conferences, and arbitration treaties, viz. a powerful army, and a sufficient navy according to her needs.

That China is slowly awakening I believe, and understand that she has now over one hundred thousand troops by way of being properly trained and armed, also I fully expect to see this number rapidly increasing, but several years must elapse before she can defy either of her eastern rivals to encroach on her dominions.

As I observed on p. 342, it is China really who has been wronged by the forced intrusion of alien nations, among whom England's share is by no means the smallest. The more one reads and knows about China, the more one sees and understands why the Chinese both call and regard us all as ' foreign devils' ; which I do not wonder at, China herself being the least aggressive nation that I know of.

That a powerful China would be a danger or a menace to the western world I do not believe.

She would be a rival to Japan, and might thus help by the balance of power in the Far East to promote peace in those regions.

Her feeling towards Japan is, at least now, not one of special affection, and the ' yellow peril ' is I believe a bogey yet very far distant.

John Chinaman is a born trader, and on the whole a honest one : he likes a good bargain of course—who does not?—but when the deal is arranged, he will keep to it.

I do not say it is beyond the power, or the mistaken diplomacy, of one or more of the western nations to cause the people of both the Middle Kingdom and of the country of the Rising Sun to combine against them, but I think it is quite uncalled for, and I am sure it is very undesirable.

When the principal years of one's life have been spent in a profession, it follows that one has both well considered that calling, and formed what are matured opinions about it. The above is my case, and I therefore wish to offer to my readers the following few remarks.

The vital importance of our Navy to England is in no way exaggerated by the well-known official preface to the Naval Articles of War, declaring it to be that on which, ' under the good Providence of God, the wealth, safety and strength of the kingdom chiefly depend.'

This, which could, perhaps, only be an actual truism of an island nation, became enhanced by our acquisition of possessions across the seas, and was completed by the increase of our population, necessitating a foreign food supply.

It is not, I think, unreasonable to say that to us, insular as we are, a strong Navy is but a defensive weapon, and may be claimed as such ; whereas when one is earnestly worked for, and achieved, by a Continental Power, the intention of aggression seems to underlie the design.

I think history shows that the increase and reduction of our Navy have synchronised with those of the chief Continental maritime powers ; in the former case following rather than preceding them.

The propulsion of ships of war by steam was a comparative drawback to our Navy, because during the last century there is not a doubt that, on the whole, we had more skilful seamen than other nations possessed.

And though ' seamanship ' of all kinds must be an art to be acquired by careful observation and long experience, yet the handling of a steamer can never need the practised eye and skilful, almost sympathetic, direction of the true sailor, who has been trained in ships under canvas only.

As in many other things, our neighbours the French were the pioneers of ironclad ships. It is true that floating batteries had existed before, and been used on various occasions ; but *La Gloire*, launched in 1860, was, I consider, the first real armoured *ship* afloat.

In the early years of ' ironclads ' then so called, the French were more addicted to ships of the same type than we were. Our idea seemed more to devise various sorts of protected ships, as experiments, thereby showing we were still quite uncertain which was the best type.

For example, in the Mediterranean Fleet for some years in the 'eighties, we had not two ironclad ships out there of a similar class. Sails died hard; perhaps turrets may be said to have had the immediate hand in their abolition.

The ill-fated *Captain* was the first ship actually built to carry out the designs of the clever and enthusiastic Cooper Coles, and to conform likewise to the then desire to have a turret ship that could sail also; and this object, up to her most tragic loss in 1870, her designer believed to be more or less accomplished.

It was soon very evident that the heavily armoured ships, however rigged, could not sail as ships had formerly done; and this became more evident not only as the armour increased in weight, but after the introduction of twin screws.

Indeed, as concerns these last, the *Alexandra*, completed in 1877, had two sets of small engines, on purpose to turn her twin screws as required, when she was under sail and her main engines were disconnected from her propellers. The *Devastation*, designed in 1869, was our first mastless sea-going ship.

Twin screws once introduced were continued, and their necessity not only for handiness, but for safety in unrigged ships, insured their general adoption.

The broadside armed ironclad slid gradually into the central box citadel; till the desire to mount heavier guns, and because they must be fewer in number to gain for them a larger arc of fire, was probably what caused the invention of the turret system, which is the undoubted parent of what now prevails in all ' capital ships,' or powerful cruisers, whether as barbette or turret.

It is perhaps curious to reflect how the ancient ram was revived in our days, but is now fast disappearing after a career in which it may almost be said only to have sunk its friends ; and with its abolition, we are again placing less comparative value on fore and aft fire.

The Whitehead torpedo-tubes have except in very small ships disappeared below the water line, but there as submerged ones they continue to be valued.

As regards the personnel of the Navy, it may be interesting to note that in 1844, though the list of flag-officers was numerically large, out of 211 (active and retired) admirals on the list only twenty-five rear-admirals were under sixty-five years of age, and only fifteen under sixty. Also that at that date we had only *one* line-of-battle ship in the Mediterranean, and it was with some difficulty, and after consulting the French Foreign Office, that the Admiralty obtained Lord Aberdeen's sanction that the flagship of the Commander-in-Chief on the above station should be a three- instead of a two-decked ship.

I think it is no matter of fancy to say that a naval officer is supposed to know more than it is possible for him to know. He must be first a seaman and a navigator, then very much of an artillerist and an infantry soldier, to which he should add a knowledge of naval construction, electricity as applied to all ship's uses, and the telegraph; of torpedoes, both motive and stationary; of all forms of signalling; of international law and of foreign tongues, at least French, being that of diplomacy: to these add, an engineer's proficiency.

To make a humorous comparison let me remind my readers of ' Rasselas,' by Dr. Johnson, and how, when Imlac was extolling the knowledge required to be a real poet, the Prince replied to him : ' Thou hast convinced me that no human being can ever be a poet.' One might say so of a naval officer, if a really complete knowledge of all branches of his profession was necessary.

To say that the personnel of the Navy has altered as much as the materiel since I entered the service would, of course, be untrue, because, as regards the latter, one may assert that the change from the war galleys of Mark Antony at Actium to the sailing line-of-battle ships in the Black Sea in 1854, was not greater than from the latter to a Dreadnought or a submarine boat.

As regards the mere numbers of officers on the Navy List; since the age-retirement scheme did not exist in 1852, the lists of officers on the active list then and now cannot well be compared, but we may compare the number of men. In 1852 the Navy vote taken was for 34,029 seamen and marines against 115,691 now, and the Navy estimates then were £5,494,888 against £44,392,500 now.

The age-retirement scheme of Mr. Childers I have mentioned previously, and given my humble judgment in its favour. Besides it, the chief change yet completely carried out, and affecting executive officers, is the abolition of the special navigating branch of the Navy.

This when proposed was, I may say, mostly objected to by the older officers of the service ; but is now I am sure very generally approved. The other great change, and still in progress, is the abolition of the engineer branch of our profession.

I have so great an opinion of the soundness and vitality of the Navy that I believe it would survive nearly everything except its actual extinction, but as regards the above change at present in progress I think as follows.

The very varied knowledge now required of a naval officer makes the present time one essentially for specialists, and certainly as engineers for that branch of the service—the multiplication and various sorts of machinery rendering this far more necessary than it was formerly.

It may naturally be remarked that in the pre-steam days all executive officers were supposed to be experts in whatever concerned the locomotion of their ship, and that they should if possible be so now. The first part would be true, and the second part desirable, but except for partial efficiency as an engineer it cannot, I think, be achieved.

The naval engineers have served us right well, as a special class ; the time may have arrived for their extinction as such, but if so their place and prospects for the future should, I believe, be the following.

1. The selection and higher training of volunteers from the executive branch, who, without being thoroughly trained practical engineers, would yet be able to occupy the higher positions as such, both afloat and in our dockyards.

2. Besides the above, to have thoroughly practical engineers, entered probably as is now done with boy artificers, and occupying virtually much the same position as was occupied by naval engineers when steamships were begun in our service.

Of course those officers diverted to the first of the above categories must give up all idea of commanding ships, or fleets ; and their separation from such ambitions should take place, at the latest, when they become commanders, better still as lieutenants. As regards the entry of naval cadets, the present regulations seem to me very good. I am sure that sailors should be ' caught ' young ; the sea is a profession to be as far as is possible bred to, or its discomforts, and still more the confinement of life on board ship, are very distasteful.

For these reasons the actual embarkation as young boys had its advantages, but the high standard of education now necessary makes their remaining for a few years at naval schools, which Osborne and Dartmouth actually are, indispensable.

It is a delicate matter to say much about the comparative efficiency of officers and men now and when I went to sea, so my remarks about this shall be few. Both officers and men are, of course, as befits present times far more generally educated, and I might add intelligent, than formerly.

As regards the officers I consider them more universally zealous—and in spite of what Talleyrand said to a diplomatist about zeal, a NAVY is nothing without it.

Comparisons are usually hazardous, often objectionable, yet I am going to make one between our two defensive services; it is this: In the Navy the officers are as a rule poorer men than in the Army, and enter their profession more with the intention of making it their home and life-career than soldiers do; and therefore I believe throw their hearts more universally into their work.

As regards the men, I doubt their physique being on the average as fine as it was formerly, but probably this can neither be proved nor disproved. If the former I do not lay it down to the loss of the work aloft, because I feel sure that the regular calisthenic exercises now practised on board our ships are far superior for the development of muscle. Our men are certainly far more sober, and better behaved when on leave; and we have no difficulty in recruiting for the service.

I cannot end my few remarks without alluding to that splendid corps, the Royal Marines, both Artillery and Light Infantry. Their history since the end of the seventeenth century may be said to be part of the history of the Navy, and their general loyalty to the officers has been, at certain times of trouble, equally creditable and efficient.

The Royal Marine Artillery emanated early last century from the request for a body of the Royal Artillery being lent to certain ships to teach the seamen gunnery. Till long after those days no naval gunnery school existed ; but the seamen certainly require now no outside assistance in that respect.

There are naval officers who are in favour of doing away with the marines, at least as embarked in ships, and I believe the United States Navy is the only large one besides our own in which marines now go afloat. I am not of the above opinion, but I should gradually let one part of the corps die out, and keep the other at least as numerous as both were a short time ago, all being under one denomination. It matters, I think, little if they are called artillery or light infantry, but I should favour the latter with extra pay for gunnery qualifications that might advance to the actual pay of the present Marine Artillery.

The reduction of the Marine Corps in numbers is, I think, a mistake. Their proportion to that of the seamen voted, when I entered the service, was then very much larger than it is now. I would not propose to restore that proportion, but I should keep the total numbers at what they were a few years ago, before their reduction commenced.

The immediate duties of the Navy now are very different from what they were at the beginning of this century even, but the reasons hardly require explanation.

When I entered the Navy certainly not more than one-third of our service afloat was in home waters, the rest being on foreign stations; now this is more than reversed, probably three-quarters of our force being in or near England.

In Chapter XXVI I have referred to the Coastguard, and I am entirely against their reduction in numbers. Besides their present important duties which Tariff Reform (if passed) would greatly augment as regards contraband goods, they are a very good recruiting body, and help to popularise the Navy, both as being visible to the shore population, and as a position to be looked forward to in the last years of their service by the men themselves: and they are a most trustworthy reserve.

Another and most important subject is that of the classes and sizes of our ships. *Dreadnoughts*, so called, are at the moment the most powerful type of fighting ship; yet many will agree with me that their origin was for us an evil, though had others begun them, we ought, of course, to have followed suit.

The nomenclature of classes of ships has entirely changed. I object to the term 'battleship' as being not distinctive; all ships meant to fight are battleships. I would restore the old term 'line-of-battle ship,' or 'ships of the line,' or perhaps say 'capital ship.'

For the rest all real ships are called cruisers of classes. I may also remark that the exact line of demarcation between a 'battleship' (so called) and a first-class cruiser is very hard to draw. The above remarks apply to 'class.'

As regards size, I think as follows. For

merchant ships no general rule can or need exist. The transatlantic liners that ply chiefly between Europe and the United States—probably to New York—may be of any size, so long as they can enter and leave the two required ports ; but for men-of-war the question is a far more involved one. When out at sea I will concede that, other things being equal, the larger ship compared with the smaller one may, and should be, the more powerful of the two ; but that by no means, in my opinion, exhausts the question.

The objections to the constant increase of the size of men-of-war seem to me to be—

1. In view of torpedoes and submarine mines, it puts too many eggs into one basket, and the great increase of the range and accuracy of Whitehead torpedoes makes their danger greater.

2. The docks able to take the largest ships in are few, especially if from injury the ship is drawing an extra draft of water.

3. You cannot tell what harbours you may require the ship to enter, and here, both as to depth of water and turning space, difficulty comes in.

4. Mishaps through grounding may occur, and certainly the larger the ship the more difficult she will be to salve.

The above are my principal arguments against the constant increase in the size of our men-of-war. I presume I need hardly say that I should have a greater number of the smaller class of ship, each carrying guns, fewer but of the same type, as those carried by their larger sisters.

Finally, I will again refer to the Navy vote and estimates quoted on p. 412, by which it will be seen that as regards the numbers of seamen and marines voted, there are now exactly 3·4 times as many as when I entered the service, or say nearly three and a half times the former numbers. And that as regards the cost of our Navy, our estimates are now eight times what they were about sixty years ago.

Could anyone then have foretold the above stupendous increases ? and what may we expect in the future ? Nobody knows—but this I think : ' Beggar my neighbour ' is a very nice game of cards for children, but when played (with ships) between first-class Powers, it is certainly costly, probably very risky ! Games usually end by one side winning, occasionally by their being drawn ; which last may have its advantages, even with nations !

Certainly our insular and geographical position is admirable for a naval war. On one side we have the open ocean, and an extent of coast line that, in the face of our Navy, the fleets of the whole world could not successfully blockade ; on the other side we are placed so near to foreign ports, that the sea-borne commerce to and from such harbours must in war time run the greatest risk of capture by us.

Nature has thus assisted us so far that only ingratitude and downright stupidity could prevent our availing ourselves to the utmost of her gifts : that is to command the sea for our own benefit, and to the destruction of our enemy's sea-borne commerce. In our past history we have done so, and the result has justified the efforts.

History should inspire as well as teach, and if so we do not lack for inspiration, but I trust we shall long be able to quote what was written and true three hundred years ago, and is true now, viz.—

'Surely at this day with us of Europe the vantage of strength at sea (which is one of the principal dowries of this Kingdom of Great Britain) is great.'

INDEX

INDEX

INDEX

INDEX

INDEX

427

INDEX

INDEX

THE END